HANDBOOK OF RETIREMENT PLANS 6TH EDITION VOLUME II

Nicholas Paleveda MBA J.D. LL.M, Adjunct Professor, Graduate Tax Program, Northeastern University

Table of Contents

INTRODUCTION

Volume II covers the other plans available for plan sponsors such as ESOPS, 409A plan or Non-Qualified Deferred Compensation, Stock Option Plans, ESPP plans, Section 79 plans, Section 83 Plans, Davis Bacon Plans, Tat Hartley Plans, VEBAs and the latest case law on such items as "Breach of Fiduciary Duty". In addition, key cases are placed in Volume II to help the reader understand the latest trends in Tax Planning.

The "Case of the Year" for 2016 is Raymound McGaugh which is a Self Directed IRA potentially ROBS case. There are other cases not in this book which are adverse in a ROBS transaction.

The "Case of the Year" for 2015 is Tibble v. Edison from the U.S. Supreme Court. In Tibble, the Supreme Court was asked to defined "Fiduciary Duty" where a plan sponsor selected a more expensive "retail" mutual fund as opposed to a less expensive fee "institutional" mutual fund.

The "Case of the Year for 2014 is Clark v. Ramaker from the U.S. Supreme Court. The Supreme Court ruled… "An inherited IRA is NOT protected from creditors".

The "Case of the Year" for 2013 is Thousand Oaks v. Commissioner from the U.S Tax Court. In Thousand Oaks, an individual sold his assets in his business-then set up a qualified plan to defer taxation on the sale-how much can he count as compensation? Great blueprint for "asset sales" of small companies.

The Case of the Year for 2012 is White v. Commissioner from the U.S. Tax Court. In White, the Tax Court struck down yet another 419 Welfare Benefit Plan funded with Life Insurance.

The Case of the Year for 2011is CIGNA v. Amara from the United States Supreme Court. Once again a very favorable case from SCOTUS concerning pensions.

The Case of the Year for 2010 is Conkright v. Frommert from the U.S. Supreme Court. Pension actuaries make mistakes…however SCOTUS will defer to the actuaries. The Supreme Court is not going to engage in actuarial calculations.

There are of course other cases published, but these cases demonstrate the importance of judicial decisions in the area of retirement plans. ISBN 13-9781545461563 ISBN 10-1515461562

ESOPS-The "PUBLIX PLAN"

Employee Stock Ownership Plans-today the largest ESOP is Publix supermarkets headquartered in Lakeland Florida and one of the top ranked supermarkets in the USA.

Publix continues to expand in other markets using this model. Employee's tend to be happy and morale is currently high considering they have over 40,000 employees.

Employee Stock Ownership Plans (ESOPs)

ESOPS

An employee stock ownership plan (ESOP) is a Code 401(a) qualified defined contribution plan that is a stock bonus plan or a stock bonus/money purchase plan. An ESOP must be designed to invest primarily in qualifying employer securities as defined by Code Section 4975 (e) (8) and meet certain requirements of the Code and regulations. The IRS and Department of Labor share jurisdiction over some ESOP features. An employee stock ownership plan (ESOP) is a retirement plan in which the company contributes its stock to the plan for the benefit of the company's employees. With an ESOP, you never buy or hold the stock directly. This type of plan should not be confused with employee stock option plans under section 423, which are not technically "retirement plans". Instead, employee stock options plans give the employee the right to buy their company's stock at a set price within a certain period of time. The U.S. Department of Labor's Employee Benefits Security Administration, not the Securities and Exchange Commission, oversees ESOPs

ESOP Rules

To be an ESOP (employee stock ownership plan), a plan described in section 4975(e) (7) (A, a plan must be formally designated as such in the plan document. The terms of an ESOP must formally provide participants with certain protections and rights with respect to plan assets acquired with the proceeds of an exempt loan. These protections and rights are those referred to in the third sentence of 54.49757(b)(4), relating to put, call, or other options and to buy-sell or similar arrangements, and in 54.49757(b) (10), (11), and (12), relating to put options. The terms of an ESOP must also formally provide that these protections and rights are nonterminable. Thus, if a plan holds or has distributed securities acquired with the proceeds of an exempt loan and either the loan is repaid or the plan ceases to be an ESOP, these protections and rights must continue to exist under the terms of the plan. However, the protections and rights will not fail to be nonterminable merely because they are not exercisable under 54.49757(b) (11) and (12) (ii). For example, if, after a plan ceases to be an ESOP, securities acquired with the proceeds of an exempt loan cease to be publicly traded, the 15-month period prescribed by 54.49757(b) (11) includes the time when the securities are publicly traded.

The formal requirements of paragraph (a) (3) (i) and (ii) of this section must be set forth in the plan. Mere reference to the third sentence of 54.49757(b) (4) and to the provisions of 54.49757(b) (10), (11), and (12) is not sufficient. Notwithstanding the limits under paragraph (a) (4) and (10) of this section on the retroactive effect of plan amendments, a remedial plan amendment adopted before December 31, 1979, to meet the requirements of paragraph (a) (3) (i) and (ii) of this section is retroactively effective as of the later of the date on which the plan was designated as an ESOP or November 1, 1977.

A plan meets the requirements of this section as of the date that it is designated as an ESOP if it is amended retroactively to meet, and in fact does meet, such requirements at any of the following times: (i) 12 months after the date on which the plan is designated as an ESOP; (ii) 90 days after a determination letter is issued with respect to the qualification of the plan as an ESOP under this section, but only if the determination is requested by the time in paragraph (a)(4)(i) of this section; or (iii) A later date approved by the district director.

An ESOP may form a portion of a plan the balance of which includes a qualified pension, profit-sharing, or stock bonus plan which is not an ESOP. A reference to an ESOP includes an ESOP that forms a portion of another plan.

If an existing pension, profit-sharing, or stock bonus plan is converted into an ESOP, the requirements of section 404 of the Employee Retirement Income Security Act of 1974 (ERISA) relating to fiduciary duties, and section 401(a) of the Code, relating to requirements for plans established for the exclusive benefit of employees, applying to such conversion. A conversion may constitute a termination of an existing plan. For definition of a termination, see the regulations under section 411(d) (3) of the Code and section 4041(f) of ERISA.

An arrangement involving an ESOP that creates a put option must not provide for the issuance of put options other than as provided under 54.49757(b) (10), (11) and (12). Also, an ESOP must not otherwise obligate itself to acquire securities from a particular security holder at an indefinite time determined upon the happening of an event such as the death of the holder.

A plan designated as an ESOP after November 1, 1977, must not be integrated directly or indirectly with contributions or benefits under title II of the Social Security Act or any other State or Federal law. ESOP's established and integrated before such date may remain integrated. However, such plans must not be amended to increase the integration level or the integration percentage. Such plans may in operation continue to increase the level of integration if under the plan such increase is limited by reference to a criterion existing apart from the plan.

An ESOP will not fail to meet the requirements of section 401(a)(2) merely because it gives plan assets as collateral for an exempt loan under 54.49757(b)(5) or uses plan assets under 54.49757(b)(6) to repay and exempt loan in the event of default.

An ESOP will not fail to meet the requirements of section 401(a) (16) merely because annual additions under section 415(c) are calculated with respect to employer contributions used to repay an exempt loan rather than with respect to securities allocated to participants. An ESOP will not fail to meet the requirements of section 401(a) merely because it provides for the current payment of income under paragraph (f) (3) of this section. A plan established before November 1, 1977 that otherwise satisfies the provisions of this section constitutes an ESOP if it is amended by December 31, 1977, to comply from November 1, 1977 with this section even though before November 1, 1977 the plan did not satisfy paragraphs (c) and (d) (2), (4), and (5) of this section.. Notwithstanding paragraph (a)(9) of this section, a plan established before November 1, 1977, that otherwise satisfies the provisions of this section constitutes an ESOP if by December 31, 1977, it is amended to comply from November 1, 1977, with this section even though before such date the plan did not satisfy the following provisions of this section: (i) Paragraph (a) (3) and (8) (iii); (ii) The last sentence of paragraph (d)(3); and (iii) Paragraph (f)(3).

A plan constitutes an ESOP only if the plan specifically states that it is designed to invest primarily in qualifying employer securities. Thus, a stock bonus plan or a money purchase pension plan constituting an ESOP may invest part of its assets in other than qualifying employer securities. Such plan will be treated the same as other stock bonus plans or money purchase pension plans qualified under section 401a with respect to those investments. All assets acquired by an ESOP with the proceeds of an exempt loan under section 4975(d) (3) must be added to and maintained in a suspense account. They are to be withdrawn from the suspense account by applying 54.49757(b) (8) and (15) as if all securities in the suspense account were encumbered. Such assets acquired before November 1, 1977, must be withdrawn by applying 54.49757(b) (8) or the provision of the loan that controls release from encumbrance. Assets in such suspense accounts are assets of the ESOP. Thus, for example, such assets are subject to section 401(a) (2).

Amounts contributed to an ESOP must be allocated as provided under 1.4011(b) (ii) and (iii) of this chapter, and securities acquired by an ESOP must be accounted for as provided under 1.402(a) 1(b) (2) (ii) of this chapter.

As of the end of each plan year, the ESOP must consistently allocate to the participants' accounts non-monetary units representing participants' interests in assets withdrawn from the suspense account. Income with respect to securities acquired with the proceeds of an exempt loan must be allocated as income of the plan except to the extent that the ESOP provides for the use of income from such securities to repay the loan. Certain income may be distributed currently under paragraph (f) (3) of this section.

 If a portion of a participant's account is forfeited, qualifying employer securities allocated under paragraph (d) (2) of this section must be forfeited only after other assets. If interests in more than one class of qualifying employer securities have been allocated to the participant's account, the participant must be treated as forfeiting the same proportion of each such class.

Valuations must be made in good faith and based on all relevant factors for determining the fair market value of securities. In the case of a transaction between a plan and a disqualified person, value must be determined as of the date of the transaction. For all other purposes under this subparagraph (5), value must be determined as of the most recent valuation date under the plan. An independent appraisal will not in itself be a good faith determination of value in the case of a transaction between a plan and a disqualified person. However, in other cases, a determination of fair market value based on at least an annual appraisal independently arrived at by a person who customarily makes such appraisals and who is independent of any party to a transaction under 54.49757(b) (9) and (12) will be deemed to be a good faith determination of value.

 An ESOP may not be considered together with another plan for purposes of applying section 401(a) (4) and (5) or section 410(b) unless: (i) The ESOP and such other plan exist on November 1, 1977, or (ii) Paragraph (e)(2) of this section is satisfied.

 Two or more ESOP's, one or more of which does not exist on November 1, 1977, may be considered together for purposes of applying section 401(a) (4) and (5) or section 410(b) only if the proportion of qualifying employer securities to total plan assets is substantially the same for each ESOP and: (i) The qualifying employer securities held by all ESOP's are all of the same class; or (ii) The ratios of each class held to all such securities held is substantially the same for each plan.

If the coverage, contribution, or benefit structure of a plan that exists on November 1, 1977 is amended after that date, as of the effective date of the amendment, the plan is no longer considered to be a plan that exists on November 1, 1977.

Except as provided in paragraph (f) (2) and (3) of this section, with respect to distributions, a portion of an ESOP consisting of stock bonus plan or a money purchase pension plan is not to be distinguished from other such plans under section 401(a).

Thus, for example, benefits distributable from the portion of an ESOP consisting of a stock bonus plan are distributable only in stock of the employer. Also, benefits distributable from the money-purchase portion of the ESOP may be, but are not required to be, distributable in qualifying employer securities. If securities acquired with the proceeds of an exempt loan available for distribution consist of more than one class, a distributee must receive substantially the same proportion of each such class. However, as indicated in paragraph (f) (1) of this section, benefits distributable from the portion of an ESOP consisting of a stock bonus plan are distributable only in stock of the employer.

Income paid with respect to qualifying employer securities acquired by an ESOP in taxable years beginning after December 31, 1974, may be distributed at any time after receipt by the plan to participants on whose behalf such securities have been allocated. However, under an ESOP that is a stock bonus plan, income held by the plan for a 2-year period or longer must be distributed under the general rules described in paragraph (f)(1) of this section.

1042 Rollovers.

1042 Rollovers have certain requirements which allow tax free distribution of the assets, however if the requirements are not met, the tax status will be denied as it was in the *Estate of John W. Clause*.

ESOP New regulations concerning Diversification of Employer Stock in an ESOP.

Certain Defined Contribution Plans or Investment Funds Not Treated as Holding Employer Securities

The proposed regulations provided that certain investment funds that include employer securities as part of a broader fund were treated as not holding employer securities. This exception was limited to the extent the employer securities were held indirectly through an investment company registered under the Investment Company Act of 1940; a common or collective trust fund or pooled investment fund maintained by a bank or trust company supervised by a State or a Federal agency; a pooled investment fund of an insurance company that is qualified to do business in a State; or any other investment fund designated by the Commissioner in revenue rulings, notices, or other guidance published in the Internal Revenue Bulletin. The proposed regulations also provided that this exception was limited to funds where the investment is independent of the employer and where the employer securities do not exceed 10 percent of the fund.

Commentators requested that this exception be broadened to include funds that are managed by an investment manager within the meaning of section 3(38) of ERISA. The final regulations do not provide for this expansion because such a fund would not necessarily be holding employer securities only as an indirect result of its investment policy.

However, the final regulations provide that, in the case of a multiemployer plan, an investment option will not be treated as holding employer securities to the extent the employer securities are held indirectly through an investment fund managed by an investment manager if the investment is independent of the employer and the percentage limitation rule is satisfied.

The final regulations replace the reference to a fund that is an investment company registered under the Investment Company Act of 1940 with a regulated investment company as described in Code section 851(a). This change extends the types of investment companies to include exchange traded funds, which are unit investment trusts if they satisfy section 851(a). The final regulations also retain the rule from the proposed regulations that allows the Commissioner to designate additional types of funds as eligible for this exception.

Commentators requested that the percentage limitation rule be eliminated. They argued that it would be difficult and costly to monitor the investment fund to ensure that the aggregate value of the employer securities held in such fund was not in excess of 10 percent of the total assets of all the fund's investments. In response to these comments, the final regulations provide that the determination of whether the value of employer securities exceeds 10 percent of the total value of the fund's investments is made for the plan year as of the end of the preceding plan year. The determination can be based on the information in the latest disclosure of the fund's portfolio holdings (for example, Form N-CSR, ``Certified Shareholder Report of Registered Management Investment Companies'') that was filed with the Securities and Exchange Commission in that preceding plan year.

The final regulations also provide that in a case where a fund that indirectly holds employer securities fails to meet the requirement that the investment be independent of the employer (including the situation where the fund no longer meets the percentage limitation rule), the plan does not fail to satisfy the diversification requirements under section 401(a) (35) merely because it does not offer those rights for up to 90 days after the investment fund is treated as holding employer securities.

Prohibition on Restrictions or Conditions

Section 401(a)(35)(D)(ii)(II) provides that a plan is not permitted to impose restrictions or conditions with respect to the investment of employer securities that are not imposed on the investment of other assets of the plan. Like the proposed regulations, the final regulations provide that the prohibition on restrictions or conditions with respect to the investment of employer securities applies to any direct or indirect restriction on an individual's right to divest an investment in employer securities that is not imposed on an investment that is not employer securities, as well as a direct or indirect benefit that is conditioned on investment in employer securities.

The proposed regulations provided for a number of permitted restrictions and conditions. The proposed regulations would have permitted a plan to impose a restriction or condition either directly or indirectly because of applicable securities laws or because the plan becomes an applicable defined contribution plan, limits investments in employer securities, limits trading frequency, does not permit investment in a frozen fund, imposes a fee on other investment options that is not imposed on the investment in employer securities or imposes a reasonable fee on the divestment of employer securities, or allows investments to be made in a stable value or similar fund more frequently than other investment funds.

A commentator requested clarification with respect to the exception for frozen funds. The commentator requested that a frozen fund include a plan that reinvests employer security dividends in additional employer securities as long as the plan does not permit any further investment in employer securities. The final regulations clarify that the plan is permitted to allow reinvestment of dividends paid on employer securities. The final regulations also clarify that the frozen fund exception is only available for a plan that does not have another employer securities fund.

Commentators requested that the list for permitted indirect restrictions or conditions be expanded to include certain defined contribution plans that make matching contributions in employer securities and allow participants to divest employer securities attributable to such contributions, but do not permit participants to later elect to reinvest any portion of their account balances in employer stock. The final regulations do not adopt this suggestion. The IRS and the Treasury Department (Treasury) have concluded that the inability to reinvest in employer securities generally acts as a material deterrent to an individual who might otherwise have elected to diversify his or her account balance of employer securities. However, the final regulations provide a transitional rule for certain leveraged ESOPs. An employer stock fund does not fail to be a frozen fund merely because of the allocation of employer securities that are released as matching contributions from the plan's suspense account that holds employer securities acquired with an exempt loan under section 4975(d)(3). This transitional rule only applies to employer securities that were acquired in a plan year beginning before January 1, 2007, with the proceeds of an exempt loan within the meaning of section 4975(d)(3) which is not refinanced after the end of the last plan year beginning before January 1, 2007. This transitional rule was added because these leveraged ESOPs cannot cease allocations of employer securities acquired with an exempt loan that are held in a suspense account without significant effect on the company's debt arrangements.

Commentators suggested that the special rule for a stable value or similar fund be expanded to allow transfers out of a stable value fund or similar fund more frequently than other funds. In response to comments, the final regulations provide that a plan is generally permitted to allow transfers to be made into or out of a stable value fund more frequently than a fund invested in employer securities. Thus, a plan that includes a broad range of investment alternatives as described in section 401(a) (35) (D) (i), including a stable value or similar fund, does not impose an impermissible restriction merely because it permits transfers into and out of the stable value or similar fund more frequently than the other funds (taking into account any restrictions or conditions imposed with respect to the other investment options under the plan).

Commentators requested clarification as to the meaning of a stable value or similar fund. The final regulations provide that a stable value or similar fund means an investment product or fund designed to preserve or guarantee principal and provide a reasonable rate of return, while providing liquidity for benefit distributions or transfers to other investment alternatives (such as a product or fund described in Department of Labor Regulation section 2550.404c-5(e) (4) (iv) (A) or (v) (A)).

One commentator noted that the Department of Labor regulations for qualified default investment alternatives (QDIAs) require QDIAs to be restriction-free for 90 days. The commentator requested clarification that the restriction-free 90-day period does not cause a plan to violate the prohibition on imposing a restriction or condition with respect to employer securities that is not imposed on other investments. However, the commentator further stated that service providers will have difficulty administering restrictions only after 90 days and therefore requested that the final regulations permit restriction-free transfers for QDIAs permanently. The final regulations expand the list of permitted indirect restrictions to provide that a plan may provide for transfers out of a QDIA (within the meaning of Department of Labor Regulation section 2550.404c-5(e)) more frequently than a fund invested in employer securities.

A commentator requested clarification concerning plans being permitted to restrict reinvestments in only one employer stock fund when the plan allows investment in another employer stock fund, provided that the stock contained in each fund has the same characteristics except for differences in the tax cost basis of the trust. The final regulations provide that any applicable tax consequences are disregarded in determining whether a plan imposes an indirect restriction or condition on an individual's right to divest an investment in employer securities. Accordingly, a plan is permitted to provide that an individual may not reinvest divested amounts in the same employer securities account but is permitted to invest such divested amounts in another employer securities account where the only relevant difference between the separate accounts is the section 402(e) (4) cost (or other basis) of the trust in the shares held in each account.

Several commentators requested clarification regarding the 7-day rule in the proposed regulations. The preamble to the proposed regulations explained that the 7-day rule was an example and not the exclusive method to limit trading frequency. The permitted restriction for trading frequency provides that a plan is permitted to impose reasonable restrictions that are designed to limit short-term trading in employer securities. Thus, the 7-day rule, which was mentioned in the preamble to the proposed regulations, is an example and other short-term trading restrictions (such as a restriction based on multiple trades within a specified period) are allowable if they meet the reasonably designed standard.

Miscellaneous

Commentators requested clarification with respect to an ESOP that has been satisfying the diversification requirements under section 401(a)(28) by distributing the portion of the participant's account covered by an election within 90 days after the period during which the election may be made, but which is now subject to the diversification requirements under section 401(a)(35). Such a distribution option does not satisfy the diversification requirements under section 401(a) (35).

These commentators were concerned that an amendment which eliminates this distribution option would be a violation of the anti-cutback rules under section 411(d) (6). Section 1107 of PPA '06 provides that any amendment which is made pursuant to a provision of PPA '06 will not fail to meet the requirements of section 411(d)(6) unless otherwise provided by the Secretary of the Treasury.\3\ Thus, an amendment to an ESOP which is now subject to the diversification requirements under section 401(a)(35) that eliminates the distribution option available for ESOPs subject to the diversification requirements under section 401(a)(28), as permitted under section 1107 of PPA '06, would not violate the anti-cutback rules under section 411(d)(6).

In addition, it is expected that guidance will be issued in the near future exercising the authority under Sec. 1.411(d)-4, A-2(d)(4), to permit elimination of such a distribution option with respect to an ESOP that is subject to section 401(a)(35) after the end of the limited period to which section 1107 of PPA '06 applies. The guidance will permit elimination of such a distribution option during the extended remedial amendment period permitted with respect to section 401(a)(35) under Notice 2009-97, that is, to the last day of the first plan year that begins on or after January 1, 2010.

Effective/Applicability Date

The final regulations are effective and applicable for plan years beginning on or after January 1, 2011.

Abuses in ESOP plans-a letter from our friends at the IRS-

Effective for years beginning after December 31, 1997, the Internal Revenue Code was amended to allow ESOPs to be shareholders in S corporations and to exempt the flow-through earnings to the ESOP from the unrelated business income tax. Accordingly, beginning in 1998, the income of an S corporation could pass through to an ESOP, and, because an ESOP is tax- exempt, no tax is paid on the income until it is distributed to the ESOP participant.

Congress intended that S corporations, like C corporations, be able to encourage employee ownership through an ESOP, but the new laws immediately led to abusive arrangements where an S corporation was used to pass corporate income to a tax-exempt ESOP where the only participants in the ESOP were the owner/employees of the business. Congress became aware that the law was subject to abuse and in 2001 amended the Code to add section 409(p) which limits the tax benefits of S corporation ESOPs unless the ESOP provides meaningful benefits to rank-and-file employees.

Change in Law

In 2001, Congress added section 409(p) to the Code. Section 409(p) was enacted to address concerns about ownership structures involving S corporations and ESOPs that concentrate the benefits of the ESOP in a small number of persons. In general, this section imposes income and excise taxes when there are prohibited allocations under an S corporation ESOP in a non-allocation year. A non-allocation year occurs when the ownership of the S corporation is so concentrated that disqualified persons own or is deemed to own at least 50 percent of the S corporation shares. Disqualified persons are persons who own at least 10 percent of S corporation stock held by the ESOP (or 20 percent with family members). For S corporation ESOPs in existence on March 14, 2001, section 409(p) is effective for plan years beginning after December 31, 2004. This delayed effective date has allowed existing S corporations that maintain ESOPs the time to restructure the stock ownership in order to avoid the tax effects of section 409(p). Temporary regulations providing guidance under section 409(p) were issued in July 2003 (2003 regulations). The IRS and Treasury have recently issued Temporary regulations providing additional guidance concerning the application of section 409(p) to S corporation ESOPs (2004 regulations). The text of both of these regulations can be found through links on the IRS web site.

The preamble to the 2004 regulations discusses ways an ESOP can prevent a non-allocation year from occurring. These methods include sale of employer securities in a participant's ESOP account, distribution of S corporation securities (if the plan allows) or transfer of S corporation securities to a non- ESOP portion of the plan or to another plan.

Abusive Transactions Involving ESOPs

In addition to section 409(p), ESOPs are subject to various requirements under the Code which must be met in order for the ESOP to be tax-exempt and to qualify for other tax benefits. Many of the existing arrangements designed to take advantage of the S corporation ESOP rules would not only violate section 409(p) when it becomes effective for these plans, but also violate other requirements of the Code. In these arrangements, taxpayers attempt to exclude the income of an operating business through the use of a combination of an S corporation and ESOP. In a typical case, an S corporation is created, with the owner of the operating business as the only employee of the S corporation. The owner of the operating business causes the two entities to enter into an agreement under which the operating business pays a fee to the S corporation in exchange for management or other services. In addition, the S management corporation purports to adopt an ESOP that is treated as the sole shareholder of the S management corporation and in which the owner is the sole participant. Taxpayers have argued that under this arrangement the operating company may deduct its payments to the S management corporation and the income of the S corporation is passed through to the purported ESOP. They further contend that because the purported ESOP is a tax-exempt entity, the income is not subject to tax until distributed from the plan. The Service has determined, however, that in many of these arrangements, the purported ESOP fails to satisfy the requirements of the Code for a valid ESOP. The following is an example of a typical abusive arrangement:

Individual A is an employee and the sole shareholder of Corporation X, a C corporation. Corporation X is an operating business with a small number of nonexcludable employees, some of who are not highly compensated employees. Corporation X does not maintain a qualified retirement plan. In 1998, Corporation X has taxable income of $500,000 and Individual A receives compensation of $200,000. The compensation is deducted by Corporation X in calculating its taxable income and is included in income by Individual A. In 1999, Corporation

Y, an S corporation, is created, and a trust purported to be an ESOP is established by Corporation Y. All of the stock of Corporation Y stock is contributed to the purported ESOP. Individual A is the sole employee of Corporation Y and the sole participant in the purported ESOP. All the stock of Corporation Y is allocated to the account of A. The purported ESOP provides for full and immediate vesting of all benefits. Although the trust is purported to be an ESOP, it is not operated in accordance with the requirements for tax qualification under section 401(a) of the Code. Also in 1999, Corporation Y enters into an agreement with Corporation X for fees to be paid in exchange for management services provided by Individual A to operation X. The principal business of Corporation Y is performing management functions for Corporation X on a regular and continuing basis. In 1999, the fees paid by Corporation X to Corporation Y equal $700,000. Corporation X deducts the full amount of the fees on its corporate tax return as a business expense and reports no taxable income. The $700,000 is reported by Corporation Y as income of the tax-exempt ESOP. Similar fees are paid in the years 2000-2003 and are reported as in 1999.

ESOP Requirements

ESOPs are subject to various requirements under the Code which must be met in order for the ESOP to be tax-exempt and to qualify for other tax benefits. For example, an ESOP must satisfy the nondiscrimination rules of section 401(a) (4) and the coverage rules of section 410(b). The nondiscrimination rules of section 401(a) (4) provide that the contributions or benefits provided under a plan may not discriminate in favor of highly compensated employees. An employee is a highly compensated employee either by being a 5-percent owner of the employer or by having compensation above a certain level. Under the coverage rules of section 410(b), an ESOP must benefit either a certain percentage of the employer's nonhighly compensated employees or a classification of employees that does not discriminate in favor of highly compensated employees. For example, an ESOP that provides benefits to an employer's highly compensated employees, but does not provide benefits to the employer's nonhighly compensated employees, will fail these coverage rules and fail to be a qualified ESOP. The plan will therefore lose any tax benefits associated with being an ESOP. Also, in determining whether these nondiscrimination and coverage rules are satisfied, section 414(m) of the Code provides that all employees of the members of an "affiliated service group" shall be treated as employed by a single employer. In that case, an employee who is a 5-percent owner of any member of the group is a highly compensated employee for the group. The term "affiliated service group" includes a group of two or more service organizations (e.g. corporations or partnerships whose principal business is the performance of services) where one of these organizations provides services to the other organization(s) in the group and there is a certain level of common ownership between the organizations. See Rev. Rul. 81-105, 1981-1 C.B. 256. In addition, the term also includes a group consisting of (1) an organization whose principal business is performing, on a regular and continuing basis, management functions for another organization (the recipient organization) and (2) the recipient organization (the organization for which such management functions are performed).

Accordingly, where an affiliated service group exists, an ESOP maintained by one of the organizations in that group may violate the coverage and nondiscrimination rules of the Code even if that organization's only employee is covered by the plan. In the example provided above, Corporations X and Y form an affiliated service group because the principal business of Corporation Y is performing, on a regular and continuing basis, management functions for Corporation X. The purported ESOP of Corporation Y violates the coverage rules under section 410(b) because only Individual A is covered by the purported ESOP, and there are other non-excludible employees of Corporations X and Y who are non-highly compensated employees. As a 5-percent owner of Corporation Y, A is a highly compensated employee with respect to the affiliated service group of Corporations X and Y.

Tax Consequences of Abusive ESOPs

If an abuse is found to exist that is similar to the one described above, there are tax consequences for the management corporation (Corporation Y, in the above example) and for the ESOP participant (Individual A). With respect to the management corporation, because the trust of the purported ESOP is nonqualified, it may not be a shareholder of an S corporation. Accordingly, the income will not pass through to the trust, but will instead be taxable to the management corporation as a C corporation. As a result, the management corporation will be taxed at the corporate level on all of its taxable income for all open years. With respect to the ESOP participant, the tax liability will vary depending on whether or not a violation of the coverage rules is found. Section 402(b) provides generally that contributions to an employees' trust under a nonqualified plan are includible in the employee's income to the extent the employee is vested in those amounts. Section 402(b) further provides that any amount (other than an employee's investment in the contract if any) actually distributed or made available to an employee from an employees' trust under a nonqualified plan is includible in income when distributed or made available. However, section 402(b) (4) includes a special rule for an employees' trust where one of the reasons for disqualification of a plan is a coverage violation under section 410(b). In that case, under section 402(b)(4) of the Code, any highly compensated employee covered by the nonqualified plan is taxable on the value of his or her vested accrued benefit under the trust (other than his or her investment in the contract, if any). Thus, in the above example, because the purported ESOP fails to satisfy the coverage rules, the amount includible in A's income for each open year would be the value of A's account balance in the trust of the purported ESOP for that year (other than A's investment in the contract if any). The value of A's account balance would include the fair market value of the shares of Corporation Y stock allocated to the account.

What you should do if you are involved with an abusive ESOP If you believe your arrangement may be considered an abusive transaction, you should immediately consult your tax advisor. If your tax adviser determines that your arrangement is, in fact, abusive, you should immediately file an amended return for all open years affected by the arrangement. This issue may not be resolved under the Employee Plans Resolution Compliance System (EPCRS). Employee Plans anticipates initiating a compliance program to review a large number of S corporation ESOPs with a small number of participants.

Qualified Amended Returns

Internal Revenue Code § 6662(a) imposes a penalty equal to 20 percent of any underpayment of tax required to be shown on a return if it is the result of negligence or a substantial understatement of income tax. An individual substantially understates his or her income tax when the reported tax is understated by the greater of 10 percent of the tax required to be shown on the return or $5,000. For corporations, other than an S corporation or a personal holding company, the understatement is measured by 10 percent of the tax required to be shown or $10,000. In determining the amount of "underpayment" that exists for purposes of the application of the penalty, the "amount shown as the tax by the taxpayer upon the return" includes or is adjusted by the amount which is shown as additional tax on a later "qualified amended return". Thus, in some instances, a taxpayer may be able to avoid or mitigate the application of the penalty if the taxpayer files a qualified amended return *before* the IRS takes certain actions. Under the provisions found in Treasury Regulation §1.6664-2(c)(3), a qualifying amended return is an amended return, or a timely request for an administrative adjustment under I.R.C. § 6227, which is filed after the due date of the return but before the earliest of:

(1) The date on which the taxpayer is first contacted by the IRS concerning an examination of the return;

(2) The date on which a person described in Section 6700(a) is first contacted by the Service about an examination of an activity described in Section 6700(a), if the taxpayer claimed any tax benefit on the return

either directly or indirectly related to the Section 6700 activity; or (3) For certain pass-through items, the date on which the pass-through entity, such as a partnership or S Corporation, is first contacted by the Service in connection with an examination to which the pass-through item relates.

By means of a Notice issued on April 30, 2004, the IRS announced that it intended to issue temporary and proposed regulations which would modify and narrow the definition of a qualified amended return by the identification of additional periods of time after which a taxpayer would not be permitted to file a qualified amended return. Notice 2004-38 may be found at 2004-21 I.R.B. 949. Prior to filing any document which you intend to serve as a Qualified Amended Return, you should consult with your tax advisor. Additional guidance on qualified amended returns can be found in Notice 2004-38 and Treasury regulation section 1.6664-2(c)(3).

In MICHAEL C. HOLLEN, D.D.S., P.C., Petitioner v. COMMISSIONER OF INTERNAL REVENUE, Respondent Docket No. 19618-08R. Filed January 4, 2011. T.C. Memo. 2011-2,

The court stated

"Respondent determined that the ESOP and the ESOT failed to qualify under sections 401(a) and 501(a), respectively, because:

(1) The ESOP was not timely amended to include provisions required by sections 402(c)(4)(C), 414(n)(2)(C), (q), and (u), and 415(c)(3);

(2) the ESOP failed to follow the vesting schedule required by section 411(a)(2)(B);

(3) the ESOP failed to use an independent appraiser to appraise employer securities as required by section 401(a)(28)(C); and

(4) the beneficiary account of Dr. Hollen exceeded the allowable amount of annual additions for the 1989 plan year.

Respondent's determination is presumed to be correct, and the burden of proof is on petitioner. See Rule 142(a); Welch v Helvering, 290 U.S. 111, 115 (1933). To prevail, petitioner must prove that respondent abused his discretion. Under this standard, petitioner must persuade the Court that respondent's determination was unreasonable, arbitrary, or capricious. See Buzzetta Constr. Corp. v. Commissioner, 92 T.C. 641, 648 (1989). Petitioner has failed to do so. Section 401(a) lists requirements which must be met in order for a trust to be considered a qualified trust entitled to preferential tax treatment under section 501(a). See generally Ronald R. Pawlak, P.C. v. Commissioner, T.C. Memo. 1995-7 (discussing the types of preferential tax treatment under section 501(a)). In addition, the Employee Retirement Income Security

Act of 1974, Pub. L. 93-406, sec. 402(a) (1), 88 Stat. 875, requires that the plan be in writing. See also sec. 1.401-1(a) (2), Income Tax Regs. Congress established the writing requirement so that every employee may, on examining the plan document, determine exactly what his or her rights and obligations are under the plan and who is responsible for operating the plan. See Curtiss-Wright Corp. v. Schoonejongen, 514 U.S. 73, 83 (1995); H. Conf. Rept. 93-1280, at 297 (1974), 1974-3 C.B. 415, 458. With these basic principles in mind, we turn to analyzing respondent's determination as to the ESOP's qualification under section 401(a). We do not specifically discuss the qualification of the ESOT under section 501(a) because the exemption of the ESOT under section 501(a) follows from the qualification of the ESOP under section 401(a). See Ronald R. Pawlak, P.C. v. Commissioner, supra. Disqualifying Reason

1: ESOP Not Properly Amended

The Small Business Job Protection Act of 1996, Pub. L. 104-188, 110 Stat. 1755, and the Internal Revenue Service Restructuring and Reform Act of 1998, Pub. L. 105-206, 112 Stat. 685, amended the plan qualification requirements under sections 402(c) (4) (C) (eligible rollover distributions), 414(n) (2) (C) (definition of employee leasing), 414(q) (definition of highly compensated employee), 414(u) (special rules for veterans), and 415(c) (3) (D) (participants' compensation). Respondent determined that the ESOP did not qualify under section 401(a) because it was not timely amended to reflect these laws. Petitioner did not amend the ESOP in accordance with the effective dates set forth in the referenced statutes. All the same, the ESOP may retroactively qualify under section 401(a) if remedial amendments were made during the remedial amendment period described in section 1.401(b)-1, Income Tax Regs.

The National Center for Employee Ownership publishes great material in this area. Professional companies generally cannot establish an ESOP as the stock must be owned by individuals who maintain professional licenses. Small companies do not want to engage in the cost of valuations and administration of an ESOP. The ESOP works well for business transitions of companies with 5 million or more in valuation who do not mind the employee/owner concept.

409A PLANS NON-QUALIFIED DEFERRED COMPENSATION

A PLAN FOR THE CEO

THE PLAN OF THE FORMER CEO OF COCA-COLA-ROBERTA GOIZUEA WHO HAD NEARLY ONE BILLION IN HIS 409A PLAN

"I think some bonuses need to be reduced, I think some bonuses should be cut entirely."

Michael Melbinger J.D. Adjunct Professor of Law, Northwestern University, Partner Winston and Strawn LLP and author of "Executive Compensation" as quoted in the PBS Newshour.

NON-QUALIFIED PLANS

Michael Melbinger, Adjunct Professor of Law at Northwestern University, (whose billing rate exceeds $750.00 per hour) in his book **"Executive Compensation"** Second edition, extensively covers nonqualified plans. The most important part of nonqualified arrangements revolve Code section 409A which was added to the law by the American Jobs Creation Act of 2004. A nonqualified plan that does not abide by 409A becomes immediately taxable subject to a 20% penalty. 409A does not cover qualified plans, incentive stock options under section 422, options granted under section 423, certain stock appreciation rights, section 4039b0 plans, and welfare plans such as VEBA, section 457(b) plans. However, this section does cover initial deferral elections, short term deferrals, employment and change of control and severance plans etc.

There are many other plans that come under this new regulation including nonqualified deferred compensation arrangements, section 83 plans, corporate owned life insurance otherwise known as COLI, Bank owned life insurance otherwise known as BOLI. Non-qualified plans generally produce no significant tax advantage to a small business if the business is a professional corporation. However, if the business is a non-service related business, there may be a small savings in taking advantage of lower marginal corporate rates. In practice most of the non-qualified plans are generally used in large corporations where the executive does not need to pay the tax and the tax burden is shifted to large corporation which absorbs the tax. In addition, many of the Non-profits also establish non-qualified plans as the tax burden to the tax exempt corporation means nothing.

With an immediate tax due and a 205 penalty, knowing the rules that relate to 409A is extremely important.

What is §409A?

§409A was enacted in October 2004 and was generally effective on January 1, 2005. It applies to compensation that workers earn in one year, but that is paid in a future year. This is referred to as nonqualified deferred compensation. This is different from deferred compensation in the form of elective deferrals to qualified plans (such as a 401(k) plan) or to a 403(b) or 457(b) plan.

How does coverage under §409A affect an employee's taxes?

If deferred compensation meets the requirements of §409A, then there is no effect on the employee's taxes. The compensation is taxed in the same manner as it would be taxed if it were not covered by §409A. If the arrangement does not meet the requirements of §409A, the compensation is subject to certain additional taxes, including a 20% additional income tax. §409A has no effect on FICA (Social Security and Medicare) tax.

How does §409A apply to the 10 and 12-month pay election?

At issue is how the 2004 law change applies to people who have compensation deferred from one year to a future year. Under the new law, when teachers and other employees are compensated on a 12-month pay period in lieu of the 9 or 10-month actual work period, they are deferring part of their income from one year to the next. For instance, a teacher who is paid over a 12-month period, running from August of one year through July of the next year, rather than over the August to May school year, a 10-month period, falls under this law.

Does §409A require that an employee be provided an election?

No, §409A does not require that an employee be provided any election regarding how the employee is paid. For example, a school district may provide that all teachers will have their pay spread over 12 months, without providing any election to the teachers. In that case, the rules under §409A would not apply and no additional taxes would be imposed.

What was the effect of Notice 2008-62 for most public school employees?

Released on July 3, 2008, the Treasury Department and IRS issued Interim Guidance with Notice 2008-62. If the criteria in the Notice is met, it is expected that regulations under §§457(f) and 409A would not apply to arrangements of electing 12-months over 10-months of pay.

What if the criteria in Notice 2008-62 are not met?

On August 7, 2007, the IRS established assistance through Frequently Asked Questions on §409A and Deferred Compensation which provides guidance on how to establish the deferred election within the provisions of §409A.

Definition of Nonqualified Deferred Compensation Plan-Final regulations

A. Excluded plans

The final regulations exclude the types of plans described in section 409A(d)(1) from the definition of a nonqualified deferred compensation plan, as well as certain other arrangements that were also set forth in the proposed regulations. Accordingly, the final regulations generally provide that a nonqualified deferred compensation plan for purposes of section 409A does not include a qualified plan, a *bona fide* sick leave or vacation plan, a disability plan, a death benefit plan, or certain medical expense reimbursement arrangements.

The final regulations clarify that the exemption from coverage under section 409A for certain welfare plans does not apply to medical expense reimbursements that constitute taxable income to the service provider. The coverage exemption applies only to arrangements that provide benefits that are excludable from gross income under section 105 or section 106.

Several commentators requested clarification of when a leave program will be treated as a *bona fide* sick leave or vacation leave plan for purposes of section 409A. Another commentator requested a clarification of the definition of a compensatory time plan. Because the definitions of these terms may raise issues and require coordination with the provisions of section 451, section 125, and, with respect to certain taxpayers, section 457, the final regulations do not address these issues.

Notice 2005-1, Q&A-6 provides that, until further guidance, taxpayers whose participation in a nonqualified deferred compensation plan would be subject to section 457(f) may rely on the definitions of *bona fide* vacation leave, sick leave, compensatory time, disability pay, or death benefit plan applicable for purposes of section 457(f) as also being applicable for purposes of section 409A. Until further guidance, such taxpayers may continue to rely on such definitions for purposes of section 409A.

One commentator requested that a qualified employer plan for purposes of the exclusion from section 409A include certain plans covered by section 402(d) (certain plans with a foreign-situs trust treated as qualified plans with respect to the taxation of the participants and beneficiaries) and retirement plans described in section 1022(i) (2) of the Employee Retirement Income Security Act of 1974, as amended (certain Puerto Rican retirement plans). The final regulations adopt this suggestion.

B. Section 457 plans

The final regulations provide that section 409A is not applicable to an eligible deferred compensation plan under section 457(b), but may be applicable to a deferred compensation plan that is subject to section 457(f). Commentators requested clarification of the application of the exception in the proposed regulations from the definition of deferred compensation referred to as the short-term deferral rule (described in section III.C.1 of this preamble) to a section 457(f) plan. As discussed below, a right to deferred compensation generally refers to a legally binding right in one taxable year to compensation that is or may be payable in a subsequent taxable year. For purposes of determining the time of payment, the term "payment" generally refers to an actual or constructive payment of cash or property. However, the final regulations provide that for purposes of the short-term deferral rule, an amount is treated as paid when it is included in income under section 457(f) whether or not an actual or constructive payment occurs. Accordingly, where the income inclusion under section 457(f) stems from the lapse of a substantial risk of forfeiture that is also treated as a substantial risk of forfeiture for purposes of section 409A, the amount included in income will be considered a short-term deferral for purposes of section 409A. However, the right to earnings on amounts that have previously been included under section 457(f) will be deferred compensation for purposes of section 409A unless the right to the earnings independently satisfies the requirements for an exclusion.

C. Arrangements with independent contractors

The final regulations provide that section 409A generally does not apply to an amount deferred under an arrangement between a service provider and an unrelated service recipient if during the service provider's taxable year in which the service provider obtains a legally binding right to the deferred amount the service provider is actively engaged in the trade or business of providing services (other than as an employee or as a director of a corporation), and provides significant services to two or more service recipients to which the service provider is not related and that are not related to one another.

The final regulations retain the safe harbor in the proposed regulations, under which a service provider is deemed to be providing significant services to two or more such service recipients for this purpose if the revenues generated from the services provided to any service recipient or group of related service recipients during such taxable year do not exceed 70 percent of the total revenues generated by the service provider from the trade or business of providing such services. Commentators expressed concern that the safe harbor did not permit independent contractors to know in advance whether the arrangements under which an independent contractor deferred compensation during a taxable year would be subject to section 409A. Commentators requested certain look-back periods, including the ability to use averaging over the previous three to five years, or to satisfy the 70 percent threshold over a certain portion of the previous three to five years. The Treasury Department and the IRS are concerned that the suggested rules would allow service providers to engage in strategic behavior to ensure that activity in certain years would be exempt from section 409A. Accordingly, the final regulations adopt an additional safe harbor that provides that a service provider that has actually met the 70 percent threshold in the three immediately previous years is deemed to meet the 70 percent threshold for the current year, but only if at the time the amount is deferred the service provider does not know or have reason to anticipate that the service provider will fail to meet the threshold in the current year.

In response to comments, the final regulations provide that if an independent contractor qualifies for the safe harbor for exclusion from coverage under section 409A with respect to arrangements with unrelated service recipients, an arrangement between the independent contractor and a service recipient related to the independent contractor will not be subject to section 409A if the arrangement, and the practices under the arrangement, are *bona fide*, arise in the ordinary course of business, and are substantially the same as the arrangements and practices (such as billing and collection practices) applicable to one or more unrelated service recipients to whom the independent contractor provides substantial services and that produce a majority of the total revenue that the independent contractor earns from the trade or business of providing such services during the year.

The final regulations further clarify that if at the time the legally binding right to the payment arose, the arrangement was not subject to section 409A because the service provider was an independent contractor that was eligible for this exclusion from coverage under section 409A, the amount deferred under the arrangement during that taxable year (and earnings credited to the deferred amount) will not become subject to section 409A in a later year if the service provider becomes an employee, independent contractor, or other type of service provider subject to the rules of section 409A.

Commentators also requested that a service recipient be permitted to rely upon a representation of an independent contractor that the independent contractor meets the exclusion requirements, so that a service recipient will know whether it is subject to the reporting requirements with respect to amounts deferred subject to section 409A. The Treasury Department and the IRS are continuing to study this issue.

STOCK OPTIONS- I.R.C

SECTION 422

The MICROSOFT PLAN

STOCK OPTIONS

Stock options are the darling of high technology, start-ups and fast moving companies. Many millionaires were made in the Seattle area when Microsoft granted stock options as a benefit program for their software developers. Stock options can also become worthless if the stock does not appreciate, or goes down in value during the time the grant of the option to the time of exercising the option.

A stock option gives an employee the right to purchase shares at a fixed price for a certain period of time. For example, a stock is trading at $100.00 a share and you have the right to buy that share for $100.00 for the next 5 years. In year 2, the share goes to $200.00 and you exercise the option making a quick $100.00. Simple. There are two basic types of stock options ISO or incentive stock options and NQSOs or nonqualified stock options. ISO must meet the rules under section 422 and Reg. 1.422-2. The ISO must be nontransferable, exercised within 10 years and have an exercise price not less than the FMV of the stock at the time the ISO was granted to the employee. The employee realizes no income upon the receipt of the grant, and is taxed only upon exercise or disposition of the option. The employer does not receive a deduction upon the grant or exercise of the option. Neither the employer nor employee pays FICA or FUTA taxes when the option is granted. When an employee exercises the option after the holding period, all the gain is capital gain measured by the option price and the sales price. The holding period on an ISO is two years.

If you receive an option to buy stock, you may have income when you receive the option, when you exercise the option, or when you dispose of the option or stock received when you exercise the option. There are two types of stock options: statutory stock options and non-statutory stock options. Generally, options granted under an employee stock purchase plan or an incentive stock option (ISO) plan are considered statutory stock options. Non-statutory stock options are not granted under an employee stock purchase plan or an ISO plan

If you are granted a statutory stock option you generally do not include any amount in your gross income when you are granted or exercise an option. However, you may be subject to Alternative Minimum Tax in the year you exercise an ISO. You have taxable income or deductible loss when you sell the stock you received by exercising the option. You generally treat this amount as a capital gain or loss. However, if you do not meet special holding period requirements, you will have to treat income from the sale as ordinary income.

If you are granted a non-statutory stock option, the amount of income to include and the time to include it depends on whether the fair market value of the option can be readily determined. If an option is actively traded on an established market, the fair market value of the option can be readily determined. Refer to Publication 525 for other circumstances under which the fair market value of an option can be readily determined and the rules for when income is reported for an option with a readily determinable fair market value. Most non-statutory options do not have a readily determinable fair market value. For non-statutory options without a readily determinable fair market value, there is no taxable event when the option is granted but the fair market value of the stock received on exercise, less the amount paid, is included in income when the option is exercised. You have taxable income or deductible loss when you sell the stock you received by exercising the option. You generally treat this amount as a capital gain or loss.

EMPLOYEE STOCK PURCHASE PLAN

THE WAL-MART PLAN

ESPP–SECTION 423

<u>Employee Stock Purchase plans under section 423 allow an employee of a company to purchase stock at a discount and not pay tax until the sale of the stock, provided the company follows prescribed IRS regulations.</u> The Wal-Mart company has adopted this plan for their employees-for those who can take advantage of the plan-+15% return each year assuming the Wal-Mart stock goes nowhere. The problem is most employees are so financially strapped they do not take advantage of the plan.

Proposed regulations. Under §1.423-2(a) (1) of the proposed regulations, an employee stock purchase plan must meet the requirements of paragraphs (i) through (ix) of §1.423-2(a)(2). The terms of the plan, or an offering under the plan, must satisfy the requirements of paragraphs (iii) through (ix) of §1.423-2(a)(2). Consistent with §1.422-2(b)(1), §1.423-2(a)(1) the regulations would provide that the plan and the terms of an offering must be in writing or electronic form, provided that such writing or electronic form is adequate to establish the terms of the plan or offering.

Section 1.423-2(a)(2) of the regulations lists the requirements that must be met for qualification as an employee stock purchase plan and provides cross references to the specific section of these regulations that addresses each requirement.

Under §1.423-2(a)(3) of the regulations, if the terms of an option are inconsistent with the terms of the employee stock purchase plan or an offering under the plan, then the option will not be treated as granted under an employee stock purchase plan. (Section 1.423-2(a)(2) of the existing regulations has been re-numbered as §1.423-2(a)(3).) If an option with terms that are inconsistent with the terms of the plan or an offering under the plan is granted to an employee who is entitled to the grant of an option under the terms of the plan or offering, and the employee is not granted an option under the offering that qualifies as an option granted under an employee stock purchase plan, then the offering will not meet the requirements of §1.423-2(e) of the regulations, which generally requires that options be granted to all employees of any corporation whose employees are granted options under an employee stock purchase plan. As a result, none of the options granted under the offering will be eligible for the special tax treatment of section 421. *Example 1* in §1.423-2(a)(4) illustrates this principle. Section 1.423-2(a)(4) of the regulations contains additional examples to illustrate the principles of §1.423-2(a)(3).

If an option with terms that are inconsistent with the terms of the plan or an offering under the plan is granted to an individual who is not entitled to the grant of an option under the terms of the plan or offering, then the option will not be treated as an option granted under an employee stock purchase plan, and the grant of the option will not disqualify the options granted under the offering. *Examples 2 and 3* in §1.423-2(a)(4) of the regulations illustrate this principle.

If, at the time of grant, an option qualifies as an option granted under an employee stock purchase plan, but the terms of the option are not satisfied, then the option will not be treated as granted under an employee stock purchase plan. However, this failure to comply with the terms of the option will not disqualify the options granted under the plan or offering. *Example 4* in §1.423-2(a)(4) of the regulations illustrates this principle.

Stockholder approval of the employee stock purchase plan. To qualify as an employee stock purchase plan, section 423(b)(2) requires that the plan be approved by the stockholders of the granting corporation within 12 months before or after the date the plan is adopted. The regulations would provide the same basic requirements for stockholder approval as those included in the existing regulations. Consistent with §1.422-2(b)(2), the regulations would provide additional guidance concerning the circumstances under which stockholder approval is required. The regulations, like the existing regulations, would require stockholder approval if there is a change in the aggregate number of shares or in the employees eligible to be granted options under the plan. The standard for determining when stockholder approval is required under these regulations generally is the same as under the existing regulations. These regulations would clarify the requirements for stockholder approval and would provide a more comprehensive list of situations that require new stockholder approval of the plan. In particular, these proposed regulations would clarify that new stockholder approval is required if there is a change in the shares with respect to which options are issued or a change in the granting corporation. For example, assume that S, a wholly owned subsidiary of P, **adopts an employee stock purchase plan under which options for** S stock will be granted to S employees, and the plan is approved by the stockholder of S (in this case, P) within the applicable 24-month period. If S later amends the plan to provide for the grant of options to acquire P stock (rather than S stock), S must obtain approval from the stockholders of S (in this case, P) within 12 months before or after the date of the amendment of the plan because the amendment of the plan to allow the grant of options for P stock is considered the adoption of a new plan. See paragraph (iii) of *Example 1* in §1.423-2(c)(5) of these proposed regulations. This conclusion differs from that in paragraph (iii) of *Example 1* under §1.422-2(b)(6), which concludes that the stockholders of P rather than the stockholders of S must approve the plan as a result of its amendment to provide for the grant of options to acquire P stock. The IRS and the Treasury Department invite comment on this result and are proposing a conforming change to *Example 1*, paragraph (iii) under §1.422-2(b)(6). These regulations also provide guidance regarding the application of the stockholder approval requirements where an employee stock purchase plan is assumed in connection with a corporate transaction. *Example 3* in §1.423-2(c)(5) illustrates this principle.

Maximum aggregate number of shares. Section 1.423-2(c)(3) of the existing regulations provides that an employee stock purchase plan must designate the maximum aggregate number of shares that may be issued under the plan. Consistent with §1.422-2(b)(3)(ii), these regulations would provide that the plan may specify that the maximum aggregate number of shares available for grants under the plan may increase annually by a specified percentage of the authorized, issued, or outstanding shares at the date of the adoption of the plan. Further, a plan providing that the maximum aggregate number of shares issued subject to options under the plan may change based on any other specific circumstances will satisfy the requirements of §1.423-2(c)(3) only if the stockholders approve an immediately determinable maximum number of shares that may be issued under the plan in any event. *Examples 4 and 5* in §1.423-2(c)(5) of the regulations illustrate these principles.

Employees covered by the plan. Section 423(b)(4) permits an employer to exclude from participation one or more of the following categories of employees: Employees who have been employed less than two years; Employees who customarily work 20 hours or less per week; Employees who customarily work not more than five months in any calendar year; and Highly compensated employees (HCEs) within the meaning of section 414(q). Section 1.423-1(e)(1) of the regulations has been updated to reflect the 1986 amendment of section 423(b)(4)(D) to substitute "highly compensated employees (within the meaning of section 414(q))" for "officers, persons whose principal duties consist of supervising the work of other employees, or highly compensated employees." See Public Law 99-514, section 1114(b)(13).

One commentator suggested that the regulations clarify that an employer may exclude from participation a subset of one of the groups set forth in section 423(b)(4). For example, an employer should be permitted to exclude a subset of HCEs, such as officers, from participation in the plan. The commentator further suggested that the regulations clarify that an employer may impose shorter service requirements than those permitted. For example, an employer should be permitted to exclude employees who have been employed less than one year from participation in the plan.

The IRS and the Treasury Department agree that a more inclusive application of the rules of section 423(b)(4) is consistent with the intent of section 423. Accordingly, §1.423-2(e)(2) of the regulations provide that an employee stock purchase plan does not fail to satisfy the coverage provision of section 423(b)(4) merely because the plan excludes employees who have completed a shorter period of service or whose customary employment is for fewer hours per week or fewer months in a calendar year than is specified in subparts (A), (B) and (C) of section 423(b)(4), provided the exclusion is applied in an identical manner to all employees of every corporation whose employees are granted options under the plan. In addition, the regulations would provide that the terms of an employee stock purchase plan may exclude HCEs: (a) with compensation above a certain level, or (b) who are officers or subject to the disclosure requirements of section 16(a) of the Securities Exchange Act of 1934, provided the exclusion is applied in an identical manner to all HCEs of every corporation whose employees are granted options under the plan. *Examples 3, 4, 5, 6, and 7* in §1.423-2(e)(6) of the regulations illustrate these principles. A commentator suggested the regulations permit employers to exclude from plan participation employees who are nonresident aliens and who receive no earned income that constitutes income from sources within the United States. The IRS and the Treasury Department agree that it may be appropriate to exclude foreign employees from plan participation in certain circumstances.

However, unlike section 410(b), section 423 does not provide an exclusion for such nonresident aliens. Accordingly, the IRS and the Treasury Department are constrained by statutory authority from providing a general exclusion from plan participation for employees who are nonresident aliens and who receive no United States source income. Therefore, §1.423-2(e)(3) of these proposed regulations provide that employees who are citizens or residents of a foreign jurisdiction (without regard to whether they are also citizens of the United States or resident aliens (within the meaning of §7701(b)(1)(A))) may be excluded from the coverage of an employee stock purchase plan only if the grant of an option under the plan to a citizen or resident of the foreign jurisdiction is prohibited under the laws of such jurisdiction or if compliance with the laws of the foreign jurisdiction would cause the plan to violate the requirements of section 423. *Example 8* in §1.423-2(e)(6) of the regulations.

Another commentator suggested that the regulations permit employers to exclude collectively bargained employees from plan participation. However, unlike section 410(b), section 423 does not provide an exclusion for collectively bargained employees. Accordingly, the IRS and the Treasury Department are again constrained by statutory authority from providing a general exclusion from plan participation for collectively bargained employees.

One commentator suggested that the regulations be amended to provide that an offering will not lose its tax-favored status due to the inadvertent exclusion of employees from plan participation. Rather, the commentator suggested that the granting corporation be permitted to correct certain errors in plan administration through a corrections program that would permit the excluded employees to participate in past offerings under a plan. Such a corrections program is beyond the scope of these regulations. However, the IRS and the Treasury Department invite comments on whether such a program is appropriate (including the statutory authority for such a program) and suggestions for the types of violations that might be covered and the methods of correction.

Section 1.423-2(e)(4) of these proposed regulations includes language that appears under §1.423-2(e)(1) of the existing regulations. Section 1.423-2(e)(2) of the existing regulations has been re-numbered as §1.423-2(e)(5) of these proposed regulations.

Equal rights and privileges. Section 423(b)(5) requires that, subject to certain exceptions, an employee stock purchase plan, by its terms, provide that all employees granted options under the plan have the same rights and privileges.

Section 1.423-2(f)(3) of these proposed regulations includes language that appears in §1.423-2(f)(1) of the existing regulations. (The examples in §1.423-2(f)(2) of the existing regulations have been relocated to *Examples 1 and 2* of §1.423-2(f)(7) of these proposed regulations. The example in §1.423-2(f)(4) of the existing regulations has been relocated to *Example 3* of §1.423-2(f)(7). Section 1.423-2(f)(4) of the existing regulations is re-numbered under these proposed regulations as §1.423-2(f)(6)).

One commentator suggested that a plan or offering should not fail to satisfy the equal rights and privileges provision of section 423(b)(5) if the provisions of the plan or offering applied to foreign employees are reasonably designed to avoid adverse consequences for such employee under foreign law as a result of plan participation. The IRS and the Treasury Department agree that in certain limited circumstances it may be appropriate for the terms of an employee stock purchase plan to be less favorable with respect to foreign employees than those terms are with respect to employees resident in the United States. Accordingly, §1.423-2(f)(4) of these proposed regulations would provide that a plan or offering will not fail to satisfy the requirements of section 423(b)(5) if, in order to comply with the laws of a foreign jurisdiction, the terms of an option granted under a plan or offering to citizens or residents of such foreign jurisdiction (without regard to whether they are also citizens of the United States or resident aliens (within the meaning of §7701(b)(1)(A))) are less favorable than the terms of options granted under the same plan or offering to employees resident in the United States. *Example 4* in §1.423-2(f)(7) of these proposed regulations illustrates this principle.

A plan or offering will not satisfy the requirements of section 423(b)(5), however, if, in order to comply with the laws of a foreign jurisdiction, the terms of the plan or offering are more favorable with respect to citizens or residents of such foreign jurisdiction than the terms of the plan or offering are with respect to employees resident in the United States.

Another commentator suggested that the regulations addressing the carryover of amounts from one offering to another be clarified. In response to this comment, these proposed regulations would clarify §1.423-2(f)(3) of the existing regulations (which has been re-numbered as §1.423-2(f)(5)). Generally, a plan permitting one or more employees to carry forward amounts that were withheld but not applied toward the purchase of stock under an earlier plan or offering and apply such amounts toward the purchase of additional stock under a subsequent plan or offering will be a violation of the equal rights and privileges requirement under section 423(b)(5). However, the carry forward of amounts withheld but not applied toward the purchase of stock under an earlier plan or offering will not violate the equal rights and privileges requirement of section 423(b)(5) if all other employees participating in the current plan or offering are permitted to make direct payments toward the purchase of shares under a subsequent plan or offering in an amount equal to the excess of: (a) the greatest amount that any employee is allowed to carry forward from an earlier plan or offering over (b) the amount, if any, the employee will carry forward from an earlier plan or offering. *Example 5* in §1.423-2(f)(7) of these proposed regulations illustrates this principle.

Further, a plan will not fail to satisfy the equal rights and privileges requirement of section 423(b)(5) merely because employees are permitted to carry forward amounts representing a fractional share which were withheld but not applied toward the purchase of stock under an earlier plan or offering and apply such amounts toward the purchase of additional stock under a subsequent plan or offering.

Option price. Under section 423(b)(6), the option price must not be less than the lesser of: (a) an amount equal to 85 percent of the fair market value of the stock at the time the option is granted, and (b) an amount not less than 85 percent of the fair market value of the stock at the time the option is exercised. Consistent with §1.422-2(e)(1), §1.423-2(g)(1) of these proposed regulations would provide that the option price may be determined in any reasonable manner, including the valuation methods permitted under §20.2031-2 (Estate Tax Regulations), so long as the option price meets the minimum pricing requirements of section 423(b)(6).

Date of grant. Section 1.421-1(c) provides, that for purposes of §§1.421-2 through 1.424-1, the language "the date of the granting of the option" and "the time such option is granted" and similar phrases refer to the date or time when the granting corporation completes the corporate action constituting an offer of stock for sale to an individual under the terms and conditions of a statutory option. The date of grant for an option granted under an employee stock purchase plan is important for several reasons. First, the favorable tax consequences under section 421 apply to the shares acquired pursuant to the exercise of an option granted under an employee stock purchase plan if the shares are not disposed of within two years from the date of grant of the option or within one year from the date of exercise of the option. Second, the $25,000 limitation under section 423(b)(8) is determined based on the fair market value of the stock measured on the date of grant of the option. The date of grant is also important for purposes of determining the employees eligible to participate in the plan and, in certain cases, determining the purchase price of stock under the plan.

Section 1.421-1(c) further provides that a corporate action constituting an offer of stock for sale is not considered complete until the date on which the maximum number of shares that can be purchased under the option and the minimum option price are fixed or determinable. Because options under an employee stock purchase plan may be priced at the lesser of an amount equal to 85 percent of the fair market value of the stock at the time the option is granted, and an amount not less than 85 percent of the fair market value of the stock at the time the option is exercised, it is not always possible to determine the minimum option price on the first day of an offering. However, many granting corporations intend for the first day of an offering to be the date of grant.

Accordingly, §1.423-2(h)(2) of these proposed regulations would provide that, for purposes of options granted under an employee stock purchase plan, the principles of §1.421-1(c) shall be applied without regard to the requirement that the minimum option price be fixed or determinable in order for the corporate action constituting an offer of stock to be considered complete. As a result, the first day of an offering could be the date of grant for an option issued under an employee stock purchase plan even though the minimum option price is not fixed or determinable on the first day of the offering. These proposed regulations include an amendment to §1.421-1(c).

One commentator questioned whether it is necessary for a plan to contain a limit on the number of shares that can be purchased by each participant during an offering in order for the date of grant of the option to be the first day of an offering. Section 1.423-2(h)(3) of these proposed regulations would provide that the date of grant will be the first day of an offering if the terms of an employee stock purchase plan or offering designate a maximum number of shares that may be purchased by each participant during the offering. Similarly, the date of grant will be the first day of an offering if the terms of the plan or offering require the application of a formula to establish, on the first day of the offering, the maximum number of shares that may be purchased by each participant during the offering.

However, §1.423-2(h)(3) of these proposed regulations does not require that an employee stock purchase plan or offering designate a maximum number of shares that may be purchased by each participant during the offering or incorporate a formula to establish a maximum number of shares that may be purchased by each participant during the offering. If the maximum number of shares that can be purchased under an option is not fixed or determinable until the date the option is exercised, then the date of exercise will be the date of grant of the option. The $25,000 limit under section 423(b)(8) and the limit on the aggregate number of shares that may be issued under an employee stock purchase plan are not sufficient to establish the maximum number of shares that can be purchased under an option so that the date of grant will be the first day of the offering. *Examples 1, 2, 3 and 4* in §1.423-2(h)(4) of these proposed regulations illustrate these principles.

Section 1.423-2(h) of the existing regulations is re-numbered as §1.423-2(h)(1) of these proposed regulations.

Annual $25,000 limitation. Section 423(b)(8) provides that an employee stock purchase plan must, by its terms, provide that no employee may be permitted to purchase stock under all the employee stock purchase plans of his or her employer corporation and its related corporations at a rate which exceeds $25,000 in fair market value of the stock (determined on the date of grant) for each calendar year in which an option granted to the employee is outstanding and exercisable. Section 1.423-2(i) of these proposed regulations would provide guidance on the operation of the $25,000 limitation that incorporates and clarifies the guidance provided in the existing regulations.

One commentator suggested that the calculation of the amount of stock that may be purchased under an employee stock purchase plan be determined in a manner consistent with the $100,000 limitation for incentive stock options described in §1.422-4. The proposed regulations generally adopt this suggestion and would provide that the $25,000 limit for employee stock purchase plans is, to the extent possible, calculated in a manner consistent with the $100,000 limitation for incentive stock options. The timing of both measures is based on when the option first becomes exercisable and both measures are made based on the fair market value of the stock determined at the date of grant. Section 1.423-2(i) of these proposed regulations emphasizes that an employee may purchase up to $25,000 of stock (based on the fair market value of such stock on the date of grant) in each calendar year during which an option granted to the employee under an employee stock purchase plan is not only outstanding, but also exercisable. *Example 5* in §1.423-2(i)(5) of these proposed regulations illustrates this principle.

For clarification, *Example 1* in §1.423-2(i)(4) of the existing regulations has been separated into *Example 1* and *Example 4* in §1.423-2(i)(5) of these proposed regulations.

Special rule where option price is between 85 percent and 100 percent of the value of the stock

Section 423(c) provides a special rule for calculating the timing and amount of compensation income that must be recognized when the option price for a share is between 85 and 100 percent of the value of the share on the date of grant. Generally, the income recognized is the lesser of: (a) the excess of the fair market value of the share on the date of grant over the option price, and (b) the excess of the fair market value of the share at the time of disposition (or death) over the option price. The flush language of section 423(c) provides that if the exercise price is not known on the date of grant, the exercise price shall be determined as if the option were exercised on the date of grant.

One commentator suggested that it is unclear how this special rule and the flush language of section 423(c) apply when the option price is determined based on some percentage of the value of a share on the last day of an offering. *Example 3* of §1.423-2(k)(3) of the existing regulations specifically addresses this issue and has been retained in §1.423-2(k)(3) of these proposed regulations. *Example 4* has been added under §1.423-2(k)(3) to illustrate the tax consequences under an employee stock purchase plan that uses a look-back feature to determine the exercise price of the option.

SECTION 79 PLANS

GROUP TERM LIFE-NOW A RETIREMENT PLAN?

A PLAN FOR THE LIFE INSURANCE INDUSTRY.

SECTION 79 PLANS

Total Amount of Coverage

IRC section 79 provides an exclusion for the first $50,000 of group-term life insurance coverage provided under a policy carried directly or indirectly by an employer. There are no tax consequences if the total amount of such policies does not exceed $50,000. The imputed cost of coverage in excess of $50,000 must be included in income, using the IRS Premium Table, and are subject to social security and Medicare taxes. Today many of the pachydermatous insurance salesmen have been promoting section 79 as a retirement plan.

Carried Directly or Indirectly by the Employer

A taxable fringe benefit arises if coverage exceeds $50,000 and the policy is considered carried directly or indirectly by the employer. A policy is considered carried directly or indirectly by the employer if:

1. The employer pays any cost of the life insurance, or
2. The employer arranges for the premium payments and the premiums paid by at least one employee subsidize those paid by at least one other employee (the "straddle" rule).

The determination of whether the premium charges straddle the costs is based on the IRS Premium Table rates, not the actual cost. You can view the Premium Table in the group-term life insurance discussion in Publication B. Because the employer is affecting the premium cost through its subsidizing and/or redistributing role, there is a benefit to employees. This benefit is taxable even if the employees are paying the full cost they are charged. You must calculate the taxable portion of the premiums for coverage that exceeds $50,000.

Not Carried Directly or Indirectly by the Employer

A policy that is not considered carried directly or indirectly by the employer has no tax consequences to the employee. Because the employees are paying the cost and the employer is not redistributing the cost of the premiums through an insurance system, the employer has no reporting requirements.

Example 1 - All employees for Employer X are in the 40 to 44 year age group. According to the IRS Premium Table, the cost per thousand is .10. The employer pays the full cost of the insurance. If at least one employee is charged more than .10 per thousand of coverage, and at least one is charged less than .10, the coverage is considered carried by the employer. Therefore, each employee is subject to social security and Medicare tax on the cost of coverage over $50,000.

Example 2 - The facts are the same as Example 1, except all employees are charged the same rate, which is set by the third-party insurer. The employer pays nothing toward the cost. Therefore there is no taxable income to the employees. It does not matter what the rate is, as the employer does not subsidize the cost or redistribute it between employees.

Coverage Provided by More Than One Insurer

Generally, if there is more than one policy from the same insurer providing coverage to employees, a combined test is used to determine whether it is carried directly or indirectly by the employer. However, the Regulations provide exceptions that allow the policies to be tested separately if the costs and coverage can be clearly allocated between the two policies. See Regulation 1.79 for more information. If coverage is provided by more than one insurer, each policy must be tested separately to determine whether it is carried directly or indirectly by the employer. The cost of employer-provided group-term life insurance on the life of an employee's spouse or dependent, paid by the employer, is not taxable to the employee if the face amount of the coverage does not exceed $2,000. This coverage is excluded as a *de minimis* fringe benefit. Whether a benefit provided is considered *de minimis* depends on all the facts and circumstances. In some cases, an amount greater than $2,000 of coverage could be considered a *de minimis* benefit. See Notice 89-110 for more information. If part of the coverage for a spouse or dependents is taxable, the same Premium Table is used as for the employee. The entire amount is taxable, not just the amount that exceeds $2,000.

Example 3 - A 47-year old employee receives $40,000 of coverage per year under a policy carried directly or indirectly by her employer. She is also entitled to $100,000 of optional insurance at her own expense. This amount is also considered carried by the employer. The cost of $10,000 of this amount is excludable; the cost of the remaining $90,000 is included in income. If the optional policy were not considered carried by the employer, none of the $100,000 coverage would be included in income.

Today, most insurance companies no longer offer Section 79 plans due to IRS audits and potential litigation. The industry has come out with a "Restrictive Property Trust" which purportedly mimics a Section 79 plan-however there is no case law supporting this theory as of today.

SECTION 83 PLANS

CALL THE ATTORNEY FOR THIS PLAN

SECTION 83 PLANS

Section 83 is a favorable election you can make for your client and you do not want to miss out on this opportunity.

Section 83(b) of the Internal Revenue Code permits the taxpayer to change the tax treatment of their Restricted Stock Awards. Employees choosing to make the Special Tax 83(b) election are electing to include the fair market value of the stock at the time of the grant minus the amount paid for the shares (if any) as part of their income (without regard to the restrictions). They will be subject to required tax withholding at the time the Restricted Stock Award is received. In addition to the immediate income inclusion, a Special Tax 83(b) election will cause the stock's holding period to begin immediately after the award is granted.

Also with a Special Tax 83(b) election, employees will not be subject to income tax when the shares vest (regardless of the fair market value at the time of vesting), and they will not be subject to further tax until the shares are sold. Subsequent gains or losses of the stock would be capital gains or losses (assuming the stock is held as a capital asset). However, if an employee were to leave the company prior to vesting, he would not be entitled to any refund of taxes previously paid or a tax loss with respect to the stock forfeited.

Under § 83(a), if, in connection with the performance of services, property is transferred to any person other than the person for whom such services are performed, then the excess of the fair market value of the property (determined without regard to any restriction other than a restriction which by its terms will never lapse) as of the first day that the transferee's rights in the property are transferable or are not subject to a substantial risk of forfeiture, whichever occurs earlier, over the amount (if any) paid for the property is included in the service provider's gross income for the taxable year which includes that day.

Section 83(b) and §1.83-2(a) of the Income Tax Regulations permit the service provider to elect to include in gross income the excess (if any) of the fair market value of the property at the time of transfer (determined without regard to any lapse restriction, as defined in § 1.83-3(i)) over the amount (if any) paid for the property, as compensation for services. If this election is made, the substantial vesting rules of § 83(a) and the regulations thereunder do not apply to the property, and, assuming there is no compensatory cancellation of a non-lapse restriction, any subsequent appreciation in the value of the property is not taxable as compensation to the service provider.

Under § 83(b)(2), an election made under § 83(b) must be made in accordance with the regulations thereunder and must be filed with the Internal Revenue Service no later than 30 days after the date that the property is transferred to the service provider.

Section 83(b) (2) and § 1.83-2(f) provide that an election under § 83(b) may not be revoked without the consent of the Commissioner. The regulations also provide that such consent will only be granted where the person filing the election is under a mistake of fact as to the underlying transaction and must be requested within 60 days of the date on which the mistake of fact first became known to the person who made the election. Neither a mistake as to the value (or decline in the value) of the property for which the election was made nor the failure of anyone to perform an act that was contemplated at the time of transfer of the property constitute a mistake of fact for this purpose.

The mistake of fact exception in § 1.83-2(f) is narrow in its scope. A mistake of fact is an unconscious ignorance of a fact that is material to the transaction. See 27A AmJur 2d, Equity § 10. By contrast, a mistake of law occurs where a person is ignorant of, or comes to an erroneous conclusion as to, the legal effect of the facts. See 27A AmJur 2d, Equity § 15.

The failure of a service provider to understand the substantial risk of forfeiture associated with the transferred property is not a mistake of fact under § 1.83-2(f).

The failure of a service provider to understand the tax consequences of making an election under § 83(b) is not a mistake of fact under § 1.83-2(f).

The Internal Revenue Service has recognized the principle that an election made under the Code or regulations may be revoked on or before the due date for making the election. See Rev. Rul. 56-67, 1956-1 C.B. 437, dist. by Rev. Rul. 76-393, 1976-2 C.B. 255. See also Rev. Rul. 78-295, 1978-2 C.B. 165. Accordingly, a request for consent to revoke a § 83(b) election will generally be granted if the request is filed on or before the due date for making that § 83(b) election.

.09 If consent to revoke an election under § 83(b) is granted, it will be effective as of the date of the § 83(b) election.

PROCEDURE

A request for consent to revoke an election made under § 83(b) must be made under the procedures for requesting a letter ruling. See Rev. Proc. 2006-1, 2006-1 I.R.B. 1, or its successor.

In addition to a complete description of the facts and the other information and documents required under section 7.01 of Rev. Proc. 2006-1, or its successor, the request must contain: the date the § 83(b) election was made; a copy of the § 83(b) election; a description of the mistake of fact as to the underlying transaction; and the date on which the mistake of fact first became known to the person making the election.

If the request to revoke an election under § 83(b) is being made on or before the due date for making the election, this fact must be included in the request for revocation.

EXAMPLES

Example 1. On July 10, 2006, in connection with the performance of services, Company M transfers 100 shares of substantially non-vested Company M stock to A, its employee. The restricted stock agreement provides that the stock will revert to Company M if A's employment is terminated for any reason before July 10, 2010. A pays $50X for the shares, which have an aggregate fair market value of $100X on July 10, 2006. On that same day, A files a valid election under § 83(b). On July 28, 2006, A learns that the forfeiture provision in the stock agreement means A will forfeit the stock even if Company M terminates A's employment without cause. In addition, A realizes that A misunderstood the tax results of filing the election. On August 16, 2006, A files a request for a ruling from the Internal Revenue Service for consent to revoke A's § 83(b) election. The request cites A's misunderstanding of the forfeiture provision and A's misunderstanding of the tax results as the basis for the ruling request. While A's request for a ruling is made within 60 days of the date A learns the full meaning of the forfeiture provision and when A realizes the tax results of filing the election, neither reason for which A requests the revocation is a "mistake of fact as to the underlying transaction." The underlying transaction is A's receipt of the restricted stock transferred pursuant to the employment agreement. A's misunderstanding of the forfeiture provision is not a mistake of fact as to the underlying transaction. Rather, it is a failure to understand the substantial risk of forfeiture set forth in the restricted stock agreement. Additionally, A's misunderstanding of the tax results of the election is a mistake of law and not a mistake of fact. Accordingly, consent to revoke the § 83(b) election will not be granted.

Example 2. The facts are the same as in *Example 1*, except that the request for a ruling is filed on August 4, 2006. Because the request is filed within the 30-day period during which the § 83(b) election could be made, consent to revoke the § 83(b) election will be granted, regardless of the reason for which it is filed.

Example 3. On August 31, 2006, B begins employment with Company O under an employment contract that provides that B will receive Company O Class A common stock. On September 1, 2006, Company O transfers 50X shares of substantially non-vested Company O Class B common stock to B in accordance with the employment contract. B pays $100X for the shares, which have an aggregate fair market value of $100X on that date. On September 15, 2006, B makes a valid election under § 83(b) with respect to the stock transfer. On September 29, 2006, B discovers that Company O has two classes of common stock and that Company O transferred Class B common stock to B instead of Class A common stock. On November 1, 2006, B files a request for a ruling from the Internal Revenue Service to revoke the election. B's request for consent to revoke the § 83(b) election is timely, and it is based on a mistake of fact as to the underlying transaction because B did not receive the property B expected to receive in the transfer. Based on these facts, and absent any other facts to the contrary, consent to revoke the § 83(b) election will be granted because the stock B received was transferred under a mistake of fact as to the underlying transaction.

Example 4. The facts are the same as in *Example 3*, except that B files the request for the ruling on December 15, 2006. Because the request for revocation was not requested within 60 days of the date B discovered the mistake of fact as to the underlying transaction, B's request will not be granted.

.DAVIS BACON PLANS

a/k/a Prevailing Wage Plan FOR GOVERNMENT CONTRACTORS

DAVIS BACON PLANS

What are the Davis-Bacon and Related Acts?

The Davis Bacon Act, as amended, requires that each contract over $2,000 to which the United States or the District of Columbia is a party for the construction, alteration, or repair of public buildings or public works shall contain a clause setting forth the minimum wages to be paid to various classes of laborers and mechanics employed under the contract. Under the provisions of the Act, contractors or their subcontractors are to pay workers employed directly upon the site of the work no less than the locally prevailing wages and fringe benefits paid on projects of a similar character. The Davis-Bacon Act directs the Secretary of Labor to determine such local prevailing wage rates.

In addition to the Davis-Bacon Act itself, Congress has added prevailing wage provisions to approximately 60 statutes which assist construction projects through grants, loans, loan guarantees, and insurance. These "related Acts" involve construction in such areas as transportation, housing, air and water pollution reduction, and health. If a construction project is funded or assisted under more than one Federal statute, the Davis-Bacon prevailing wage provisions may apply to the project if any of the applicable statutes requires payment of Davis-Bacon wage rates.

The geographic scope of the Davis-Bacon Act is limited, by its terms, to the 50 States and the District of Columbia. By the same token, the scope of each of the related Acts is determined by the terms of the particular statute under which the Federal assistance is provided. For example, Davis-Bacon prevailing wage provisions would apply to a construction contract located in Guam or the Virgin Islands funded under the Housing and Community Development Act of 1974, even though the Davis-Bacon Act itself does not apply to Federal construction contracts to be performed outside the 50 States and the District of Columbia. Under the Davis-Bacon and Related Acts (DBRA), covered contractors must maintain payrolls and basic records and submit certified weekly payrolls. Although use of Form WH-347 is optional, the form will satisfy the requirements of Regulations, Parts 3 and 5 (29 CFR, Subtitle A), as to payrolls submitted in connection with contracts subject to the DBRA. Records to be maintained include:

- Name, address, and social security number of each employee;
- Each employee's work classification(s);
- Hourly rate(s) of pay (including rates of contributions or costs anticipated for bona fide fringe benefits or cash equivalents thereof);
- Daily and weekly numbers of hours worked;
- Deductions made; and
- Actual wages paid.

Davis-Bacon Labor Standards Provisions

Pursuant to the American Recovery and Reinvestment Act, Division B, section 1601, Davis-Bacon labor standards must be applied to projects financed with the proceeds of the following tax-favored bonds:

1. Any new clean renewable energy bond (as defined in section 54C of the Internal Revenue Code of 1986) issued after February 17, 2009,
2. Any qualified energy conservation bond (as defined in section 54D of the Internal Revenue Code of 1986) issued after February 17, 2009,
3. Any qualified zone academy bond (as defined in section 54E of the Internal Revenue Code of 1986) issued after February 17, 2009,
4. Any qualified school construction bond (as defined in section 54F of the Internal Revenue Code of 1986), and

5. Any recovery zone economic development bond (as defined in section 1400U–2 of the Internal Revenue Code of 1986).

The Department of Labor, Wage and Hour Division has issued guidance in All agency memorandum number 208, concerning applicability of Davis-Bacon labor standards to construction financed with the proceeds of these tax-favored bonds under ARRA Division B, section 1601.

The Davis-Bacon contract clauses stated in 29 CFR 5.5(a) (1) through (10) must be incorporated into covered contracts for construction, alteration, or repair work. Additional information regarding the application of Davis-Bacon labor standards is available at the U.S. Department of Labor Wage and Hour Division website.

Davis-Bacon Poster (Government Construction)

Every employer performing work covered by the labor standards of The Davis-Bacon and Related Acts shall post a notice (including any applicable wage determination) at the site of the work in a prominent and accessible place where it may be easily seen by employees.

TAFT HARTLEY PLANS-

THE UNION PLAN

.IRS Guidance on Taft Hartley

The Labor Management Relations Act (LMRA), commonly known as the Taft-Hartley Act, was enacted in 1947 to regulate relations between unions and employers. Section 302(c)(5) of Taft-Hartley (section 186(c)(5) of the National Labor Relations Act as amended by the LMRA) governs the establishment of multiemployer benefit plans including retirement plans that are qualified under the Internal Revenue Code.

In general, Taft-Hartley strictly prohibits employers from making payments to union representatives. However, section 302(c)(5)(NLRA section 186(c)(5)) provides an exception to this rule for trust funds established by the union for the exclusive benefit of the employer's employees and their beneficiaries, if certain conditions are met. These include requirements that the payments be held in trust; that the detailed basis on which payments are to be made be specified in a written agreement with the employer; that employees and employers be equally represented in the administration of the trust; and that payments intended to be used for providing pensions be paid to a separate trust which provides that those funds cannot be used for any other purpose.

1. Typically, the joint employer-union board of trustees described in Taft-Hartley is the group that establishes a multiemployer trust, adopts the multiemployer plan associated with the trust, and sets the terms of the plan including the benefits to be provided.

2. The trust document may contain key provisions that govern the relationship of participating employers and the union to the plan. These frequently include a statement that the board of trustees may reject a collective bargaining agreement providing for the signatory employer's participation in the plan if the agreement contradicts plan provisions. This is important because any document augmenting the terms of the basic plan document (such as a collective bargaining agreement, side agreement with a participating employer, or reciprocity agreement with another plan) must not conflict with the terms of the plan document or else the plan may not satisfy the definite written program or definitely determinable benefit requirements of Regs. section 1.401-1. Another key provision in the trust document is a requirement that employers allow the trustees access to records relevant to administering the trust and maintaining the qualified status of the plan.

3. In some cases, adherence to the trust agreement by a signatory employer is prescribed by standard language that the trustees require be added to any collective bargaining agreement providing for participation in the plan. In other cases, such adherence is effected through a participation agreement between the employer and the union which must be approved by the board of trustees. In most cases, the employer agrees to be bound by the trust agreement, by actions of the employer trustees, and by actions of the board of trustees pursuant to the trust agreement.

Collective Bargaining Agreements

1. The collective bargaining agreement that a union enters into with an employer satisfies the Taft-Hartley requirement that there be a written agreement that specifies the detailed basis on which the payments are to be made to the trust. In addition to labor matters unrelated to retirement benefits, a collective bargaining agreement establishes the obligation of the signatory employer to contribute to the plan on behalf of its employees; identifies the class of employees covered by the plan ("collectively bargained employees"); and in a multiemployer plan sets the rate of contribution.

2. Collective bargaining agreements are usually entered into for a finite period, generally from one to five years. Termination of an agreement without renewal or replacement is generally considered a withdrawal by the employer from the plan with regard to work performed after the termination. If the parties bargain to renew or replace a terminating agreement, the old agreement (including the obligation to contribute to the plan) remains in effect until the parties have bargained to an impasse. In some cases, a collective bargaining agreement or the trust document may require an employer to continue participation in the plan until the employer has affirmatively notified the board of trustees of its intention to withdraw.

3. Collective bargaining agreements are negotiated between a local, regional, or national union and individual employers or an association bargaining for a group of employers. Contributing employers may each negotiate individual bargaining agreements, or they may sign a single agreement as a group. Collective bargaining agreements serve essentially the same purpose as corporate board resolutions adopting plans.

4. The contribution rate specified in the collective bargaining agreement may be for a sum per hour (or unit of time or work) per employee that is deposited directly in the multiemployer retirement trust. Alternatively, the required contribution for the retirement plan, along with contributions or payments for other purposes discussed in the collective bargaining agreement may be paid to a conduit trust, the funds of which are then allocated for the several different purposes including payment to the retirement trust. Other purposes may include health, apprenticeship, severance, or vacation funds.

Participation and Reciprocity Agreements

1. Multiemployer retirement plans may cover employees who are not collectively bargained employees, such as employees of the union, of the retirement fund and affiliated funds, or of the signatory employers. Participation by noncollectively bargained employees must be provided for in the plan document. The plan terms enabling coverage of noncollectively bargained employees must require the employer of such employees to enter into a "participation agreement," or "side agreement," with the trustees of the plan.

2. Multiemployer plans may enter into reciprocity agreements with other multiemployer plans, usually ones in different locations that cover similar type jobs and with affiliated

chapters of the home fund's union. The terms of the plan must permit such agreements. These agreements allow participants to aggregate their service under several plans to qualify for a benefit from a plan, or spell out how much of the benefit is paid by each multiemployer plan. Reciprocity agreements are discussed at IRM 4.72.14.3.5.9.

Administrative Features of Multiemployer Plans

1. Multiemployer plans can vary greatly in size. Smaller plans are known as "locals" because they cover collectively bargained employees of a local chapter of a union. There are also "regional" and "national" plans, and even "international" plans that cover both U.S. residents and workers in other countries where the union has a presence, such as Canada. There can be significant administrative differences between locals and larger multiemployer plans.

2. Like other plans, multiemployer plans can be either defined benefit or defined contribution plans. Once rare, multiemployer 401(k) plans are being established at an increasing rate. Only defined benefit plans are covered by Title IV of ERISA and the Pension Benefit Guaranty Corporation's guarantee program. The PBGC maintains a separate trust fund for multiemployer plans, funded under a different premium scale than the single-employer trust fund. Sponsors of plans that cover any employees that are collectively bargained must use Form 5303 to apply for determination letters.

3. A multiemployer plan files only one annual information return, Form 5500, not one for each employer. The Form 5500 instructions contain more detailed information on multiemployer plan reporting requirements.

4. In examining multiemployer plans, an agent will encounter an administrative structure that differs in many ways from its counterpart in single-employer plans. A multiemployer plan differs from a single-employer plan in that it is adopted and administered by a joint union/employer board of trustees, pursuant to Taft-Hartley, to provide benefits or contributions negotiated under a collective bargaining agreement between one or more unions and at least two employers. Under labor law, benefits are a mandatory subject of collective bargaining.

5. Trustees are typically union officials and officers of the employers who meet to hear reports, discuss policies, and vote on matters requiring formal board action. The minutes

of these meetings are an excellent source of information on service crediting practices, benefit payments, partial termination events, employer or participant suits, and other matters that may relate to a plan's qualification. Section 3(16) of Title I of ERISA specifies that the trustees are the plan sponsors and that, unless the plan document designates another, the trustees also serve as the plan administrator. Administrative duties may be performed by a joint labor-management committee or by a professional plan administrator (often called a "fund manager"). In larger plans, the board may empower committees of one or more trustees to make certain binding decisions or to oversee various ongoing activities. Examples include a retirement committee empowered to act on retirement applications, or an investment committee formed to monitor the performance of trust assets and make buy/sell decisions in accordance with the full board's general investment policy.

6. Many multiemployer plans grant past service credit to employees for service with the employer in order to encourage an employer who is not yet contributing to the plan to join. A multiemployer plan may grant past service for work in similar jobs before the plan began, or participants may claim prior service for an employer who has since gone out of business. To help verify the claim, multiemployer plans may obtain participants' permission to check their social security records as additional proof of this service.

7. In single-employer plans, employee payroll data may feed automatically into the plan's participant database; in contrast, administrators of multiemployer plans must solicit that data from the employers. Due to multiple contributing employers, the unique portability of service, and the adversarial relationship between the employers and the union and among competing employers, multiemployer plan administrators must take extra care that the contributing employers provide the proper participant information. Multiemployer plans may use the monthly billings to solicit information from each employer; along with remitting the contribution owed, the employer provides the name, social security number, hours worked, date of birth, and other information for each employee for that period. In most multiemployer plans, service credit may not be determined until an employee actually applies for the benefit.

8. Since obtaining correct information is essential for maintaining qualified status, multiemployer plans may also use field auditors to check on the accuracy of the

employer's information. Field auditors visit the contributing employers to compare the remittance reports with their payroll and other personnel records, and with union dues and other records maintained by the union or affiliated health and welfare plans. Another verification method used by plans is to send monthly reports of credited service to the participants themselves, for their concurrence.

VEBA- SECTION 501(c)-9

WELFARE BENEFITS-HEALTH, DEATH, DIABILITY

VEBA

History of VEBA section 501(c) (9)

The History of Section 501(c)(9) is sketchy at best. This provision was first enacted as Section 103(16) of the Revenue Act of 1928, ch. 852, 45 Stat. 791. The Ways and Means Committee Report simply states that the exemption was granted because "[v]oluntary employees' beneficiary associations providing for the payment of life, sick, accident or other benefits to members and their dependents are common to-day and it appears desirable to provide specifically for their exemption from the ordinary corporation tax...." H.R.Rep. No. 2, 70th Cong., 1st Sess. at 17, 1939-1 C.B. (Part 2) 384, 395. See also S.Rep. No. 960, 70th Cong., 1st Sess. at 25, 1939-1 C.B. (Part 2) 409, 426 (same as Ways and Means Committee Report except for clerical changes). The legislative history accompanying each re-enactment of the exemption is equally unhelpful as concerns the issue before us and provides no insight as to its raison d'etre. That the exemption elicited no more than cursory legislative explanation is not surprising; the accounts of the initial enactment and re-enactment of most of today's exemptions are equally silent. See Bittker & Rahdert, The Exemption of Nonprofit Organizations from Federal Income Taxation, 85 Yale L.J. 299, 301 (1976). A similar lack of commentary on the subject has led two commentators to speculate that this scholarly silence "may have reflected a conviction that the wisdom of tax exemption was self-evident, that the basic policy was politically invulnerable to change, or that taxation in this area would bring in little revenue." Id.

But the absence of historical notes on the exemption's meaning and scope does not end the matter. The Section 501(c)(9) exemption does not exist in a vacuum; rather it co-exists with a number of other quite diverse organizations that Congress saw fit to exempt from the federal income tax. See 26 U.S.C. Sec. 501(c). " 'The true meaning of a single section of a statute in a setting as complex as that of the revenue acts, however precise its language, cannot be ascertained if it be considered apart from related sections, or if the mind be isolated from the history of the income tax legislation of which it is an integral part.' "Commissioner v. Engle, 464 U.S. 206, 223, 104 S.Ct. 597, 607, 78 L.Ed.2d 420 quoting Helvering v. Morgan's, Inc., 293 U.S. 121, 126, 55 S.Ct. 60, 62, 79 L.Ed. 232.

Of particular note is an exemption that Congress created on the heels of that for VEBAs. Section 103(17) of the Revenue Act of 1928, ch. 852, 45 Stat. 791, "introduce[d] into the law a new kind of exempt organization, namely, teachers' retirement fund associations of a purely local character." H.R.Conf.Rep. No. 1882, 70th Cong., 1st Sess. at 13-14, 1939-1 C.B. (Part 2) 444, 447 (emphasis added). See 26 U.S.C. Sec. 501(c)(11).5 As with the enactment of the exemption for VEBAs, we have not been able to locate any reference to the purpose of the exemption. Still, it is significant that Congress chose to define by geographic limitation those teacher retirement funds which are eligible for exempt status while at the same time choosing not so to limit VEBAs.

VEBA is an acronym for "voluntary employees' beneficiary association." They are trusts that are exempt from tax under the provisions of IRC section 501(c) (9). A VEBA is a "welfare benefit fund" to which sections 419 and 419A will apply if it is part of a plan of an employer through which the employer provides welfare benefits to employees and their beneficiaries. While welfare benefit funds can also be taxable trusts, most welfare benefit funds apply for exempt status as VEBAs in order to reduce or eliminate income taxes at the trust level. VEBA's file Form 990, whereas taxable trusts file Form 1041.

A "welfare benefit" is an employee benefit other than those to which IRC sections 83(h), 404, and 404A apply. The most common types of welfare benefits are medical, dental, disability, severance and life insurance benefits. It is important to remember that an examination of an employer's deduction for its contribution to a welfare benefit fund is not an examination of the trust itself. The actual examination of a VEBA trust itself must be handled by an agent from the Tax Exempt and Government Entities division.

There are many closely-held businesses claiming deductions for contributions to welfare benefit funds that claim to be exempted from the deduction limitations of sections 419 and 419A because they meet the requirements of sections 419A(f)(5) (for separate funds under collective bargaining agreements) or 419A(f)(6) (for 10-or-more employer plans). In 1995, the Service issued Notice 95-34 warning taxpayers about potential problems with promoter claims regarding 10-or-more employer plans. In 2000, the Service issued Notice 2000-15 classifying such arrangements as abusive corporate tax shelters. Treasury issued Proposed Regulations covering 10-or-more employer plans on July 11, 2002. The most recent Tax Court case involving such plans, Neonatology Associates, P.A., et al., v. Commissioner, 115 T.C 43 (2000) aff'd 299 F. 3d 221 (3rd Cir. 2002), found that the majority of the contributions to one such plan were actually constructive dividends and thus nondeductible to the corporation and currently includible in the shareholder's income. The Court upheld the Service's imposition of penalties on both the corporate and individual entities. Since promoters of these arrangements tend to promise business owners current deductions for benefits to be received in the future, we expect that the popularity of these products will increase if Congress enacts tax legislation prospectively reducing the individual federal income tax rates. For more information on the types of plans being marketed, you can go to any Internet search engine and search under the terms: "welfare benefit funds," "VEBA," "Section 419A (f) (6)" or "Section 419A (f) (5)."

Technicalities

In general, sections 419 and 419A limit an employer's deduction for contributions to a welfare benefit fund to the amount of the benefits actually paid during the year by the fund (determined using the cash-basis method of accounting) plus a limited allowance for reserves for incurred but unpaid claims and post-retirement medical and life insurance benefits. Section 419A(c)(1) allows a limited reserve for incurred but unpaid claims for disability, medical, SUB or severance pay and life insurance benefits.

If the fund qualifies as a separate fund under a collective bargaining agreement, in general, section 419A (f) (5) provides that there is no "account limit" for such reserves. Section 419A (f) (6) provides, in general, that the deduction limitations under sections 419 and 419A do not apply if the fund qualifies as a 10-or-more employer plan. In order to qualify, the plan must not maintain "experience-rating arrangements" with respect to individual employers, nor can any employer normally contribute more than 10% of the total contributions made by all employers.

Sections 419 and 419A are not applicable if the benefits provided by the plan are determined to be deferred compensation. In these situations IRC section 404 controls. In general, section 404(a) (5) provides that an employer's deduction takes place in the year in which the amount attributable to the contribution is includible in the employees' gross income. However, if more than one employee participates in the plan, an employer can only take a deduction if separate accounts are maintained for each employee.

In all situations, sections 419 and 419A comes into play only if the contributions to the fund are otherwise deductible under the Code. For example, if the contribution was determined to be a constructive dividend, and thus not otherwise deductible, then sections 419 and 419A would not be applicable.

In practice 419 plans are routinely disqualified by the IRS in a cat and mouse game where the rules are confusing and never followed at least according to our friends at the IRS. The Tax Court has often stated, "The IRS determination is presumed to be correct and the burden of proof is on the taxpayer".

In the case, Mark Curcio and Barbara Curcio, v. Commissioner of Internal Revenue, T.C. Memo. 2010-115 (U.S. Tax Court 2010), Ira B. Stechel and John T. Morin, for petitioners.

The Court stated: "Section 419(a) provides that an employer's contributions to a welfare benefit fund are deductible, but only if they are otherwise deductible under chapter 1 of the Code. The deductibility of an employer's contributions to a welfare benefit fund is further limited by section 419(b) to the fund's qualified cost for the taxable year. Section 419A(f)(6) provides that contributions paid by an employer to a multiple-employer welfare benefit fund are not subject to the deduction limitation of section 419(b). Petitioners argue that (1) contributions to Benistar Plan are ordinary and necessary business expenses deductible under section 162(a) (which is in chapter 1 of the Code) and (2) Benistar Plan is a multiple-employer welfare benefit plan under section 419A(f)(6), so that the deduction limits of section 419(b) are not applicable. We first consider whether the contributions made by the participating companies are ordinary and necessary business expenses deductible under section 162(a). We conclude that the contributions are not ordinary and necessary business expenses deductible under section 162(a). Our decision turns on our factual findings regarding the mechanics of Benistar Plan and our conclusion that petitioners had the right to receive the value reflected in the underlying insurance policies purchased by Benistar Plan. Petitioners used Benistar Plan to funnel pretax business profits into cash-laden life insurance policies over which they retained effective control. As a result, contributions to Benistar Plan are more properly viewed as constructive dividends to petitioners and are not ordinary and necessary business expenses under section 162(a).

We acknowledge that the evidence at trial and the arguments in the briefs in large part deal with Carpenter's attempts to fashion the Benistar Plan to qualify as a welfare benefit plan under section 419. Carpenter was trained as a tax lawyer and studied the evolving regulations issued or proposed under section 419 and the developing caselaw and amended the plan in attempts to secure deductions for the premiums paid by petitioners. He published a book in an attempt to explain the provisions of section 419 to insurance brokers. The parties presented expert testimony and opinions about the nature of Benistar Plan and the underlying policies. Petitioners' expert, however, relied solely on representations by Carpenter, some of which were contradicted by the evidence at trial. Under the circumstances of these cases, exploration of the intricacies of section 419 would not be productive and might be misleading as applied to future cases where the benefits provided did not so clearly exceed ordinary and necessary expenses deductible under section 162. Because we do not interpret section 419A(f)(6), we do not address petitioners' contention that section 1.419A(f)(6)-1, Income Tax Regs., is invalid."

This case began a series of cases which struck down 419A (f) 6 plans a/k/a "VEBA".

Concerning Section 419A(f)(6) Plans.

In G. Mason Cadwell, Jr., Petitioner v. Commissioner of Internal Revenue, 136 T.C. No. 2 (U.S. Tax Court 2011), the court stated:

"The issues we must decide concern the income tax consequences of employee welfare benefits. Generally, contributions to welfare benefit plans are deductible by an employer when paid if they qualify as ordinary and necessary business expenses, but only to the extent allowed by sections 419 and 419A. Secs. 162(a), 419, 419A(f)(6). In recent years, adopted multiemployer plans have been claiming to satisfy section 419A(f)(6) and purporting to generate deductions for the insurance benefits provided under the plans. Notice 95-34, supra. This Court has decided several cases regarding purported section 419A(f)(6) plans. In Booth v. Commissioner, 108 T.C. 524, 565 (1997), we held that the plan in issue did not meet the requirements of section 419A(f)(6) because it was "an aggregation of separate welfare benefit plans, each of which has an experience-rating arrangement with the contributing employer." In Neonatology Associates P.A. v. Commissioner, 115 T.C. 43 (2000), affd. 299 F.3d 221 (3d Cir. 2002), without deciding whether the plans in issue met the requirements of section 419A(f)(6), we held that the corporate employer/participants may not deduct contributions in excess of the cost of term life insurance. We also held that the disallowed deductions should be treated as dividend distributions to the employee-owners of the C corporations to the extent of earnings and profits. Id. at 96-97. In V.R. DeAngelis M.D.P.C. v. Commissioner, T.C. Memo. 2007-360, affd. per curiam 574 F.3d 789 (2d Cir. 2009), similarly without ruling on whether the plan met the requirements of section 419A(f)(6), we held that payments for life insurance were essentially a distribution of S corporation profits rather than payments made with compensatory intent. In Curcio v. Commissioner, T.C. Memo. 2010-115, again without ruling on whether the plan met the requirements of section 419A(f)(6), we held that contributions were distributions of profits to the employee-owners and not deductible pursuant to section 162(a). We did not address in any of the foregoing cases the tax consequences to a non-owner employee for contributions to a plan that purportedly met the requirements of section 419A(f)(6) and subsequently was converted into a plan that no longer qualified.

We must decide the consequences to petitioner of contributions to such a plan."

Which, of course, was included in income with taxes and penalties applied to the employee.

FIDUCIARY DUTY

FIDUCIARY DUTY

Fiduciary duty is now a "buzzword" in the retirement planning industry. Plan sponsors have in many cases unknowingly have carried this liability for years-but in the recent case *Tibble v. Edison,* (Docket No. 13-550, 2015) the U.S. Supreme Court has once again given little guidance in this area. In *Tibble*, the plaintiff argued the plan sponsor "breached their fiduciary duty" by not opting for the lowest cost mutual funds. The plan sponsor may have opted for the higher cost funds as they were bundled with administrative services, but in the world of litigation facts like this may be shoved into a corner and ignored. So what did the Supreme Court say?

In *Tibble*, the Supreme Court ruled in a 9-0 decision (in part):

"The parties now agree that the <u>duty of prudence involves a continuing duty to monitor investments and remove imprudent ones under trust law.</u> Brief for Petitioners 24 ("Trust law imposes a duty to examine the prudence of existing investments periodically and to remove imprudent investments"); Brief for Respondents 3 ("All agree that a fiduciary has an ongoing duty to monitor trust investments to ensure that they remain prudent"); Brief for United States as Amicus Curiae 7 ("The duty of prudence under ERISA, as under trust law, requires plan fiduciaries with <u>investment responsibility to examine periodically the prudence of existing investments and to remove imprudent investments within a reasonable period of time</u>"). <u>The parties disagree, however, with respect to the scope of that responsibility.</u> Did it require a review of the contested mutual funds here, and if so, just what kind of review did it require? A fiduciary must discharge his responsibilities "with the care, skill, prudence, and diligence" that a prudent person "acting in a like capacity and familiar with such matters" would use. §1104(a)(1). ***We express no view on the scope of respondents' fiduciary duty in this case.*** We remand for the Ninth Circuit to consider petitioners' claims that respondents breached their duties within the relevant 6-year period under §1113, recognizing the importance of analogous trust law. (emphasis added)."

It is clear that the Supreme Court "punted" back to the 9th circuit as to **the scope of "fiduciary duty'.** Now it becomes interesting-if the U.S. Supreme Court does not know or express views on **the scope of "fiduciary duty"** how can an advisor be expected to know what that duty is when recommending an investment to a qualified plan? The Department of Labor has drafted "proposed rules" which would make advisors "fiduciaries" subject to a scope of duties not answered by the U.S. Supreme Court. The DOL Rule found in CFR 29 2509, 2510 states in part:

"If adopted, the proposal would treat persons who provide investment advice or recommendations to an employee benefit plan, plan fiduciary, plan participant or beneficiary, IRA, or IRA owner as fiduciaries under ERISA and the Code in a wider array of advice relationships than the existing ERISA and Code regulations, which would be replaced.

So now you have it-(assuming the rule is enacted) -advisors become fiduciaries which the scope of their fiduciary duty remains undefined until the 9th Circuit renders an opinion which the Supreme Court may review.

CASE OF THE YEAR

When I was in law practice at a tax law firm, one of the attorney's was always looking for the "key case" that could be placed before a judge to help him or her make their decision. The "key case" was like a "magic potion" a "keystone". In law school, professors also have their favorite cases and courts which they tend to quote over and over again. In tax practice, so much work is compliance and filling out forms, we tend to forget the area is constantly interpreted by the courts-especially on "reasonable compensation" (what is that?-how do you calculate that?) and Fiduciary duty (am I a fiduciary?).

The cases give insight to how the courts operate. The primary court that reviews tax cases is the U.S. Tax Court but they can be overruled by the Court of Appeals and the U.S. Supreme Court. Higher courts do not like overruling a lower court decision and the odds are about 75% that the lower court decision will stand.

The "Case of the Year" are what I would call key cases in certain area of the tax law that make a difference in practice. Granted, there are other good cases out there-but like a Hollywood movie-we only select one per year. Each case tells a story-usually a good story or it would not reach the U.S. Supreme Court or U.S. Tax Court in a published opinion.

I also have a case of the Century and case of the decade. Last Century it was Texas v. Florida-and you must read the footnotes where an estate was entirely consumed by death taxes. This century it not over with….takes time.

CASE OF THE YEAR FOR 2015

INTRODUCTION

Tibble represents the problem with an ERISA fiduciary. The Fiduciary scope is not defined in this case and that issue is sent back to the 9th Circuit. In the meantime, the Department of Labor is attempting to classify anyone who sells a product to a qualified plan to be an ERISA Fiduciary. In May of 2015 I met with U.S. Senators Burr and Tillis to discuss the implication of the rule. If the U.S. Supreme Court does not know the scope of fiduciary duty-how can you expect an insurance agent to know this? I highlighted this in the text.

TIBBLE ET AL. v. EDISON INTERNATIONAL ET AL. CERTIORARI TO THE UNITED STATES COURT OF APPEALS FOR THE NINTH CIRCUIT No. 13–550. Argued February 24, 2015—Decided May 18, 2015 In 2007, petitioners, beneficiaries of the Edison 401(k) Savings Plan (Plan), sued Plan fiduciaries, respondents Edison International and others, to recover damages for alleged losses suffered by the Plan from alleged breaches of respondents' fiduciary duties. As relevant here, petitioners argued that respondents violated their fiduciary duties with respect to three mutual funds added to the Plan in 1999 and three mutual funds added to the Plan in 2002. Petitioners argued that respondents acted imprudently by offering six higher priced retail-class mutual funds as Plan investments when materially identical lower priced institutional-class mutual funds were available. Because ERISA requires a breach of fiduciary duty complaint to be filed no more than six years after "the date of the last action which constitutes a part of the breach or violation" or "in the case of an omission the latest date on which the fiduciary could have cured the breach or violation," 29 U. S. C. §1113, the District Court held that petitioners' complaint as to the 1999 funds was untimely because they were included in the Plan more than six years before the complaint was filed, and the circumstances had not changed enough within the 6year statutory period to place respondents under an obligation to review the mutual funds and to convert them to lower priced institutional-class funds. The Ninth Circuit affirmed, concluding that petitioners had not established a change in circumstances that might trigger an obligation to conduct a full due diligence review of the 1999 funds within the 6-year statutory period. Held: The Ninth Circuit erred by applying §1113's statutory bar to a breach of fiduciary duty claim based on the initial selection of the investments without considering the contours of the alleged breach of fiduciary duty. ERISA's fiduciary duty is "derived from the common law of trusts," Central States, Southeast & Southwest Areas Pension Fund v. Central Transport, Inc., 472 U. S. 559, 570, which provides that a trustee has a continuing duty—separate and apart from the duty to exercise prudence in selecting investments at the outset—to monitor, and remove imprudent, trust investments. So long as a plaintiff's claim alleging breach of the continuing duty of prudence occurred within six years of suit, the claim is timely. This Court expresses no view on the scope of respondents' fiduciary duty in this case, e.g., whether a review of the contested mutual funds is required, and, if so, just what kind of review. A fiduciary must discharge his responsibilities "with the care, skill, prudence, and diligence" that a prudent person "acting in a like capacity and familiar with such matters" would use. §1104(a)(1). The case is remanded for the Ninth Circuit to consider petitioners' claims that respondents breached their duties within the relevant 6-year statutory period under §1113, recognizing the importance of analogous trust law. Pp. 4–8. 729 F. 3d 1110, vacated and remanded. BREYER, J., delivered the opinion for a unanimous Court.

No. 13–550

GLENN TIBBLE, ET AL., PETITIONERS v.

EDISON INTERNATIONAL ET AL.

ON WRIT OF CERTIORARI TO THE UNITED STATES COURT OF

APPEALS FOR THE NINTH CIRCUIT

[May 18, 2015]

JUSTICE BREYER delivered the opinion of the Court. Under the Employee Retirement Income Security Act of 1974 (ERISA), 88 Stat. 829 et seq., as amended, a breach of fiduciary duty complaint is timely if filed no more than six years after "the date of the last action which constituted a part of the breach or violation" or "in the case of an omission the latest date on which the fiduciary could have cured the breach or violation." 29 U. S. C. §1113. The question before us concerns application of this provision to the timeliness of a fiduciary duty complaint. It requires us to consider whether a fiduciary's allegedly imprudent retention of an investment is an "action" or "omission" that triggers the running of the 6-year limitations period. In 2007, several individual beneficiaries of the Edison 401(k) Savings Plan (Plan) filed a lawsuit on behalf of the Plan and all similarly situated beneficiaries (collectively, petitioners) against Edison International and others (collectively, respondents). Petitioners sought to recover damages for alleged losses suffered by the Plan, in addition to injunctive and other equitable relief based on alleged breaches of respondents' fiduciary duties. The Plan is a defined-contribution plan, meaning that participants' retirement benefits are limited to the value of their own individual investment accounts, which is determined by the market performance of employee and employer contributions, less expenses. Expenses, such as management or administrative fees, can sometimes significantly reduce the value of an account in a defined contribution plan. As relevant here, petitioners argued that respondents violated their fiduciary duties with respect to three mutual funds added to the Plan in 1999 and three mutual funds added to the Plan in 2002. Petitioners argued that respondents acted imprudently by offering six higher priced retail-class mutual funds as Plan investments when materially identical lower priced institutional-class mutual funds were available (the lower price reflects lower administrative costs). Specifically, petitioners claimed that a large institutional investor with billions of dollars, like the Plan, can obtain materially identical lower priced institutional class mutual funds that are not available to a retail investor. Petitioners asked, how could respondents have acted prudently in offering the six higher priced retail-class mutual funds when respondents could have offered them effectively the same six mutual funds at the lower price offered to institutional investors like the Plan? As to the three funds added to the Plan in 2002, the District Court agreed. It wrote that respondents had "not offered any credible explanation" for offering retail-class, i.e., higher priced mutual funds that "cost the Plan participants wholly unnecessary [administrative] fees," and it concluded that, with respect to those mutual funds, respondents had failed to exercise "the care, skill, prudence and diligence under the circumstances" that ERISA demands of fiduciaries. No. CV 07–5359 (CD Cal., July 8, 2010), App. to Pet. for Cert. 65, 130, 142, 109.

As to the three funds added to the Plan in 1999, however, the District Court held that petitioners' claims were untimely because, unlike the other contested mutual funds, these mutual funds were included in the Plan more than six years before the complaint was filed in 2007. 639 F. Supp. 2d 1074, 1119–1120 (CD Cal. 2009). As a result, the 6-year statutory period had run. The District Court allowed petitioners to argue that, despite the 1999 selection of the three mutual funds, their complaint was nevertheless timely because these funds underwent significant changes within the 6-year statutory period that should have prompted respondents to undertake a full due-diligence review and convert the higher priced retail-class mutual funds to lower priced institutional class mutual funds. App. to Pet. for Cert. 142–150. The District Court concluded, however, that petitioners had not met their burden of showing that a prudent fiduciary would have undertaken a full due-diligence review of these funds as a result of the alleged changed circumstances. According to the District Court, the circumstances had not changed enough to place respondents under an obligation to review the mutual funds and to convert them to lower priced institutional-class mutual funds. Ibid. The Ninth Circuit affirmed the District Court as to the six mutual funds. 729 F. 3d 1110 (2013). With respect to the three mutual funds added in 1999, the Ninth Circuit held that petitioners' claims were untimely because petitioners had not established a change in circumstances that might trigger an obligation to review and to change investments within the 6-year statutory period. Petitioners filed a petition for certiorari asking us to review this latter holding. We agreed to do so. Section 1113 reads, in relevant part, that "[n]o action may be commenced with respect to a fiduciary's breach of any responsibility, duty, or obligation" after the earlier of

"six years after (A) the date of the last action which constituted a part of the breach or violation, or (B) in the case of an omission the latest date on which the fiduciary could have cured the breach or violation." Both clauses of that provision require only a "breach or violation" to start the 6-year period. Petitioners contend that respondents breached the duty of prudence by offering higher priced retail-class mutual funds when the same investments were available as lower priced institutional-class mutual funds. The Ninth Circuit, without considering the role of the fiduciary's duty of prudence under trust law, rejected petitioners' claims as untimely under §1113 on the basis that respondents had selected the three mutual funds more than six years before petitioners brought this action. The Ninth Circuit correctly asked whether the "last action which constituted a part of the breach or violation" of respondents' duty of prudence occurred within the relevant 6-year period. It focused, however, upon the act of "designating an investment for inclusion" to start the 6year period. 729 F. 3d, at 1119. The Ninth Circuit stated that "[c]characterizing the mere continued offering of a plan option, without more, as a subsequent breach would render" the statute meaningless and could even expose present fiduciaries to liability for decisions made decades ago. Id., at 1120. But the Ninth Circuit jumped from this observation to the conclusion that only a significant change in circumstances could engender a new breach of a fiduciary duty, stating that the District Court was "entirely correct" to have entertained the "possibility" that "significant changes" occurring "within the limitations period" might require "'a full due diligence review of the funds,'" equivalent to the diligence review that respondents conduct when adding new funds to the Plan. Ibid. We believe the Ninth Circuit erred by applying a statutory bar to a claim of a "breach or violation" of a fiduciary duty without considering the nature of the fiduciary duty. The Ninth Circuit did not recognize that under trust law a fiduciary is required to conduct a regular review of its investment with the nature and timing of the review contingent on the circumstances. Of course, after the Ninth Circuit considers trust-law principles, it is possible that it will conclude that respondents did indeed conduct the sort of review that a prudent fiduciary would have conducted absent a significant change in circumstances. An ERISA fiduciary must discharge his responsibility "with the care, skill, prudence, and diligence" that a prudent person "acting in a like capacity and familiar with such matters" would use. §1104(a)(1); see also Fifth Third Bancorp v. Dudenhoeffer, 573 U. S. ___ (2014). We have often noted that an ERISA fiduciary's duty is "derived from the common law of trusts." Central States, Southeast & Southwest Areas Pension Fund v. Central Transport, Inc., 472 U. S. 559, 570 (1985). In determining the contours of an ERISA fiduciary's duty, courts often must look to the law of trusts. We are aware of no reason why the Ninth Circuit should not do so here. Under trust law, a trustee has a continuing duty to monitor trust investments and remove imprudent ones. This continuing duty exists separate and apart from the trustee's duty to exercise prudence in selecting investments at the outset. The Bogert treatise states that "[t]he trustee cannot assume that if investments are legal and proper for retention at the beginning of the trust, or when purchased, they will remain so indefinitely." A. Hess, G. Bogert, & G. Bogert, Law of Trusts and Trustees §684, pp. 145–146 (3d ed. 2009)

(Bogert 3d). Rather, the trustee must "systematic[ally] consider[r] all the investments of the trust at regular intervals" to ensure that they are appropriate. Bogert 3d §684, at 147–148; see also In re Stark's Estate, 15 N. Y. S. 729, 731 (Surr. Ct. 1891) (stating that a

trustee must "exercise[e] a reasonable degree of diligence in looking after the security after the investment had been made"); Johns v. Herbert, 2 App. D. C. 485, 499 (1894) (holding trustee liable for failure to discharge his "duty to watch the investment with reasonable care and diligence"). The Restatement (Third) of Trusts states the following: "[A] trustee's duties apply not only in making investments but also in monitoring and reviewing investments, which is to be done in a manner that is reasonable and appropriate to the particular investments, courses of action, and strategies involved." §90, Comment b, p. 295 (2007). The Uniform Prudent Investor Act confirms that "[m]managing embraces monitoring" and that a trustee has "continuing responsibility for oversight of the suitability of the investments already made." §2, Comment, 7B U. L. A. 21 (1995) (internal quotation marks omitted). Scott on Trusts implies as much by stating that, "[w]hen the trust estate includes assets that are inappropriate as trust investments, the trustee is ordinarily under a duty to dispose of them within a reasonable time." 4 A. Scott, W. Fratcher, & M. Ascher, Scott and Ascher on Trusts §19.3.1, p. 1439 (5th ed. 2007). Bogert says the same. Bogert 3d §685, at 156–157 (explaining that if an investment is determined to be imprudent, the trustee "must dispose of it within a reasonable time"); see, e.g., State Street Trust Co. v. DeKalb, 259 Mass. 578, 583, 157 N. E. 334, 336 (1927) (trustee was required to take action to "protect the rights of the beneficiaries" when the value of trust assets declined). In short, under trust law, a fiduciary normally has a continuing duty of some kind to monitor investments and remove imprudent ones. A plaintiff may allege that a fiduciary breached the duty of prudence by failing to properly monitor investments and remove imprudent ones. In such a case, so long as the alleged breach of the continuing duty occurred within six years of suit, the claim is timely. The Ninth Circuit erred by applying a 6year statutory bar based solely on the initial selection of the three funds without considering the contours of the alleged breach of fiduciary duty. The parties now agree that the duty of prudence involves a continuing duty to monitor investments and remove imprudent ones under trust law. Brief for Petitioners 24 ("Trust law imposes a duty to examine the prudence of existing investments periodically and to remove imprudent investments"); Brief for Respondents 3 ("All agree that a fiduciary has an ongoing duty to monitor trust investments to ensure that they remain prudent"); Brief for United States as Amicus Curiae 7 ("The duty of prudence under ERISA, as under trust law, requires plan fiduciaries with investment responsibility to examine periodically the prudence of existing investments and to remove imprudent investments within a reasonable period of time"). The parties disagree, however, with respect to the scope of that responsibility. Did it require a review of the contested mutual funds here, and if so, just what kind of review did it require? A fiduciary must discharge his responsibilities "with the care, skill, prudence, and diligence" that a prudent person "acting in a like capacity and familiar with such matters" would use. §1104(a)(1). We express no view on the scope of respondents' fiduciary duty in this case. We remand for the Ninth Circuit to consider petitioners' claims that respondents breached their duties within the relevant 6-year period under §1113, recognizing the importance of analogous trust law. A final point: Respondents argue that petitioners did not raise the claim below that respondents committed new breaches of the duty of prudence by failing to monitor their investments and remove imprudent ones absent a significant change in circumstances. We leave any questions of forfeiture for the Ninth Circuit on remand. The Ninth Circuit's judgment is vacated, and the case is remanded for further proceedings consistent with this opinion. It is so ordered.

CASE OF THE YEAR 2014

INTRODUCTION

This case is popular among estate planning attorneys who are now setting up conduit and accumulation trust for inherited IRAs. The theory is to rely on state "spendthrift laws" to protect the assets as opposed to "federal bankruptcy law" that does not. We await the test of this legal theory.

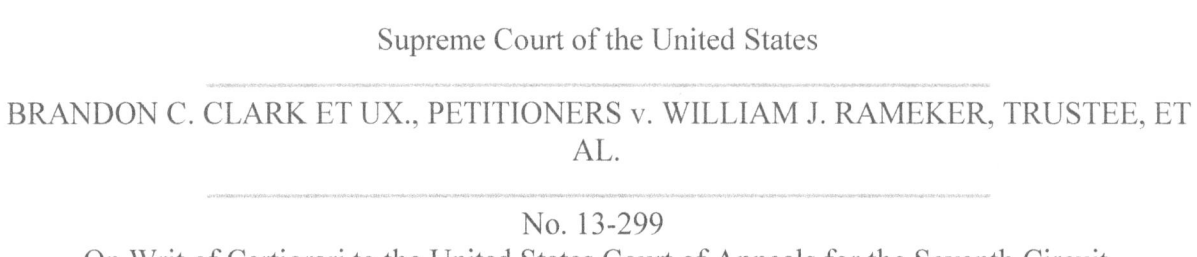

Supreme Court of the United States

BRANDON C. CLARK ET UX., PETITIONERS v. WILLIAM J. RAMEKER, TRUSTEE, ET AL.

No. 13-299
On Writ of Certiorari to the United States Court of Appeals for the Seventh Circuit.
Argued March 24, 2014, Decided June 12, 2014 October TERM, 2013

Syllabus

When petitioners filed for Chapter 7 bankruptcy, they sought to exclude roughly $300,000 in an inherited individual retirement account (IRA) from the bankruptcy estate using the "retirement funds" exemption. See **11 U. S. C. § 522**(b)(3)(C). The Bankruptcy Court concluded that an inherited IRA does not share the same characteristics as a traditional IRA and disallowed the exemption. The District Court reversed, explaining that the exemption covers any account in which the funds were originally accumulated for retirement purposes. The Seventh Circuit disagreed and reversed the District Court.

Held: Funds held in inherited IRAs are not "retirement funds" within the meaning of § 522(b)(3)(C). Pp. 4-11.

(a) The ordinary meaning of "retirement funds" is properly understood to be sums of money set aside for the day an individual stops working. Three legal characteristics of inherited IRAs provide objective evidence that they do not contain such funds. First, the holder of an inherited IRA may never invest additional money in the account. **26 U. S. C. § 219**(d) (4). Second, holders of inherited IRAs are required to withdraw money from the accounts, no matter how far they are from retirement. §§ 408(a)(6), 401(a)(9)(B). Finally, the holder of an inherited IRA may withdraw the entire balance of the account at any time — and use it for any purpose — without penalty. Pp. 4-6.

(b) This reading is consistent with the purpose of the Bankruptcy Code's exemption provisions, which effectuate a careful balance between the creditor's interest in recovering assets and the debtor's interest in protecting essential needs. Allowing debtors to protect funds in traditional and Roth IRAs ensures that debtors will be able to meet their basic needs during their retirement years. By contrast, nothing about an inherited IRA's legal characteristics prevent or discourage an individual from using the entire balance immediately after bankruptcy for purposes of current consumption. The "retirement funds" exemption should not be read in a manner that would convert the bankruptcy objective of protecting debtors' basic needs into a "free pass," *Schwab* v. *Reilly*, **560 U. S. 770, 791**. Pp. 6-7.

(c) Petitioners' counterarguments do not overcome the statute's text and purpose. Their claim that funds in an inherited IRA are retirement funds because, at some point, they were set aside for retirement, conflicts with ordinary usage and would render the term "retirement funds," as used in § 522(b)(3)(C), superfluous. Congress could have achieved the exact same result without specifying the funds as "retirement funds." And the absence of the phrase "debtor's interest," which appears in many other § 522 exemptions, does not indicate that § 522(b)(3)(C) covers funds intended for someone else's retirement. Where used, that phrase works to limit the value of the asset that the debtor may exempt from her estate, not to distinguish between a debtor's assets and the assets of another. Also unpersuasive is petitioners' argument that § 522(b)(3)(C)'s sentence structure —*i.e.*, a broad category, here, "retirement funds," followed by limiting language, here, "to the extent that" — prevents the broad category from performing any independent limiting work. This is not the only way in which the phrase "to the extent that" may be read, and this argument reintroduces the problem that makes the term "retirement funds" superfluous. Finally, the possibility that an account holder can leave an inherited IRA intact until retirement and take only the required minimum distributions does not mean that an inherited IRA bears the legal characteristics of retirement funds. Pp. 8-11.

714 F. 3d 559, affirmed.

SOTOMAYOR, J., delivered the opinion for a unanimous Court.

JUSTICE SOTOMAYOR delivered the opinion of the Court.

When an individual files for bankruptcy, she may exempt particular categories of assets from the bankruptcy estate. One such category includes certain "retirement funds." **11 U. S. C. § 522**(b)(3)(C). The question presented is whether funds contained in an inherited individual retirement account (IRA) qualify as "retirement funds" within the meaning of this bankruptcy exemption. We hold that they do not.

I

A

When an individual debtor files a bankruptcy petition, her "legal or equitable interests . . . in property" become part of the bankruptcy estate. **§ 541(a)(1)**. "To help the debtor obtain a fresh start," however the Bankruptcy Code allows debtors to exempt from the estate limited interests in certain kinds of property. *Rousey* v. *Jacoway,***544 U. S. 320, 325** (2005). The exemption at issue in this case allows debtors to protect "retirement funds to the extent those funds are in a fund or account that is exempt from taxation under **section 401, 403, 408, 408A, 414,457, or 501(a)** of the **[*2245]** Internal Revenue Code." **§§ 522(b) (3) (C), (d) (12).[fn1]** The enumerated sections of the Internal Revenue Code cover many types of accounts, three of which are relevant here.

The first two are traditional and Roth IRAs, which are created by **26 U. S. C. § 408** and § **408A**, respectively. Both types of accounts offer tax advantages to encourage individuals to save for retirement. Qualified contributions to traditional IRAs, for example, are tax-deductible. **§ 219(a)**. Roth IRAs offer the opposite benefit: Although contributions are not tax-deductible, qualified distributions are tax-free. **§§ 408A(c)(1), (d)(1)**. To ensure that both types of IRAs are used for retirement purposes and not as general tax-advantaged savings vehicles, Congress made certain withdrawals from both types of accounts subject to a 10 percent penalty if taken before an accountholder reaches the age of 59½. See **§§ 72(t)(1)-(2)**; see also n. 4, *infra*.

The third type of account relevant here is an inherited IRA. An inherited IRA is a traditional or Roth IRA that has been inherited after its owner's death. See **§§ 408(d)(3)(C)(ii), 408A(a)**. If the heir is the owner's spouse, as is often the case, the spouse has a choice: He or she may "roll over" the IRA funds into his or her own IRA, or he or she may keep the IRA as an inherited IRA (subject to the rules discussed below). See Internal Revenue Service, Publication 590: Individual Retirement Arrangements (IRAs), p. 18 (Jan. 5, 2014). When anyone other than the owner's spouse inherits the IRA, he or she may not roll over the funds; the only option is to hold the IRA as an inherited account.

Inherited IRAs do not operate like ordinary IRAs. Unlike with a traditional or Roth IRA, an individual may withdraw funds from an inherited IRA at any time, without paying a tax penalty. **§ 72(t)(2)(A)(ii)**. Indeed, the owner of an inherited IRA not only may but *must* withdraw its funds: The owner must either withdraw the entire balance in the account within five years of the original owner's death or take minimum distributions on an annual basis. See **§§ 408(a)(6), [**164] 401(a)(9)(B); 26 CFR § 1.408-8** (2013) (Q-1 and A-1(a) incorporating **§ 1.401(a)(9)-3** (Q-1 and A-1(a))); see generally D. Cartano, Taxation of Individual Retirement Accounts § 32.02[A] (2013). And unlike with a traditional or Roth IRA, the owner of an inherited IRA may never make contributions to the account. **26 U. S. C. § 219**(d)(4).

B

In 2000, Ruth Heffron established a traditional IRA and named her daughter, Heidi Heffron-Clark, as the sole beneficiary of the account. When Ms. Heffron died in 2001, her IRA — which was then worth just over $450,000 — passed to her daughter and became an inherited IRA. Ms. Heffron-Clark elected to take monthly distributions from the account.

In October 2010, Ms. Heffron-Clark and her husband, petitioners in this Court, filed a Chapter 7 bankruptcy petition. They identified the inherited IRA, by then worth roughly $300,000, as exempt from the bankruptcy estate under **11 U. S. C. § 522**(b)(3)(C). Respondents, the bankruptcy trustee and unsecured creditors of the estate, objected to the claimed exemption on the ground that the funds in the inherited IRA were not "retirement funds" within the meaning of the statute.

The Bankruptcy Court agreed, disallowing the exemption. *In re Clark*, **450 B. R. 858**, **866** (WD Wisc. 2011). Relying on the "plain language of **§ 522(b)(3)(C)**," the court concluded that an inherited IRA "does not contain *anyone's* `retirement funds,'" because unlike with a traditional IRA, the funds are not "segregated to meet the needs of, nor distributed on the occasion of, any person's retirement." **Id., at 863.[fn2]** The District Court reversed, explaining that the exemption covers any account containing funds "originally" "accumulated for retirement purposes." *In re Clark*, **466 B. R. 135**, **139** (WD Wisc. 2012). The Seventh Circuit reversed the District Court's judgment. *In re Clark*, **714 F. 3d 559** (2013). Pointing to the "different rules governing inherited" and non-inherited IRAs, the court concluded that "inherited IRAs represent an opportunity for current consumption, not a fund of retirement savings." **Id., at 560**, **562**.

We granted certiorari to resolve a conflict between the Seventh Circuit's ruling and the Fifth Circuit's decision in *In re Chilton*, **674 F. 3d 486** (2012). **571 U. S. ___** (2013). We now affirm.

II

The text and purpose of the Bankruptcy Code make clear that funds held in inherited IRAs are not "retirement funds" within the meaning of § **522(b)(3)(C)**'s bankruptcy exemption.

A

The Bankruptcy Code does not define "retirement funds," so we give the term its ordinary meaning. See *Octane Fitness, LLC* v. *ICON Health & Fitness, Inc.*, **572 U. S. ___**, ___ (2014) **(slip op., at 7)**. [**165] The ordinary meaning of "fund[s]" is "sum[s] of money . . . set aside for a specific purpose." American Heritage Dictionary 712 (4th ed. 2000). And "retirement" means "[w]ithdrawal from one's occupation, business, or office." *Id.*, at 1489. **Section 522(b)(3)(C)**'s reference to "retirement funds" is therefore properly understood to mean sums of money set aside for the day an individual stops working.

The parties agree that, in deciding whether a given set of funds falls within this definition, the inquiry must be an objective one, not one that "turns on the debtor's subjective purpose." Brief for Petitioners 43-44; see also Brief for Respondents 26. In other words, to determine whether funds in an account qualify as "retirement funds," courts should not engage in a case-by-case, fact-intensive examination into whether the debtor actually planned to use the funds for retirement purposes as opposed to current consumption. Instead, we look to the legal characteristics of the account in which the funds are held, asking whether, as an objective matter, the account is one set aside for the day when an individual stops working. Cf. *Rousey*, **544 U. S., at 332** (holding that traditional IRAs are included within **§ 522(d)(10)(E)**'s exemption for "a payment under a stock bonus, pension, profit sharing, annuity, or similar plan or contract on account of . . . age" based on the legal characteristics of traditional IRAs). **[*2247]**

Three legal characteristics of inherited IRAs lead us to conclude that funds held in such accounts are not objectively set aside for the purpose of retirement. First, the holder of an inherited IRA may never invest additional money in the account. **26 U. S. C. § 219**(d)(4). Inherited IRAs are thus unlike traditional and Roth IRAs, both of which are quintessential "retirement funds." For where inherited IRAs categorically prohibit contributions, the entire purpose of traditional and Roth IRAs is to provide tax incentives for accountholders to contribute regularly and over time to their retirement savings.

Second, holders of inherited IRAs are required to withdraw money from such accounts, no matter how many years they may be from retirement. Under the Tax Code, the beneficiary of an inherited IRA must either withdraw all of the funds in the IRA within five years after the year of the owner's death or take minimum annual distributions every year. See **§ 408(a)(6)**; **§ 401(a)(9)(B)**; **26 CFR § 1.408-8** (Q-1 and A-1(a) incorporating **§ 1.401(a)(9)-3** (Q-1 and A-1(a))). Here, for example, petitioners elected to take yearly distributions from the inherited IRA; as a result, the account decreased in value from roughly $450,000 to less than $300,000 within 10 years. That the tax rules governing inherited IRAs routinely lead to their diminution over time, regardless of their holders' proximity to retirement, is hardly a feature one would expect of an account set aside for retirement.

Finally, the holder of an inherited IRA may withdraw the entire balance of the account at any time — and for any purpose — without penalty. Whereas a withdrawal from a traditional or Roth IRA prior to the age of 59½ triggers a 10 percent tax penalty subject to narrow exceptions, see n. 4, *infra* — a rule that encourages individuals to leave such funds untouched until retirement age — there is no similar limit on the holder of an inherited IRA. Funds held in inherited IRAs accordingly constitute "a pot of money that can be freely used for current consumption," **714 F. 3d., at 561**, not funds objectively set aside for one's retirement.

B

Our reading of the text is consistent with the purpose of the Bankruptcy Code's exemption provisions. As a general matter, those provisions effectuate a careful balance between the interests of creditors and debtors. On the one hand, we have noted that "every asset the Code permits a debtor to withdraw from the estate is an asset that is not available to . . . creditors." *Schwab* v. *Reilly*, **560 U. S. 770, 791** (2010). On the other hand, exemptions serve the important purpose of "protect[ing] the debtor's essential needs." *United States* v. *Security Industrial Bank*, **459 U. S. 70, 83** (1982) (Blackmun, J., concurring in judgment).**[fn3]**

Allowing debtors to protect funds held in traditional and Roth IRAs comports with this purpose by helping to ensure that debtors will be able to meet their basic needs during their retirement years. At the same time, the legal limitations on traditional and Roth IRAs ensure that debtors who hold such accounts (but who have not yet reached retirement age) do not enjoy a cash windfall by virtue of the exemption — such debtors are instead**[*2248]** required to wait until age 59½ before they may withdraw the funds penalty-free.

The same cannot be said of an inherited IRA. For if an individual is allowed to exempt an inherited IRA from her bankruptcy estate, nothing about the inherited IRA's legal characteristics would prevent (or even discourage) the individual from using the entire balance of the account on a vacation home or sports car immediately after her bankruptcy proceedings are complete. Allowing that kind of exemption would convert the Bankruptcy Code's purposes of preserving debtors' ability to meet their basic needs and ensuring that they have a "fresh start," *Rousey*, **544 U. S., at 325**, into a "free pass," *Schwab*, **560 U. S., at 791**. We decline to read the retirement funds provision in that manner.

III

Although petitioners' counterarguments are not without force, they do not overcome the statute's text and purpose.

Petitioners' primary argument is that funds in an inherited IRA are retirement funds because — regardless of whether they currently sit in an account bearing the legal characteristics of a fund set aside for retirement — they did so at an earlier moment in time. After all, petitioners point out, "the initial owner" of the account "set aside the funds in question for retirement by depositing them in a" traditional or Roth IRA. Brief for Petitioners 21. And "[t]he [initial] owner's death does not in any way affect the funds in the account." *Ibid.*

We disagree. In ordinary usage, to speak of a person's "retirement funds" implies that the funds are currently in an account set aside for retirement, not that they were set aside for that purpose at some prior date by an entirely different person. Under petitioners' contrary logic, if an individual withdraws money from a traditional IRA and gives it to a friend who then deposits it into a checking **[***6]** account, that money should be forever deemed "retirement funds" because it was originally set aside for retirement. That is plainly incorrect.

More fundamentally, the backward-looking inquiry urged by petitioners would render a substantial portion of **11 U. S. C. § 522**(b)(3)(C)'s text superfluous. The funds contained in every individual-held account exempt from taxation under the Tax Code provisions enumerated in **§ 522(b)(3)(C)** have been, at some point in time, "retirement funds." So on petitioners' view, rather than defining the exemption to cover "retirement funds to the extent that those funds are in a fund or account that is exempt from taxation under [the enumerated sections] of the Internal Revenue Code," Congress could have achieved the exact same result through a provision covering any "fund or account that is exempt from taxation under [the enumerated sections]." In other words, **§ 522(b)(3)(C)** requires that funds satisfy not one but two conditions in order to be exempt: the funds must be "retirement funds," and they must be held in a covered account. Petitioners' reading would write out of the statute the first element. It therefore flouts the rule that "'a statute should be construed so that effect is given to all its provisions, so that no part will be inoperative or superfluous.'" *Corley* v. *United States*, **556 U. S. 303, 314**(2009).

Petitioners respond that many of § 522's other exemptions refer to the "debtor's interest" in various kinds of property. See, *e.g.*, **§ 522(d)(2)** (exempting "[t]he debtor's interest, not to exceed [$3,675] in value, in one motor vehicle"). **Section 522(b)(3)(C)**'s retirement funds exemption, **[*2249]** by contrast, includes no such reference. As a result, petitioners surmise, Congress must have meant the provision to cover funds that were at one time retirement accounts, even if they were for someone else's retirement. Brief for Petitioners 33-34. But Congress used the phrase "debtor's interest" in the other exemptions in a different manner — not to distinguish between a debtor's assets and the assets of another person but to set a limit on the value of the particular asset that a debtor may exempt. For example, the statute allows a debtor to protect "[t]he debtor's aggregate interest, not to exceed [$1,550] in value, in jewelry." **§ 522(d)(4)**. The phrase "[t]he debtor's aggregate interest" in this provision is just a means of introducing the $1,550 limit; it is not a means of preventing debtors from exempting other persons' jewelry from their own bankruptcy proceedings (an interpretation that would serve little apparent purpose). And Congress had no need to use the same "debtor's interest" formulation in **§ 522(b)(3)(C)** for the simple reason that it imposed a value limitation on the amount of exemptible retirement funds in a separate provision, **§ 522(n)**.

Petitioners next contend that even if their interpretation of "'retirement funds' does not independently *exclude* anything from the scope of the statute," that poses no problem because Congress actually intended that result. Reply Brief 5-6. In particular, petitioners suggest that when a sentence is structured as **§ 522(b)(3)(C)**is — starting with a broad category ("retirement funds"), then winnowing it down through limiting language ("to the extent that" the funds are held in a particular type of account) — it is often the case that the broad category does no independent limiting work. As counsel for petitioners noted at oral argument, if a tax were to apply to "sports teams to the extent that they are members of the major professional sports leagues," the phrase "sports teams" would not provide any additional limitation on the covered entities. Tr. of Oral Arg. 15.

There are two problems with this argument. First, while it is possible to conceive of sentences that use **§ 522(b)(3)(C)**'s "to the extent that" construction in a manner where the initial broad category serves no exclusionary purpose, that is not the only way in which the phrase may be used. For example, a tax break that applies to "nonprofit organizations to the extent that they are medical or scientific" would not apply to a for-profit pharmaceutical company because the initial broad category ("nonprofit organizations") provides its own limitation. Just so here; in order to qualify for bankruptcy protection under **§ 522(b)(3)(C)**, funds must be both "retirement funds" and in an account exempt from taxation under one of the enumerated Tax Code sections.

Second, to accept petitioners' argument would reintroduce the surplusage problem already discussed. *Supra*, at 8-9. And although petitioners are correct that "the only effect of respondents' interpretation of `retirement funds' would seemingly be to deny bankruptcy exemption to inherited IRAs," Reply Brief 2, as between one interpretation that would render statutory text superfluous and another that would render it meaningful yet limited, we think the latter more faithful to the statute Congress wrote.

Finally, petitioners argue that even under the inquiry we have described, funds in inherited IRAs should still qualify as "retirement funds" because the holder of such an account can leave much of its value intact until her retirement if she invests wisely and chooses to take only the minimum annual distributions required by law. See Brief for Petitioners 27-28. But **[*2250]** the possibility that some investors may use their inherited IRAs for retirement purposes does not mean that inherited IRAs bear the defining legal characteristics of retirement funds. Were it any other way, money in an ordinary checking account (or, for that matter, an envelope of $20 bills) would also amount to "retirement funds" because it is possible for an owner to use those funds for retirement.**[fn4]**

* * *

For the foregoing reasons, the judgment of the United States Court of Appeals for the Seventh Circuit is affirmed.

It is so ordered.

[fn1] Under **§ 522**, debtors may elect to claim exemptions either under federal law, see **§ 522(b)(2)**, or state law, see **§ 522(b)(3)**. Both tracks permit debtors to exempt "retirement funds." See **§ 522(b)(3)(C)** (retirement funds exemption for debtors proceeding under state law); **§ 522(d)(12)** (identical exemption for debtors proceeding under federal law). Petitioners elected to proceed under state law, so we refer to **§ 522(b)(3)(C)**throughout.

[fn2] The Bankruptcy Court also concluded in the alternative that, even if funds in an inherited IRA qualify as retirement funds within the meaning of **§ 522(b) (3) (C)**, an inherited IRA is not exempt from taxation under any of the Internal Revenue Code sections listed in the provision. See **450 B. R., at 865**. Because we hold that inherited IRAs are not retirement funds to begin with, we have no occasion to pass on the Bankruptcy Court's alternative ground for disallowing petitioners' exemption.

[fn3] As the House Judiciary Committee explained in the process of enacting **§ 522**, "[t]he historical purpose" of bankruptcy exemptions has been to provide a debtor "with the basic necessities of life" so that she "will not be left destitute and a public charge." H. R. Rep. No. 95-595, p. 126 (1977).

[fn4] Petitioners also argue that inherited IRAs are similar enough to Roth IRAs to qualify as retirement funds because "the owner of a Roth IRA may withdraw his contributions . . . without penalty." Brief for Petitioners 44. But that argument fails to recognize that withdrawals of contributions to a Roth IRA are not subject to the 10 percent tax penalty for the unique reason that the contributions have already been taxed. By contrast, all capital gains and investment income in a Roth IRA are subject to the pre-59½ withdrawal penalty (with narrow exceptions for, for example, medical expenses), which incentivizes use of those funds only in one's retirement years.

CASE OF THE YEAR 2013

INTRODUCTION

I started working in this area prior to Thousand Oaks-a/k/a sell a business via an asset sale then create a pension for the owners who still hold the stock-but no employees are in the plan. The Judge Robert Wherry who wrote the decision I actually worked for when he was in a law firm in Denver. I even had dinner at his house once-just a good guy. This was over 30 years ago.-but his writing style is somewhat unique-notice-Carrying the Torch etc. He writes like this in quite a few of his cases. This case is a blueprint on asset sale-then set up a pension to defer the tax-except be careful on "reasonable compensation".

CASE OF THE YEAR 2013

T.C. Memo. 2013-10

UNITED STATES TAX COURT

THOUSAND OAKS RESIDENTIAL CARE HOME I, INC., ET AL.,1 Petitioners v. COMMISSIONER OF INTERNAL REVENUE, Respondent

Docket Nos. 1448-10, 1480-10,   Filed January 14, 2013.   1481-10.

R determined that a corporation's compensation packages for its owner-employees were unreasonable and disallowed deductions for compensation paid for the 2003 through 2005 tax years.

Held: The compensation packages paid to the corporation's owner-employees were reasonable and deductible under I.R.C. sec. 162, for the 2003, 2004, and 2005 tax years to the extent determined herein. The compensation paid to the owner-employees' daughter, Grace-Ann Strick, was unreasonable.

1Cases of the following petitioners are consolidated herewith: Thousand Oaks Residential Care Home I, Inc., docket No. 1480-10; and Robert A. Fletcher and Pearl Fletcher, docket No. 1481-10. On December 15, 2011, we granted motions to change the captions in docket Nos. 1448-10 and 1480-10.

Held, further, the corporation is liable for the I.R.C. sec. 4972 excise tax to the extent determined herein. It is not liable for the I.R.C. sec. 6651(a)(1) and (2) additions to tax. Ps are liable for a portion of the I.R.C. sec. 6662(a) penalties as redetermined in this opinion.

Matthew Taggart, Ryan Andrews, Michael B. Luftman, and Charles Kolstad, for petitioners.

Kris H. An, for respondent.

MEMORANDUM FINDINGS OF FACT AND OPINION

WHERRY, Judge: These cases are before the Court on petitions for redetermination of income tax and excise tax deficiencies, additions to tax, and penalties respondent determined for petitioners' 2002 through 2005 tax years.2

After concessions the issues remaining are:3

2Unless otherwise indicated, all section references are to the Internal Revenue Code of 1986 (Code), as amended and in effect for the taxable years at issue. All Rule references are to the Tax Court Rules of Practice and Procedure.

3Petitioners Robert A. Fletcher and Pearl Fletcher concede with respect to their personal Federal income tax returns that they are not entitled to a deduction for depreciation expenses of $5,800 reported on Schedules E, Supplemental Income and Loss, for each of the 2003, 2004, and 2005 tax years. They also concede that they are not entitled to deduct certain taxes of $1,670, $1,605, and $1,714 for the 2003, 2004, and 2005 tax years, respectively, reported on Schedule E, and respondent (continued...)

VI.   Whether the compensation Thousand Oaks Residential Care Home I, Inc.

(TORCH), paid to Robert A. and Pearl Fletcher was reasonable under section 162..... (Cont'd)

3(...continued) concedes that they are entitled to deduct those expenses on Schedules A, Itemized Deductions, for the applicable years. The Fletchers concede that they are also not entitled to deduct other Schedule E taxes of $709, $668, and $1,916 for the 2003, 2004, and 2005, tax years, respectively, and respondent concedes that they are entitled to deduct those expenses on Schedule A. The Fletchers concede that they are not entitled to deduct Schedule E insurance expenses of $520, $500, and $505 for the 2003, 2004, and 2005 tax years, respectively. The parties agree that Schedule E warehouse rental income should be decreased by $1,200 and $2,400 for the 2003 and 2005 tax years, respectively. The Fletchers concede that they received unreported rental income of $4,400, $6,000, and $5,800 for the 2003, 2004, and 2005 tax years, respectively. The Fletchers concede that they are liable for the sec. 6662 accuracy-related penalty with respect to the disallowed Schedule E expenses and unreported 67 Erbes property rental income.

Petitioner Thousand Oaks Residential Care Home I, Inc., concedes that it is not entitled to deduct repairs and maintenance expenses of $2,954 for the 2003 tax year. This petitioner concedes that it is not entitled to deduct rental expenses of $2,800 and $7,100 for the 2003 and 2005 tax years, respectively. Respondent concedes that this petitioner is entitled to deduct taxes and licenses expenses of $19,198, $19,110, and $6,009 for the 2003, 2004, and 2005 tax years, respectively. This petitioner concedes that it is not entitled to deduct expenses of $56 and $103 for the 2003 and 2005 tax years, respectively. It also concedes that it is not entitled to other deductions of $26,464, $15,432, and $8,924 for the 2003, 2004, and 2005 tax years. This petitioner concedes that it is not entitled to deduct advertising expenses of $45 or employee benefit programs expenses of $2,852 for the 2003 tax year. Respondent concedes that this petitioner is entitled to deduct $20 for the disallowed contribution for the 2003 tax year, and this petitioner concedes that it is not entitled to deduct $150 of the same for the 2003 tax year. This petitioner concedes that it is liable for the sec. 6662 accuracy-related penalty with respect to all of its concessions listed in this paragraph.

…..for the 2003, 2004, and 2005 tax years, including the pension plan contributions paid on behalf of Robert A. and Pearl Fletcher for the 2003 and 2004 tax years,

(2) whether the compensation TORCH paid to the Fletchers' daughter, Grace-Ann Strick, was reasonable under section 162 for the 2003, 2004, and 2005 tax years,

(3) whether TORCH is liable for excise tax of $44,710.90 and $91,128.30 under section 4972 for the 2003 and 2004 tax years, respectively,

(4) whether TORCH is liable for section 6651(a)(1) failure to file additions to tax of $10,050.95 and $20,503.87 for the 2003 and 2004 tax years, respectively,

(5) whether TORCH is liable for section 6651(a)(2) failure to pay additions to tax of $11,177.73 and $22,326.43 for the 2003 and 2004 tax years, respectively, and

(6) whether petitioners Robert A. and Pearl Fletcher are liable for the section 6662(a) accuracy-related penalty for the 2003, 2004, and 2005 tax years and whether TORCH is liable for the section 6662(a) accuracy-related penalty for the 2002, 2003, 2004, and 2005 tax years.

FINDINGS OF FACT

The parties' stipulation of facts and supplemental stipulation of facts, with accompanying exhibits, and the stipulations of settled issues are incorporated herein by this reference. At the time they filed their respective Tax Court petitions, the individual petitioners resided in California and the corporate petitioner maintained its principal place of business in California.

Robert and Pearl Fletcher's Background–Lighting the Torch

Dr. Robert A. Fletcher began his career as an accountant for the Salvation Army Grace Hospital in Windsor, Ontario. He received formal training by taking charter accountant's courses offered by an accountant's association in Windsor, Ontario. He then became the business manager of the office staff at Leamington Memorial Hospital in Leamington, Ontario. Dr. Fletcher then moved to the United States in 1962 and began working at Seaside Oil, which merged with Tidewater Flying A Oil Co. that then merged with Getty Oil Co. He then became the chief accountant for Getty Oil. After leaving Getty Oil Dr. Fletcher decided to attend Cleveland Chiropractic College in Los Angeles. After graduation Dr. Fletcher became a California licensed chiropractor and began a chiropractic business in 1969. Starting in 1974 Dr. Fletcher operated his chiropractic practice as an owner employee of Robert A. Fletcher Chiropractic Corp., which was incorporated on October 30, 1974. Dr. Fletcher spent approximately 30 hours per week at his chiropractic practice until he retired from practicing chiropractic medicine in 1995. Ms. Fletcher is a registered nurse. She went through three years of training at the Grace Hospital in Toronto and received a nursing degree in 1959. After receiving her nursing degree, Ms. Fletcher's first job was at Hotel Dieu Hospital in Windsor, Canada, working in the operating room for about six months. After that, she worked at Leamington Memorial Hospital in Ontario, where she ran the recovery room. After the Fletchers moved to California Ms. Fletcher began working at the St. Francis Hospital in Santa Barbara in the intensive care unit and in the labor and delivery room. After a few years Ms. Fletcher then went to work at the Granada Hills Community Hospital, where she ran one of the shifts in the large extended care unit. Her duties there included: overseeing the nurse's aides, dispensing medication, writing all of the reports and recordings on patients' charts, overseeing lab results, calling doctors, taking orders, and interacting with patients' families.

Thousand Oaks Residential Care I (Corporation)–Carrying the Torch

On June 30, 1973, the Fletchers purchased a struggling corporation called Thousand Oaks Residential Care I from John and Edith Breen. Dr. Fletcher explained that they paid $25,000 and assumed the debt obligations of the corporation, which were several hundreds of thousands of dollars, including the real property mortgage.4 The corporation owned and operated TORCH an assisted living facility in Thousand Oaks, California.5 Dr. Fletcher was the corporation's sole shareholder. From 1973 to 2005 the corporation's board of directors consisted of three members: Robert A. Fletcher, Pearl Fletcher, and Lorne Muth, Pearl Fletcher's brother. Dr. Fletcher oversaw TORCH's general operations, handled its finances, and supervised its maintenance workers. He also performed substantial maintenance work himself. After Dr. Fletcher retired from his chiropractic practice in 1995 he

---

4Although Dr. Fletcher's testimony was that they paid $25,000 and assumed the debt obligations, the corporation's Federal Form 1120, U.S. Corporation Income Tax Return, page 4 balance sheet for 2005 shows a common stock balance of $24,000, and the record does not reveal any stock redemptions. We believe Dr. Fletcher's testimony that they initially paid $25,000 for the corporation.

worked full time for TORCH. Ms. Fletcher worked on and managed the assisted care personnel aspects of TORCH. She worked with residents, learned of their diagnoses, handicaps and illnesses, handled family matters, communicated with the nurses and nurses' aides, communicated with doctors and pharmacists, worked with dietitians, and supervised the housekeeping staff. The Fletchers received Forms W-2, Wage and Tax Statement, from TORCH reporting the following incomes:6 Year Ms. Fletcher Dr. Fletcher 1973-1983 -0- -01984 $6,000 -01985 13,000 $12,923 1986 15,521 18,764 1987 26,769 29,077 1988 36,000 36,000 1989 36,000 36,000 1990 4,154 4,154 1991 -0- -01992 20,800 -0 1993 20,800 -0

6All amounts have been rounded to the nearest whole number. No Forms W2 were presented for any year where the amount paid was "-0-".

1994 23,331 -01995 25,885 -01996 26,500 -01997 26,500 -01998 26,500 -01999 26,112 3,112 2000 25,072 19,669 2001 25,011 26,000 2002 129,030 130,000 Total 512,985 315,699

The corporation did not begin to cover its expenses and was losing money until the Fletchers had owned it for 18 months. The corporation paid all of its other employees at the market rate for their services. The corporation reported the following revenue information on its Forms 1120 for the 1987 through 2005 tax years:

Year

Gross receipts

Taxable income

Depreciation expense

Taxable income before deprecation1 1987 $863,021 $35,863 $24,277 $60,140 1988 864,899 24,754 31,133 55,887 1989 826,847 (8,748) 25,907 17,159 1990 679,545 (28,066) 15,636 (12,430) 1991 840,221 3,075 19,586 22,661 1992 894,853 (26,117) 25,441 (676) 1993 957,930 (8,463) 31,601 23,138 1994 982,305 34,585 32,410 66,995 1995 1,066,006 22,767 20,702 43,469 1996 1,127,454 16,063 33,092 49,155 1997 1,169,540 22,903 18,346 41,249 1998 1,238,596 44,632 30,033 74,665 1999 1,265,554 81,916 12,980 94,896 2000 1,250,983 29,479 10,380 39,859 2001 1,327,452 (27,516) 15,546 (11,970) 2002 1,001,110 297,798 13,949 311,747 20032 -0- 925,640 1,072 926,712 2004 -0- (917,045) -0- (917,045) 2005 -0- (3,943) -0- (3,943) Total 16,356,316 519,577 362,091 881,668 1The Court has derived this column of information from the reported taxable income and depreciation amounts on the Forms

1120. 2The facility was sold in 2002, and thereafter the corporation did not receive any gross receipts.

In July 2002 the corporation hired the Fletchers' daughter, Grace-Ann Strick, at $10 per hour. Beginning in October 2002 (after the sale of TORCH, see infra), the corporation paid Ms. Strick $2,000 per month.

Passing the Torch

On October 1, 2002, the corporation sold its sole asset, the assisted living facility, in an installment sale for $3,400,000 to Inga Jakobavich.7 The corporation allocated the $3,400,000 sale proceeds as follows: (1) $83,000 to furniture, equipment and machines, (2) $17,000 to a 1999 Windstar Van, (3) $200,000 to goodwill, and (4) $3,100,000 to building and land. Ms. Jakobavich has owned and operated an assisted living facility called Hillcrest Royale Retirement Community (Hillcrest) since 1989. After the purchase Ms. Jakobavich changed the name from TORCH to Thousand Oaks Royale Retirement Community. Since 2003 Ms. Jakobavich has paid herself $240,000 a year as the owner-operator of Hillcrest. When TORCH was sold it had about 85 residents and between 45 and 50 employees on staff. As part of the sale agreement, Dr. Fletcher entered into an interim lease back and management agreement starting on October 1, 2002, and ending on the earlier of April 30, 2003, or when Ms. Jakobovich obtained her own

---

7Ms. Jakobovich agreed to pay the following amounts: (i) $700,000 at 8% interest with a monthly payment of $5,402.71 from November 1, 2002, to October 1, 2007; and (ii) $2,120,000 at 7% interest with a monthly payment of $14,983.72 from November 1, 2002, to April 1, 2003, when the entire principal balance together with interest was due.

License. The Fletchers continued to work at TORCH for nine months following its sale.

After the Sale of TORCH

The corporation created a defined benefit plan (pension plan), effective January 1, 2003_. **_The Fletchers and Ms. Strick were the only participants of the plan._** The corporation paid Dr. Fletcher Form W-2 wages of $200,000, $200,000, and $30,000 in 2003, 2004, and 2005, respectively. It also contributed $191,433 and $259,506 to the pension plan for the benefit of Dr. Fletcher in 2003 and 2004, respectively, for a total compensation package of $880,939. The corporation paid Ms. Fletcher Form W-2 wages of $200,000, $200,000, and $30,000 in 2003, 2004, and 2005, respectively.8 It also contributed $191,433 and $198,915 to the pension plan for the benefit of Ms. Fletcher in 2003 and 2004, respectively for a total compensation package of $820,348.

The corporation's annual board minutes dated November 28, 2003, state:

"Compensation to Administrators was approved for payment of back salaries that

---

8The Schedules E for 2004 and 2005 appear to mistakenly leave off the $200,000 and $30,000 of executive compensation for each of the Fletchers. The Fletchers do not dispute receiving this income, and their accountant explained at trial that the expense for the Fletchers' compensation was included in the cost of labor elsewhere on the return.

Were not paid in prior years due to insufficient cash flow." The corporation's annual board minutes dated November 26, 2004, reiterated that the salaries approved in the prior year would remain the same, and the annual board minutes dated December 26, 2005, again state that the compensation paid to the Fletchers was intended as catchup compensation for inadequate compensation from prior years. In 1987 the long-term debt of the corporation was $758,071. In 2002 the long-term debt was $16,228, but the corporation owed $141,167 to its shareholders. The corporation's 2005 Form 1120 page 4 shows that at the end of the year the corporation had assets of $151,734 in cash on hand, $200 in current assets, and $700,000 in mortgage and real estate loans. It also shows that the corporation had liabilities of $149,262 in loans from shareholders, $515,987 in mortgages, notes, bonds payable in a year or more, $24,000 in common stock, and $162,685 in retained earnings. Ragnar Storm-Larsen's accounting firm, Storm-Larsen & Co., Inc., has prepared petitioners' returns and accounting records since the early 1990s. Mr. Storm-Larsen is an enrolled agent and has an M.B.A. degree from the California Lutheran University. It was Mr. Storm-Larsen's regular business practice to ask the taxpayer to review and approve a return before it was filed.

Dr. Fletcher approached Mr. Storm-Larsen when he believed that the sale of TORCH was imminent and that he and Ms. Fletcher would be paying a large amount of tax. Mr. Storm-Larsen researched catchup compensation and explained to Dr. Fletcher that if he had not been paid reasonable compensation in the past then he could make an adjustment and pay himself more. Mr. Storm-Larsen also advised Dr. Fletcher that a contribution to the pension plan was a benefit and that he could include it as compensation not previously received. Mr. Storm-Larsen advised the Fletchers that the compensation was reasonable.

Expert Report–Elizabeth Newlon, Ph.D.

Respondent commissioned Elizabeth Newlon, Ph.D., a senior consultant of National Economic Research Associates, Inc., to assess the compensation Dr. and Ms. Fletcher could reasonably expect for work performed at TORCH. Dr. Newlon has a B.S. degree in economics from Ohio State University and an M.A. degree and a Ph.D. in economics from Carnegie Mellon University. She is a published writer and has worked on discrimination, wage-and-hour, and wrongful termination suits and provided compensation estimates for medical directors. In order to compare the Fletchers' compensation with the nationwide data available, Dr. Newlon first determined that Ms. Fletcher's responsibilities were those of a medical and health services manager and that Dr. Fletcher's responsibilities were those of a general and operations manager, although she questioned "that there was a need for a full-time manager of this type". Dr. Newlon then compared the Fletchers' compensation with that of individuals doing similar types of work at residential care facilities in California. Dr. Newlon used labor rates from the Bureau of Labor Statistics' Occupational Employment Statistics program. That data is available only for 2002 2010; therefore Dr. Newlon deflated the compensation back to 1973 using the average decrease in compensation year to year, working backwards from 2010 to 2002. Dr. Newlon also adjusted the data to control for differences in the prevailing wages in California. She increased the national figures using the ratio of the median California medical and health services manager wages for Ms. Fletcher and the median general and operations manager wages for Dr. Fletcher to the national median wages for those positions (which worked out to be 118% for both). Dr. Newlon then decreased Dr. Fletcher's estimated compensation to reflect the amount she believed he was working, i.e. to 25% of the estimated amount for the years his tax statements stated that he worked 25% of his time at TORCH, 100% for the years after his retirement, and 25% for the years after the Fletchers sold TORCH. The following table shows Dr. Newlon's conclusions as to reasonable compensation for the Fletchers:

Year Ms. Fletcher % Mr. Fletcher Worked Mr. Fletcher 2003 $61,622 25% $6,952

2002 57,437

Nov. – Dec. 25 2,614 Jan. – Oct. 100 52,286 2001   55,111 100 56,526 2000   53,169 100 54,223 1999   51,296 100 52,014 1998   49,489 100 49,895 1997   47,746 100 47,862 1996   46,064 100 45,912 1995   44,441 100 44,042 1994   42,876 25 10,562 1993   41,365 25 10,132 1992   39,908 25 9,179 1991   38,502 25 9,323 1990   37,146 25 8,943 1989   35,837 25 8,579 1988   34,575 25 8,229 1987   33,357 25 7,894 1986   32,182 25 7,572 1985   31,048 25 7,264 1984   29,955 25 6,968 1983   28,899 25 6,684 1982   27,881 25 6,412

 1981   26,899 25 6,151 1980   25,952 25 5,900 1979   25,037 25 5,660 1978   24,155 25 5,429 1977   23,304 25 5,208 1976   22,484 25 4,996 1975   21,691 25 4,792 1974   20,927 25 4,597 1973   20,190 25 2,205   Total 1,130,545 565,005

Procedural Background

Respondent issued notices of deficiency on: October 21, 2009, for Dr. and Ms. Fletcher's 2003, 2004, and 2005 tax years; October 21, 2006, for Thousand Oaks Residential Home, Inc., for its tax years ended December 31, 2002, 2003, 2004, and 2005; and October 21, 2009, for Thousand Oaks Residential Care Home, for its tax years ended December 31, 2003 and 2004, showing income tax deficiencies and penalties of:[9]

[9]All values have been rounded to the nearest whole number.

Petitioner Year Deficiency

Accuracy-related penalty Sec. 6662(a)

Robert A. & Pearl Fletcher, docket   No. 1481-10 2003 $29,750 $5,950 2004   31,191 6,238 2005   16,729 3,346

Petitioner TYE Dec. 31 Deficiency

Accuracy-related penalty Sec. 6662(a)

TORCH, docket No. 480-10 2002 $99,391 $19,878 2003 526,695 105,399 2004   701   104 2005 18,916   3,783

Petitioner TYE Dec. 31 Deficiency

Additions to tax Sec. 6651(a)(1) and (2)

TORCH, docket No. 1448-10 2003 $44,711 $10,060 $11,178 2004   91,128   20,504   22,326

OPINION

VII.   Burden of Proof

The Commissioner's determination of a taxpayer's liability for an income tax deficiency is generally presumed correct, and the taxpayer bears the burden of proving that the determination is improper. See Rule 142(a); Welch v. Helvering, 290 U.S. 111, 115 (1933). However, pursuant to section 7491(a)(1), the burden of proof on factual issues that affect the taxpayer's tax liability may be shifted to the Commissioner where the "taxpayer introduces credible evidence with respect to * * * such issue." The burden will shift only if the taxpayer has, inter alia, complied with substantiation requirements pursuant to the Code and "maintained all records required under this title and has cooperated with reasonable requests by the Secretary for witnesses, information, documents, meetings, and interviews". Sec. 7491(a)(2). Because we decide these cases on the preponderance of the evidence, we need not address who bears the burden of proof.

II. Reasonable Compensation

Respondent contends that the compensation packages paid to the Fletchers were not reasonable under section 162 for the 2003, 2004, and 2005 tax years and disallowed deductions for all of the compensation.10 Petitioners contend that compensation paid in those years was reasonable and included catchup payments

---

10On brief respondent raises the issue of whether the fact that the corporation made only two payments to the defined benefit plan included in the Fletchers' compensation package makes the plan a temporary rather than a permanent one under sec. 1.401-1(b)(2) Income Tax Regs. Respondent never challenged the plan previously, and we decline to address this argument here, noting only that as petitioners correctly point out: "[t]he permanency requirement referred to in the regulations does not contemplate perpetual contributions". Estate of Benjamin v. Commissioner, 54 T.C. 953, 967 (1970), aff'd, 465 F.2d 982 (7th Cir. 1972).

---

for prior years in which they were undercompensated. In determining the reasonableness of compensation, we look at the compensation package as a whole, which includes salary and pension plan contributions. Bianchi v. Commissioner, 66 T.C. 324, 330 (1976), aff'd, 553 F.2d 93 (2d Cir. 1977).

VIII.   Overview of Section 162(a)(1)

Section 162(a) (1) provides a deduction for ordinary and necessary business expenses, including "a reasonable allowance for salaries or other compensation for personal services actually rendered". The deductibility of compensation is determined through a two-prong test: the amount of compensation must be reasonable, and the payment must be purely for services rendered. Nor-Cal Adjusters v. Commissioner, 503 F.2d 359, 362 (9th Cir. 1974), aff'g T.C. Memo. 1971-200; sec. 1.162-7, Income Tax Regs. We consider the reasonableness of the combined salary payments and the contributions to the defined benefit plan.11 See Rutter v. Commissioner, 853 F.2d 1267, 1274 (5th Cir. 1988), aff'g T.C. Memo. 1986-407; Bianchi v. Commissioner, 66 T.C. at 333-334.

11Contributions to defined benefit plans are not generally deductible under sec. 162 unless they meet the requirements of sec. 404(a). Sec. 404(a) incorporates the reasonable compensation standard of sec. 162. See LaMastro v. Commissioner, 72 T.C. 377, 381-382 (1979).

B. Catchup Compensation & Services Actually Rendered

Compensation for prior years' services is deductible in the current year as long as the employee was actually under compensated in prior years and the current payments are intended as compensation for past services. R.J. Nicoll Co. v. Commissioner, 59 T.C. 37, 50-51 (1972). When the compensation was actually for prior years of service, it need not be reasonable in the year it was paid. Devine Bros., Inc., v. Commissioner, T.C. Memo. 2003-15. Therefore, we shall evaluate the Fletchers' compensation in its entirety. In order for an employer to deduct compensation under section 162(a)(1) the compensation packages need to be both

reasonable and for services actually provided. Nor-Cal Adjusters v. Commissioner, 503 F.2d at 362; sec. 1.162-7, Income Tax Regs. The corporation's annual board minutes dated November 28, 2003, explicitly state: "Compensation to Administrators was approved for payment of back salaries that were not paid in prior years due to insufficient cash flow." The corporation's annual board minutes dated November 26, 2004, reiterated that the salaries approved in the prior year would remain the same, and we infer that this means that the board also intended those compensation packages as payment of back salaries for prior years. The corporation's annual board minutes dated December 26, 2005, again state that the compensation paid to the Fletchers was for inadequate compensation from prior years.

We found the Fletchers' testimony that the compensation was intended as catchup compensation for prior years credible and, when viewed along with the corporation's annual board minutes, we find that the compensation was intended as compensation for each of the three years at issue, respectively, and as catchup compensation for prior services actually rendered. Now we must determine whether the catchup compensation was reasonable.

C. Reasonableness of Payments

The reasonableness of the payments is considered with reference to five broad factors set forth in Elliotts, Inc. v. Commissioner, 716 F.2d 1241 (9th Cir. 1983), rev'g T.C. Memo. 1980-282. No single factor is dispositive. Id. At 1245. The relevant factors are: (1) the employee's role in the company; (2) a comparison of the employee's salary with salaries paid by similar companies for similar services; (3) the character and condition of the company; (4) potential conflicts of interest; and (5) internal consistency. Id. At 1245-1247.

The Court of Appeals for the Ninth Circuit, to which an appeal in these cases would lie absent stipulation to the contrary, adds an additional factor: whether an independent investor would be willing to compensate the employee as he was so compensated. Metro Leasing & Dev. Corp. v. Commissioner, 376 F.3d 1015, 1019 (9th Cir. 2004), aff'g 119 T.C. 8 (2002). The Court of Appeals notes that "the perspective of an independent investor is but one of many factors that are to be considered when assessing the reasonableness of an executive officer's compensation." Id. At 1021. The reasonableness of compensation is a question of fact to be determined on the basis of all the facts and circumstances. Pac. Grains, Inc. v. Commissioner, 399 F.2d 603, 606 (9th Cir. 1968), aff'g T.C. Memo. 1967-7.

IX. Employee's Role in the Company

This factor looks to the overall significance of the employee to the company. Elliotts, Inc. v. Commissioner, 716 F.2d at 1245. "Relevant considerations include the position held by the employee, hours worked, and duties performed, Am. Foundry v. Commissioner, 536 F.2d 289, 291-292 (9th Cir. 1976), as well as the general importance of the employee to the success of the company". Id. The Fletchers were hands-on owner-operators of TORCH. Although TORCH was only moderately profitable, the Fletchers explained that they bought the facility for very little cash (i.e., $25,000) plus assumed liabilities, when the revenues from the facility could not even cover its bills and that within 18 months they had turned it around. Dr. Fletcher was the president and overall manager of TORCH, and Ms. Fletcher was the head nurse and was in charge of personnel and resident relations. We find this factor weighs in favor of petitioners.

X. Comparison With Salaries Paid by Similar Companies

The next relevant factor is a comparison of the employee's salary with salaries paid by similar companies providing similar services. Elliotts, Inc. v. Commissioner, 716 F.2d at 1246; Hoffman Radio Corp. v. Commissioner, 177 F.2d 264, 266 (9th Cir. 1949). Petitioners did not provide the Court with any evidence of employees of other companies providing similar services with the exception of Ms. Jakobavich, who testified that she has paid herself $240,000 a year as the owner-operator of Hillcrest since 2003. However, we know nothing of Ms. Jakobavich's job description, duties, hours, or the profitability of Hillcrest. Respondent presented an expert witness to compare the Fletchers' compensation with nationwide data.12

12We note that we evaluate expert opinions in the light of each expert's demonstrated qualifications and all other evidence in the record. See Parker v. Commissioner, 86 T.C. 547, 561 (1986). We are not bound by an expert's opinion and may accept or reject an expert opinion in full or in part in the exercise of sound judgment. See Helvering v. Nat'l Grocery Co., 304 U.S. 282, 295 (1938); Parker v. Commissioner, 86 T.C. at 561-562. We may also reach a determination of value based on our own examination of the evidence in the record. Silverman v. Commissioner, 538 F.2d 927, 933 (2d Cir. 1976), aff'g T.C. Memo. 1974-285.

Combining two of the tables supra, we can summarize respondent's expert's findings as to the adequacy of Dr. Fletcher's and Ms. Fletcher's compensation:

Year	Ms. Fletcher (estimate)	Ms. Fletcher actual	Amount under-paid	Dr. Fletcher (estimate)	Dr. Fletcher actual	Amount underpaid
2002	$57,437	$129,030	($71,593)	$54,900	$130,000	($75,100)
2001	55,111	25,011	30,100	56,526	26,000	30,526
2000	53,169	25,072	28,097	54,223	19,669	34,554
1999	51,296	26,112	25,184	52,014	3,112	48,902
1998	49,489	26,500	22,989	49,895	-0-	49,895
1997	47,746	26,500	21,246	47,862	-0-	47,862
1996	46,064	26,500	19,564	45,912	-0-	45,912
1995	44,441	25,885	18,556	44,042	-0-	44,042
1994	42,876	23,331	19,545	10,562	-0-	10,562
1993	41,365	20,800	20,565	10,132	-0-	10,132
1992	39,908	20,800	19,108	9,179	-0-	9,179
1991	38,502	-0-	38,502	9,323	-0-	9,323
1990	37,146	4,154	32,992	8,943	4,154	4,789
1989	35,837	36,000	(163)	8,579	36,000	(27,421)
1988	34,575	36,000	(1,425)	8,229	36,000	(27,771)
1987	33,357	26,769	6,588	7,894	29,077	(21,183)
1986	32,182	15,521	16,661	7,572	18,764	(11,192)
1985	31,048	13,000	18,048	7,264	12,923	(5,659)
1984	29,955	6,000	23,955	6,968	-0-	6,968
1983	28,899	-0-	28,899	6,684	-0-	6,684
1982	27,881	-0-	27,881	6,412	-0-	6,412
1981	26,899	-0-	26,899	6,151	-0-	6,151
1980	25,952	-0-	25,952	5,900	-0-	5,900
1979	25,037	-0-	25,037	5,660	-0-	5,660
1978	24,155	-0-	24,155	5,429	-0-	5,429
1977	23,304	-0-	23,304	5,208	-0-	5,208
1976	22,484	-0-	22,484	4,996	-0-	4,996
1975	21,691	-0-	21,691	4,792	-0-	4,792
1974	20,927	-0-	20,927	4,597	-0-	4,597
1973	20,190	-0-	20,190	2,205	-0-	2,205
Total	1,068,923	512,985	555,938	558,053	315,699	242,354

For the years for which a "-0-" appears in the above table, petitioners did not supply a Form W-2. The Fletchers credibly testified that for the years for which they did not have a Form W-2 from the corporation, the corporation did not have sufficient funds to pay them a salary, making a Form W-2 unnecessary. Respondent did not establish that the Fletchers received a salary in any of those years and failed to produce any further Forms W-2. Looking at the above table, even respondent's own expert, whom the Court found knowledgeable, agrees that the Fletchers were underpaid in comparison with] data from a national survey.13 Using the data from this chart, respondent's expert shows that before the years at issue Ms. Fletcher was underpaid by $555,938 and Dr. Fletcher was underpaid by $242,354. In the years at issue, as we determined above, Dr. Fletcher received a total compensation package of $880,939 and Ms. Fletcher received a total compensation package of $820,348 for services rendered. After subtracting the amounts by which the Fletchers were underpaid in prior years as determined by respondent's expert, Dr. Fletcher's combined compensation for the years at issue was $638,585 and Ms. Fletcher's combined compensation for the years at issue was $264,410. Respondent's expert, Dr. Newlon, used labor rates from the Bureau of Labor Statistics' Occupational Employment Statistics program to determine the figures represented in the table above. That data for 2003 through 2005 shows that a combined compensation inflated for California wages and assuming full- time employment, would be $187,537.40 for Dr. Fletcher and $195,785.60 for Ms.Fletcher.14 Because of the large difference between the actual compensation and

13 We note that Dr. Newlon did not account for the time value of money. Because the Fletchers were required to wait for compensation for prior years, their catchup compensation should also have been inflated for the time value of money.

14 These figures were taken from a table included in Dr. Newlon's expert report that reported data from the Bureau of Labor Statistics' Occupational (continued...)

respondent's expert's opinion, this factor weighs in favor of finding that the Fletchers' compensation was unreasonable.

XI.   Character and Condition of the Company

Under this factor we analyze the character and condition of the company, focusing on the company's size, complexity, net income, and general economic condition. Elliotts, Inc. v. Commissioner, 716 F.2d at 1246. First, we note that one of the reasons the Fletchers determined to pay themselves catchup compensation is that in multiple years the corporation had insufficient cash flow and profit to pay them adequate compensation. However, the corporation's profitability is not the only indication of the character and condition of the company. In 1987 the long-term debt of the corporation was $758,071. By 2002 the long-term debt had been reduced to $16,228, and the corporation owed $141,167 in loans from shareholders.15 Had the Fletchers chosen to pay themselves higher salaries in years they chose to aggressively pay down the loans, the outstanding

14(...continued) Employment Statistics program. Dr. Newlon did not reach any conclusions for these numbers; however, she did not believe that the Fletchers were each fully employed by the corporation for each of years at issue.

15 With stated capital of only $25,000 the corporation was thinly capitalized and some of the loans from shareholders might arguably in substance have been capital. Respondent has never raised this issue; consequently, we shall treat the "loans" as loans.

debt would have been higher when TORCH was sold and the Fletchers would have made less on the sale. Also, as we noted above, TORCH was only moderately profitable, but the Fletchers bought the facility when the revenues it generated could not even cover its bills and within 18 months had turned it around. Although the corporation was not profitable enough to pay the Fletchers in some years, the Fletchers paid down long-term debt, and upon purchasing TORCH, managed to make it profitable enough to pay its own bills and to command a substantial price when it was sold. Therefore we find this factor slightly favors petitioners.

XII.   Potential Conflicts of Interest

This factor focuses on any indicia that there may be a conflict of interest. Id. Primarily we are concerned whether a relationship exists between the employee and the company that may permit the disguise of nondeductible corporate distributions as salary expenditures. Id. The Fletchers, as owner-operators who never received a dividend and who used all of the profits of TORCH's sale to pay themselves income, undoubtedly had a conflict of interest. Petitioners' opening brief agrees that "a conflict of interest clearly existed". With petitioners' concession we find that this factor weighs against finding that the compensation the Fletchers received was reasonable and deductible under section 162.

XIII.   Internal Consistency

"[E]vidence of an internal inconsistency in a company's treatment of payments to employees may indicate that the payments go beyond reasonable compensation." Elliotts, Inc. v. Commissioner, 716 F.2d at 1247. In most of the years before the years at issue, the Fletchers' compensation was indeed inconsistent with the payments to other employees, but the Fletchers discriminated against themselves. In years when the corporation experienced cash flow problems or was not profitable they took no, or very little, salary. Respondent correctly points out that during the years at issue the Fletchers had large salaries; however, as discussed above, we found that the Fletchers were paying themselves previously earned compensation for years in which they were under compensated. We find that this factor weights in favor of finding that the compensation the Fletchers received was reasonable and deductible under section 162.

XIV.   Additional Factor: The Independent Investor

While we found supra that the Fletchers did intend the compensation as catchup compensation for prior services rendered, paying out compensation packages that deplete the rest of the corporation's assets denies the corporation's equity owners a fair return on their capital investment. In Elliotts, Inc. v. Commissioner, 716 F.2d at 1247, the Court of Appeals for the Ninth Circuit noted that

If the bulk of the corporation's earnings are being paid out in the form of compensation, so that the corporate profits, after payment of the compensation, do not represent a reasonable return on the shareholder's equity in the corporation, then an independent shareholder would probably not approve of the compensation arrangement. If, however, that is not the case and the company's earnings on equity remain at a level that would satisfy an independent investor, there is a strong indication that management is providing compensable services and that profits are not being siphoned out of the company disguised as salary. [Fn. Ref. omitted.]

The Fletchers purchased TORCH for $25,000 in 1973, and the record does not indicate if they paid in any additional amounts.16 A reasonable investor would expect to receive a return on this initial investment and would not approve of a

---

16The record does not reveal whether the Fletchers were personally liable for the loans assumed upon the purchase of TORCH, which would warrant an increased return on the investment. And the record does not indicate whether the Fletchers contributed additional amounts to TORCH during the periods it could not cover its bills. Because the record is so sparse as to additional paid-in capital, we will assume that TORCH took loans from the shareholders and then repaid them when there was money. Also, as discussed supra note 4, Dr. Fletcher testified that the Fletchers paid $25,000 and assumed the debt obligations when they purchased the corporation; however, the corporation's Form 1120, page 4 balance sheet for 2005 shows a common stock balance of $24,000, and the record does not reveal any stock redemptions. We find Dr. Fletcher's testimony credible that they initially paid $25,000 for the corporation.

---

salary package that entirely depletes the corporation's assets. Id. (20% return on equity "would satisfy independent investor"); L & B Pipe & Supply Co. v. Commissioner, T.C. Memo. 1994-187 (investor would have been happy with either 6% dividend return plus 10% growth in retained earnings or 20% growth in shareholders' equity). As the cases above show, the Court has found a return on investment of between 10% and 20% tends to indicate compensation was reasonable.17 A 10% return on $25,000 compounded annually for 31.5 years (1973-2005) is roughly $503,300, and a 20% return is $7,800,982.18 Because TORCH was a small highly leveraged business purchased with a large amount of debt, a hypothetical investor in TORCH might be satisfied with a 10% return on this investment. Therefore the corporation should have had $503,300 left for distribution after payment of the

17We note that in June 1973 the prime interest rate was between 7.5% and 7.75% and that a 10-year Treasury note had a 6.46% interest rate. Because of the nature of TORCH an investor would have expected to earn a higher rate of return than the Treasury note.

18Although as explained in Miller & Sons Drywall, Inc. v. Commissioner, T.C. Memo. 2005-114, "this Court has generally calculated a corporation's ROE [return on equity] by dividing its net income after tax for a specific year by its shareholders equity" instead of using compound growth rates, we find that under the specific facts of these cases using compound growth rates paints a more accurate picture. As the table supra page 9 shows, the corporation had minimal income in most of the years it was in business and in both 2004 and 2005 had negative income.

---

compensation packages. Because the compensation packages did not leave enough of the corporation's assets to be paid back to the hypothetical investor as a return on investment, we find that this factor weighs against a finding of reasonable compensation.

XV.   Conclusion

After reviewing each factor discussed above, we find that the compensation packages the Fletchers received as compensation for the 2003, 2004, and 2005 tax years were unreasonable. Taking into account the rate of return a reasonable investor would have expected, we find that the Fletchers were overpaid by a total of $282,615.19 A reasonable investor would require at least this amount remain in

---

19We have found that the corporation should have had on hand $503,300 to pay the hypothetical investor, and the corporation had $162,685 in retained earnings at the end of the 2005 tax year. We disallowed Ms. Strick's compensation of $59,000 infra (that in substance amounted to a dividend or distribution to shareholders and a gift by them to their daughter), which increased the amount the corporation had left on hand. Therefore, the Fletchers were overpaid by a total of $282,615 (i.e. $503,300 - $161,685 - $59,000 = $282,615).

The Fletchers' combined total compensation for the years at issue was $1,701,287. Dr. Fletcher's combined compensation accounted for 51.8% of that amount, and Ms. Fletcher's accounted for 48.2%. Therefore we attribute $146,395 of the overpayment to Dr. Fletcher and $136,220 to Ms. Fletcher. Of Dr. Fletcher's combined compensation his salary accounted for 48.8% and the pension plan contribution accounted for 51.2%. Therefore we find that Dr. Fletcher was overpaid in salary by $71,441 (which is not deductible) and had a nondeductible pension plan (continued...)

---

the corporation to be paid out to the investor as a return on the investment. We again note that the reasonableness of compensation is a question of fact to be determined on the basis of all the facts and circumstances. Pacific Grains, Inc. v. Commissioner, 399 F.2d at 606.

III. Compensation Paid to Grace-Ann Strick

Respondent contends that the compensation paid to Ms. Strick was not reasonable under section 162 for the 2003, 2004, and 2005 tax years. As discussed supra, section 162(a)(1) provides a deduction for ordinary and necessary business expenses, including reasonable compensation for services rendered. Under the two prong test the amount of compensation must be reasonable, and the payment must be purely for services rendered. Nor-Cal Adjusters v. Commissioner, 503 F.2d at 362; sec. 1.162-7, Income Tax Regs. In July 2002 the corporation hired Ms. Strick at $10 per hour. The corporation was sold on October 1, 2002, and beginning in October 2002, the corporation paid Ms. Strick $2,000 per month.

19(...continued) contribution of $74,954. Of Ms. Fletcher's combined compensation her salary accounted for 52.4% and the pension plan contribution accounted for 47.6%. Therefore we find that Ms. Fletcher was overpaid in salary by $71,380 (which is not deductible) and had a nondeductible pension plan contribution of $64,840.

Petitioners contend that Ms. Strick was hired to handle third-party vendors and worker's compensation claims filed by former employees against the corporation. Petitioners provided documents related to worker's compensation claims filed by Paula Muriel and Amparo Villasenor to substantiate Ms. Strick's employment. Ms. Muriel's accident occurred on or about February 11, 2002, and was settled on or about March 21, 2002. As this was before Ms. Strick began working for TORCH, we do not find this evidence substantiates Ms. Strick's employment. Petitioners also provided documents related to the claim filed by Amparo Villasenor. Mr. Villasenor was injured on or about May 13, 2000. Although the file is much more extensive than that of Ms. Muriel and it appears that petitioners hired and paid attorneys through 2003 to handle the appeal of the worker's compensation claim, Ms. Strick's name does not appear on any of the documents, and she did not testify at trial to explain what services she provided. On the basis of the preponderance of the evidence we find that all of the compensation paid to Grace-Ann Stick was not reasonable under section 162 for the 2003, 2004, and 2005 tax years and the corporation is not entitled to deduct it.

IV. Section 4972 Excise Tax

Because TORCH did not file Form 5330, Return of Excise Taxes Related to Employee Benefit Plans, respondent contends that the corporation is liable for excise tax of $44,710.90 and $91,128.30 under section 4972 for the 2003 and 2004 tax years, respectively. Section 4972 imposes a 10% tax on any nondeductible contributions to qualified employer plans. See Citrus Valley Estates, Inc. v. Commissioner, 99 T.C. 379 (1992), aff'd in part, remanded in part, 49 F.3d 1410 (9th Cir. 1995). Because we found supra that a portion of TORCH's contributions to the pension plan was unreasonable compensation and therefore not deductible under section 162 (and thereby section 404), the 10% section 4972 excise tax applies to that extent.

V. Section 6651(a)(1) and (2) Additions to Tax

Respondent contends that the corporation is liable for section 6651(a)(1) failure to file additions to tax of $10,050.95 and $20,503.87 for the 2003 and 2004 tax years, respectively. As a general rule, "any person made liable for any tax * * * shall make a return or statement according to the forms and regulations prescribed by the Secretary." Sec. 6011(a); see also Citrus Valley Estates, Inc. v. Commissioner, 99 T.C. at 462 (holding section 6651(a) is applicable to the failure to file a Form 5330). Section 6651(a)(1), in the case of a failure to file a return on time, imposes an addition to tax of 5% of the tax required to be shown on the return for each month or fraction thereof for which there is a failure to file, not to exceed 25% in the aggregate.[20] The addition to tax will not apply if it is shown that such failure is due to reasonable cause and not due to willful neglect. Sec. 6651(a)(1). Respondent also contends that the corporation is liable for section 6651(a)(2) failure to pay additions to tax of $11,177.73 and $22,326.43 for the 2003 and 2004 tax years, respectively, because the corporation did not pay the excise tax due to be shown on Form 5330. Section 6651(a)(2) provides for an addition to tax of 0.5% per month up to 25% for failure to pay the amount shown on a return unless it is shown that the failure is due to reasonable cause and not due to willful neglect. Petitioners contend that they reasonably relied on the advice of Mr. Storm Larsen that the compensation package was reasonable and therefore deductible, thus TORCH need not file Form 5330. They argue that the failure to file and failure to pay were due to reasonable cause and not willful neglect. When Dr. Fletcher understood that after the sale of TORCH they would be paying a large amount of tax, he sought Mr. Storm-Larsen's advice. Mr. Storm-Larsen researched

20The sec. 6651(a)(1) addition to tax is reduced by the amount of the sec. 6651(a)(2) addition to tax for any month (or fraction thereof) to which an addition to tax applies under both sec. 6651(a)(1) and (2). See sec. 6651(c)(1).

catchup compensation and explained to Dr. Fletcher that if he had not been paid reasonable compensation in the past then he could make an adjustment and pay himself more. Mr. Storm-Larsen also told Dr. Fletcher that a contribution to the pension plan was a benefit and that he could pay himself for compensation not previously received. Mr. Storm-Larsen advised the Fletchers that the compensation was reasonable, which would therefore not require a Form 5330 filing. The Supreme Court of the United States has explained that "Courts have

frequently held that "reasonable cause" is established when a taxpayer shows that he reasonably relied on the advice of an accountant or attorney that it was unnecessary to file a return, even when such advice turned out to have been mistaken." United States v. Boyle, 469 U.S. 241, 250 (1985). We agree with petitioners that they reasonably relied on the advice of their accountant and TORCH is not liable for the section 6651(a)(1) and (2) additions to tax.

VI. Section 6662(a) Accuracy-Related Penalty

Respondent also contends that petitioners Robert A. and Pearl Fletcher are liable for the section 6662(a) accuracy-related penalty for the 2003, 2004, and 2005 tax years and petitioner TORCH is liable for the section 6662(a) accuracy-related penalty for the 2002, 2003, 2004, and 2005 tax years.

Subsection (a) of section 6662 imposes an accuracy-related penalty of 20% of any underpayment that is attributable to causes specified in subsection (b). Respondent asserts that one or both of two causes justify the imposition of the penalty for each year: a substantial understatement of income tax and negligence.

Sec. 6662(b)(1) and (2).

There is a "substantial understatement" of income tax for any tax year where, in the case of an individual, the amount of the understatement exceeds the greater of (1) 10% of the tax required to be shown on the return for the tax year or (2) $5,000. Sec. 6662(d)(1)(A). In the case of corporations (other than S corporations or personal holding companies) the amount of the understatement exceeds the greater of (1) 10% of the tax required to be shown on the return for the tax year or (2) $10,000,000.

Sec. 6662(d)(1)(B).

Section 6662(a) also imposes a penalty for negligence or disregard of the rules or regulations. Under this section "'negligence' includes any failure to make a reasonable attempt to comply with the provisions of this title". Sec. 6662(c). Under caselaw, "'Negligence is a lack of due care or the failure to do what a reasonable and ordinarily prudent person would do under the circumstances.'" Freytag v. Commissioner, 89 T.C. 849, 887 (1987) (quoting Marcello v. Commissioner, 380 F.2d 499, 506 (5th Cir. 1967), aff'g on this issue 43 T.C. 168 (1964) and T.C. Memo. 1964-299), aff'd, 904 F.2d 1011 (5th Cir. 1990), aff'd, 501 U.S. 868 (1991).

There is an exception to the section 6662(a) penalty when a taxpayer can demonstrate (1) reasonable cause for the underpayment and (2) that the taxpayer acted in good faith with respect to the underpayment. Sec. 6664(c)(1). Regulations promulgated under section 6664(c) further provide that the determination of reasonable cause and good faith "is made on a case-by-case basis, taking into account all pertinent facts and circumstances." Sec. 1.6664-4(b)(1), Income Tax Regs. Reliance on the advice of a tax professional may, but does not necessarily, establish reasonable cause and good faith for the purpose of avoiding a section 6662(a) penalty. See Boyle, 469 U.S. at 251 ("Reliance by a lay person on a lawyer [or accountant] is of course common; but that reliance cannot function as a substitute for compliance with an unambiguous statute."). The caselaw sets forth the following three requirements in order for a

taxpayer to use reliance on a tax professional to avoid liability for a section 6662(a) penalty: "(1) The adviser was a competent professional who had sufficient expertise to justify reliance, (2) the taxpayer provided necessary and accurate information to the adviser, and (3) the taxpayer actually relied in good faith on the adviser's judgment." See Neonatology Asscos., P.A. v. Commissioner, 115 T.C. 43, 99 (2000), aff'd, 299 F.3d 221 (3d Cir. 2002); see also Charlotte's Office Boutique, Inc. v. Commissioner, 425 F.3d 1203, 1212 n.8 (9th Cir. 2005) (quoting and with approval the above three-prong test), aff'g 121 T.C. 89 (2003). With respect to the employment plan contributions, we find that petitioners actually relied on the advice of their accountant, who was a competent professional, and that they provided him with the necessary and accurate information. Therefore, petitioners are not liable for the section 6662(a) accuracy-related penalty related to the contributions. However, as discussed supra, we found that the compensation paid to Ms. Strick was not for services actually rendered and therefore not reasonable compensation. We do not find that Dr. and Ms. Fletcher actually relied on the advice of their accountant with respect to those payments, and TORCH is therefore liable for the section 6662(a) accuracy-related penalty related to those amounts. The Court has considered all of the parties' contentions, arguments, requests, and statements. To the extent not discussed herein, the Court concludes that they are meritless, moot, or irrelevant.

To reflect the foregoing,

Decisions will be entered under Rule 155.

(Note-rule 155 means time to compute the damages)

CASE OF THE YEAR 2012

INTRODUCTION

The founder of xelan (seen in the case below) is Dr. Donald Guess. I talked to him many times on the phone as the IRS had shut down his operation-then came after him for tax evasion. He was convicted for filing a form late-which he legally could do-but too bad the courts would not listen. He did go to jail and is now out. Not unusual that tax evasion occurs by gifting closely held stock at high value to a charity. This also happened to a person know as Wade Cook-a great promoter in the 1980s. Kathy Barrow, an attorney mentioned in the case actually spoke at a conference we put on. The IRS did not like her involvement in 419 cases, so they placed a 6700 investigation on her. She quit 419 plans. The Corporation xelan was vindicated from tax fraud-but like Arthur Anderson it came too late.

T.C. Memo. 2012-104

UNITED STATES TAX COURT

JERALD W. WHITE AND CLAUDIA K. WHITE, Petitioners v. COMMISSIONER OF INTERNAL REVENUE, Respondent

DIOGENES HOLDINGS, INC., Petitioner v. COMMISSIONER OF INTERNAL REVENUE, Respondent

Docket Nos. 22514-07, 22515-07.   Filed April 11, 2012.

David E. Price and Adria S. Price, for petitioners.

Thomas A. Dombrowski, Anne W. Durning, and Roger P. Law, for respondent.

MEMORANDUM FINDINGS OF FACT AND OPINION

RUWE, Judge: These cases were consolidated for the purposes of trial, briefing, and opinion.

Respondent determined deficiencies and accuracy-related penalties under section 6662(a)1 with respect to petitioners' Federal income taxes as follows:

Jerald W. and Claudia K. White docket No. 22514-07

		Accuracy-related penalty
Year	Deficiency	Sec. 6662(a)
2001	$77,600	$15,520.00
2002	77,200	15,440.00
2003	294,777	58,955.40

Diogenes Holdings, Inc. docket No. 22515-07

		Accuracy-related penalty
Year	Deficiency	Sec. 6662(a)
2001	$61,635	$12,327.00
2002	61,453	12,290.60
2003	61,840	12,368.00

The deficiencies result from respondent's disallowance of deductions claimed by Diogenes Holdings, Inc. (Diogenes), for contributions to the xélan Welfare Benefit Trust (xélan 419 plan) in 2001 and 2002 and to the Millennium Multiple Welfare Benefit Trust (Millennium plan) in 2003, and respondent's

1Unless otherwise indicated, all section references are to the Internal Revenue Code (Code) in effect for the years at issue, and all Rule references are to the Tax Court Rules of Practice and Procedure.

———————————————————————————————

determination that Dr. Jerald W. White (Dr. White) and Claudia K. White (Mrs. White) must include the amount of the contributions in their income. Respondent also determined that Dr.

and Mrs. White must include the "full value" of "the arrangement" in their income for 2003 when the xélan 419 plan terminated and the assets in the xélan 419 plan were available for distribution.2

The issues we are asked to decide are:

(1) whether Diogenes' contributions to the xélan 419 plan in 2001 and 2002 and to the Millennium plan in 2003 are deductible;

(2) whether Dr. and Mrs. White must include in their income for 2001, 2002, and 2003, respectively, the contributions Diogenes made to the xélan 419 plan in 2001 and 2002 and to the Millennium plan in 2003;

(3) whether Dr. and Mrs. White must include in their 2003 income, under section 402(b)(2), an additional $642,220 because when the xélan 419 plan

_____

2Respondent gave three alternative reasons for the disallowance of the deductions Diogenes claimed for the contributions to the xélan 419 plan and the Millennium plan: (1) the contributions were not ordinary and necessary business expenses under sec. 162; (2) the contributions were limited by and subject to the rules of sec. 404(a)(5); and (3) the arrangement is a welfare benefit fund to which the exceptions under sec. 419A(f)(6) do not apply. Respondent gave alternative reasons for requiring Dr. and Mrs. White to include the contributions to the xélan 419 plan and the Millennium plan in their income: (1) the contributions were constructive dividends to Dr. and Mrs. White under secs. 301 and 61, and (2) the contributions were compensatory and includible in income as an economic benefit under sec. 61.

terminated in 2003, the insurance policies held by the xélan 419 plan were distributable to Dr. and Mrs. White; and

(4) whether petitioners are liable for accuracy-related penalties under section 6662(a) for substantial understatements of income tax, or, alternatively, negligence or disregard of rules and regulations.

FINDINGS OF FACT

Some of the facts have been stipulated and are so found. The stipulation of facts, the supplemental stipulation of facts, and the second and third supplemental stipulations of facts are incorporated herein by this reference.

Background

Dr. and Mrs. White and Diogenes At the time the petitions were filed Dr. and Mrs. White resided in Tennessee, and Diogenes' principal place of business was in Tennessee. Dr. White has practiced medicine in Tennessee since 1974. Dr. White is the sole owner and provides medical services as an employee of Brownsville Medical Clinic, P.A. (Brownsville Medical), a C corporation. Brownsville Medical owns and operates three medical facilities: Brownsville Medical Clinic, Brownsville, Tennessee; the Medical Clinic of Alamo, Alamo, Tennessee; and Old Hickory Family Medicine, Jackson, Tennessee. Dr. White practices medicine at all three locations. Mrs. White is a registered nurse licensed in Tennessee. She practices nursing at the clinics operated by Brownsville Medical. Dr. White's daughter Margaret White Nelson (Margaret) was born in 1964. Margaret obtained a medical degree from the University of Tennessee Medical School in 1991 and since 1996 has worked as a pediatrician practicing medicine at Cincinnati Children's Hospital and at a pediatric clinic in Cincinnati. Margaret occasionally performs services as a doctor at one of the clinics owned by Brownsville Medical.

Dr. and Mrs. White have a son, Eric Bristol White (Eric), who was born in1984. Eric was 15 years old in 1999. Eric became a licensed pharmacy technician in Tennessee in 2005. During the years at issue Dr. and Mrs. White owned several other corporations. Dr. White owned 67% and Mrs. White owned 33% of the shares of Brownsville Apothecary, Inc. (Brownsville Apothecary), a C corporation. Mrs. White owned 51% of the shares of Cost Plus Pharmacy, Inc. (Cost Plus), an S corporation, and Margaret and Eric each owned 24.5%. Brownsville Apothecary and Cost Plus have had very little employee turnover. Diogenes was incorporated in Tennessee on August 13, 1999. Dr. White owns 100% of the shares of Diogenes, and is its president. Mrs. White is Diogenes' secretary/treasurer.

On August 29, 1999, Diogenes entered into a management agreement with Brownsville Medical (including Brownsville Medical Clinic, Medical Clinic of Alamo, and Old Hickory Family Medicine) and Brownsville Apothecary. The agreement states that Diogenes "agrees to furnish advisory and management expertise in all aspects of business to the above."

For the years at issue Dr. and Mrs. White reported the following relevant amounts on their jointly filed Federal individual income tax returns:

	2001	2002	2003
Gross income	$1,418,560	$1,115,707	$1,142,511
Itemized deductions	122,512	110,429	27,462
Taxable income (loss)	1,296,048	1,005,278	1,115,049
Income tax	478,797	358,773	350,805

Brownsville Medical reported the following relevant amounts on its Federal income tax returns:

	2001	2002	2003
Total income1	$2,527,967	$2,316,241	$2,137,828
Less: Total deductions	2,569,771	2,274,031	2,138,283
Taxable income	(41,804)	2(223)	(455)

1Gross receipts less cost of goods sold. 2Amount includes deductions for net operating loss from 2001.

Included in total deductions for Brownsville Medical were the following relevant items:

	2001	2002	2003
Compensation of officers	$792,546	$444,397	$295,000
Salaries and wages	958,633	1,054,676	1,077,034
Pension, profit-sharing,	71,345	69,323	72,785
Employee benefit programs	--	--	-
Consultant fees	235,000	234,076	237,500

Brownsville Apothecary reported the following relevant amounts on its income tax returns:

	2001	2002	2003
Total income1	$719,437	$741,101	$881,557
Less: Total deductions	702,992	741,037	882,456
Net operating loss carryover	19,825	3,380	3,316
Taxable income	(3,380)	(3,316)	(4,215)

1Gross receipts less cost of goods sold.

Included in total deductions were the following relevant items:

	2001	2002	2003
Compensation of officers	$379,000	$411,400	$500,000
Salaries and wages	108,213	125,266	138,663
Pension, profit-sharing,	27,299	22,731	21,789
Employee benefit programs	--	--	-
Consultant fees	99,000	90,453	101,000

For the years at issue Diogenes reported the following relevant amounts on its

Federal corporate income tax returns:

	2001	2002	2003
Total income	$302,228	$300,980	$300,601
Compensation of officers	45,000	45,000	90,000

Salaries and wages	--	--	-
Pension, profit-sharing,	--	200,000	-
Employee benefit programs	200,000	--	200,000
Total deductions	300,621	300,130	298,142
Taxable income (loss)	1,607	850	2,459
Income tax	241	128	369

Tax Preparers

Kenneth Cozart is a Tennessee certified public accountant (C.P.A.) practicing with the firm Kenneth Cozart & Associates. Mr. Cozart has been providing accounting services to Dr. and Mrs. White since 1976. Mr. Cozart prepared Dr. and Mrs. White's Forms 1040, U.S. Individual Income Tax Return, Brownsville Medical and Brownsville Apothecary's Forms 1120, U.S. Corporation Income Tax Return, and Cost Plus' Forms 1120S, U.S. Income Tax Return for an S Corporation, for years 1998 through 2006. Morris A. Goldstein (M. Goldstein) and Sidney Goldstein (S. Goldstein) are Tennessee C.P.A.s practicing with the firm Goldstein & Associates. Diogenes used Goldstein & Associates to prepare its 1999 through 2003 corporate income tax returns. M. Goldstein signed Diogenes' Form 1120 for each of the years 1999 through 2003 as the paid preparer.

xélan

xélan, the Economic Association of Health Professionals, Inc. (Economic Association), was founded more than 30 years ago by L. Donald Guess as a membership organization for doctors. The Economic Association was part of a family of companies (xélan) which provided its members with a variety of insurance products offered by established companies as well as group supplemental insurance programs (e.g., disability, long-term care, malpractice) designed specifically for its members. The name "xélan" was adopted for the Economic Association in 1974 "combining 'x', the individual's savings required to finance lifestyle costs through life expectancy, with 'élan', the French word meaning a lifestyle of personal freedom."

Members of the xélan family included: the Economic Association; xélan, Inc.; the xélan Foundation, Inc.; xélan Investment Services, Inc.; xélan Pension Services, Inc.; Pyramidal Funding Systems, Inc., d.b.a. xélan Insurance Services; xélan Financial Planning, Inc.; and xélan Administrative Services, Inc. Doctors wishing to participate in xélan's programs would become members of the Economic Association by paying an initial $975 enrollment fee and an annual membership fee of $275. xélan provided its members with financial services through a network of financial counselors.

The xélan programs, services, and products, in pertinent part, included a service entitled the "xélan Tax Reduction Programs (Capital Accumulation and Distribution Phases)". There were three areas of emphasis under the xélan Tax Reduction Program, namely: Income Tax Reduction; Capital Gains Tax Elimination; and Estate Tax Elimination. Dr. and Mrs. White became involved with two products offered under the Income Tax Reduction program, the Disability Equity Trust3 and the xélan 419 plan.

3Between 1999 and 2004 Diogenes deducted $204,000 in payments made to the xélan Disability Equity Trust for Dr. White as follows:

Year	Deduction		
1999	$50,000		
2000	50,000	2001	50,000
2002	50,000	2003	-0
2004	4,000		

The xélan 419 Plan

The xélan 419 plan was established in 1997 with a trust agreement dated December 5, 1997, and was designed to be a "10 or more employer plan" within the meaning of sections 419(e)(1) and 419A(f)(6)(B). xélan's promotional materials described the xélan 419 plan as:

[A]n employee welfare benefit plan providing severance pay and preretirement death benefits to "C" corporation employees through an institutionally trusteed multiple employer trust. * * * The funding vehicle for the [xélan] 419 Plan is a specially designed life insurance investment contract that meets the minimum death benefit corridor requirement exceeding contract cash accumulations necessary to qualify the contract for tax free earnings on cash accumulations. The [xélan] 419 plan is usually administered as a 5-year funding plan and annual, deductible contributions of up to 40% of corporate earnings for 5 years are permitted.

The xélan 419 plan was amended and restated on December 30, 1999, effective January 1, 1999. The amended and restated xélan 419 plan retained the following pertinent definitions:

(A) "Annual Compensation" means the total of all compensation, reported as wages, tips, and other compensation on an Employee's Form W-2, but excluding the value of any Employer

3(...continued) The Internal Revenue Service (IRS) examined income tax returns of participants in the xélan Disability Equity Trust, including the returns of Dr. and Mrs. White and Diogenes for 2001 through 2003, with respect to participation in the program. The IRS, Dr. and Mrs. White, and Diogenes entered into a closing agreement resolving the issue pertaining to the xélan Disability Equity Trust.

---

provided taxable fringe benefits. For Shareholder Employees, however, Annual Compensation means net practice income.

*   *   *   *   *   *   *

(E) "Employee" means any person who is employed by and receives Annual Compensation from the Employer. Employee includes within its meaning a Shareholder-Employee.

(F) "Employer" means a corporate business entity which has at least one employee other than a Shareholder-Employee and executes a Participation Agreement to participate in the Trust.

*　　*　　*　　*　　*　　*　　*

(I) "Hours of Service" means and shall include each hour for which an Employee is directly or indirectly paid, or entitled to payment, for the performance of duties for the Employer.

*　　*　　*　　*　　*　　*　　*

(K) "Participant" means an Employee who meets the eligibility requirements set forth in this Trust.

*　　*　　*　　*　　*　　*　　*

(O) "Shareholder-Employee" means any employee or officer of a Corporation who owns or is attributed as owning within the meaning of §318(a)(1) of the Code, during the taxable year of such Corporation, more than five percent of the outstanding stock of the Corporation.

*　　*　　*　　*　　*　　*　　*

(Q) "Termination Date" means the date the Employer terminates its participation in the Trust in accordance with Article III. B.

*　　*　　*　　*　　*　　*　　*

(V) "Year of Service" means 1,000 Hours of Service, or more, in a Trust Year. For purposes of determining an Employee's eligibility to participate, service with the Employer by an Employee prior to the Employer's Entry Date shall be counted.

Participation

According to the amended trust agreement, in order to participate in the xélan 419 trust "an Employer must (a) execute the Participation Agreement, (b) be approved as an participating Employer by the Trust Administrator, and (c) obtain a legal opinion from tax counsel, the form and content of which must be acceptable to Xélan, regarding the tax consequences of participating in the Trust."

Contributions

According to the amended trust agreement the amount of an employer's contribution to the xélan 419 plan for each trust year depended on the amounts of the severance and death benefits provided by the employer for its participants, the funding level provided to the employer by the trust administrator, and the amount of an annual premium charged by the insurance company selected by the trust administrator for an individual life insurance policy on the life of each participant.

Once an employer identified to the trust administrator the employees who were eligible to participate in the xélan 419 plan "the Trustee will make an application with an insurance company selected by the Trust Administrator for policies of interest sensitive whole life (with a return of cash value rider attached) or universal life insurance (with Option B Rider attached) on the life of each eligible Employee."

An employer's contribution for each trust year was the sum of the premiums paid for the individual life insurance policies purchased by the trustee. Once the contribution amount was established, the annual contribution for each employer did not change unless the employer changed the benefits, added participants, or dropped participants.

In its Program Summary xélan further explained that

Contributions must also be provided on an annual basis for eligible rank and file employees. Rank and file contribution costs are usually less than 10% of the employer's contributions so long as there are less than 10 rank and file employees eligible to participate in the plan. If there are 10 or more other employees in the doctor's employer corporation that are eligible to participate, the [xélan] 419 Plan is usually not efficient as a retirement plan. In some situations when a doctor's employing corporation has more than 10 other employees, the doctor can sometimes be incorporated individually. The doctor's personal corporation then receives compensation under a contract for services from the original employing corporation that has a large number of "other employees". Under this approach doctors can receive their share of corporate earnings under a contract for services between the original employing corporation and the doctor's new 100% owned "C" corporation employer. The self-incorporated doctor needs at least one other employee for his or her "C" corporation to adopt a [xélan] 419 Plan. The other employee may be the spouse of the self-incorporated doctor. * * *

Termination

The amended trust agreement further provides that an employer's participation in the xélan 419 plan will terminate if: (1) the employer fails to make any required contributions or has otherwise failed to abide by the terms of the trust;

(2) the employer provides written notice to the trustee of the employer's intent to withdraw from the trust; (3) xélan, by action of its board of directors, determines to terminate the trust; or (4) the employer or any other party files a petition for relief under chapter 7 of the United States Bankruptcy Code.

An individual employee's participation in the xélan 419 trust terminates upon:

(1) the employer's termination of its participation; (2) the death of the employee; (3) the employee's cessation of employment for any reason, whether voluntary or involuntary, including disability; or (4) the date the employee attains age 62.

xélan's Program Summary touted that

An employer corporation has the right to terminate its participation in the multiple employer trust at any time. When an employer terminates participation, covered employees are eligible to receive distributions of their accounts of accumulated cash in the trust, or to purchase the life insurance investment contracts funding the employee's plan benefits from the trustee through administrative procedures defined in the plan document. If a participant elects the administrative option to purchase the life insurance investment contract funding their benefits from the trustee, they receive a life insurance investment contract containing cash accumulations that qualifies as a "non modified endowment contract". Non modified endowment status permits loans from the contract to the owner to be received by the owner without current income taxation. The life insurance investment contract also contains a "wash loan" provision that reduces interest costs on these loans to the borrower to zero. Upon the death of the borrower, the loans from the insurance contract are repaid to the insurance company from the income tax free death benefit component of the contract. A portion of the tax free IRC 101(a) death benefit of the contract equal to the loan balance borrowed by the doctor is paid to the lender (the insurance company) as a collateral assignee. Any death benefit exceeding the loan repayment is also received by named beneficiaries of the contract as income tax free death benefit under IRC 101(a).

xélan's Lawyers

Initially, Attorney Brant Freer, of the Detroit law firm of Miller Canfield, advised xélan with respect to the xélan 419 plan and provided legal opinions to participants until about February 1999. Beginning in or about March 1999 the law firm Williams Coulson Johnson Parker Lloyd & Tedesco L.L.C. (Williams Coulson), of Pittsburgh, Pennsylvania, became legal counsel for the xélan 419 plan. Michael E. Lloyd, one of the founding partners of Williams Coulson, is an attorney holding a juris doctor from the University of Pittsburgh and a master of laws (taxation) from Georgetown University Law Center. Before his association with Williams Coulson, Mr. Lloyd served as a senior tax attorney for the Office of Associate Chief Counsel, Employee Benefits and Exempt Organizations of the Internal Revenue Service. Mr. Lloyd participated in xélan-sponsored conferences for xélan financial counselors, xélan advisory board members, client doctors, and special guests. While at Williams Coulson, Mr. Lloyd provided xélan with advice concerning, among other things, the xélan 419 plan. Mr. Lloyd provided legal opinions for participants in the xélan 419 plan and the xélan Supplemental Disability Trust. Mr. Lloyd did not provide advice regarding or review the insurance products selected by the xélan 419 plan, nor did he review or consider the employee census submitted by employers to ascertain whether the employers were in compliance with the xélan 419 plan requirements before issuing the opinion.

Typically, whenever a new participant signed up for participation in the xélan 419 plan, xélan would request a legal opinion for the participant from Williams Coulson. Upon receipt of the information from xélan, Williams Coulson would prepare an opinion letter addressed to the participant of the xélan 419 plan. The opinion letters were based upon general facts and assumptions; if the facts and assumptions were not as stated in the letter, then the opinion and conclusions would not apply. If xélan asked, ***Williams Coulson would backdate opinion letters to make it appear that the letters had been issued in a prior tax year.***

Promotion of the xélan 419 Plan

xélan solicited new clients for its products by mailing promotional flyers to doctors and by inviting them to attend xélan seminars. At the seminars attendees heard presentations, were given sales promotional materials, and "received recommendations for 'doctors only' tax, asset protection and investment management programs that prevent losses to unnecessary taxes". As part of the seminar participants completed a xélan Loss Test which was used to identify which xélan products and programs would be most appropriate for the participant's use. The promoters indicated that one of the key aspects of the xélan program was that it "eliminates income taxes on earnings other that [sic] what you need to live on." The philosophy and programs xélan offered were extensively promoted via brochures and other promotional materials. xélan maintained a Web site, http://www.xelan.com, which contained additional information about its organization, philosophy, personnel, and programs. The mechanics and philosophy of xélan were further explained via audio and video tapes provided to its members. Many of the promotional materials touted that "In 1975 the first xélan Financial Counselors were recruited and trained to implement the xélan annual written plans for doctors. These xélan Tax Reduction Plans created individualized financial structures that limited doctors' income tax losses to lifestyle cost needs and allocated remaining pre-tax surplus earnings to deductible savings

plans." xélan marketed the xélan 419 plan as part of its tax reduction program. The tax reduction program consisted of two phases: (1) the capital accumulation phase; and (2) the capital distribution phase. During the capital accumulation phase of the tax reduction program, xélan recommended:

(1) that xélan clients ideally become employees of "C" corporations; (2) that annual taxable compensation be set at lifestyle needs plus income taxes; (3) that annual pre-tax surplus practice or business income be accumulated incrementally during the course of each tax year in a corporate or personal savings account that earns the $100,000 CD rate; (4) that the accumulated annual corporate or personal pre-tax surplus be allocated prior to 12/31 to one or more of the deductible savings plans available through the xélan Program to employees of "C" corporations: the 419 Plan, the Leveraged Split Dollar Plan, the Disability Equity Trust, the Long Term Care Equity Trust, the Malpractice Equity Trust, the Family Public Charity xélan Foundation, and/or a Qualified Retirement Plan. * * *

xélan's Program Summary described the xélan 419 plan as not only a convenient method to reduce current taxable income while providing life insurance, but also as a retirement investment vehicle. At the seminars the xélan 419 plan was described as a "non-qualified retirement plan". xélan's Program Summary states:

The significant economic and tax advantages of these specially designed insurance industry "non modified endowment" investment and death benefit contracts, as compared to traditional qualified retirement plans, is the tax free receipt by the owners of retirement funding distributions, the tax free receipt by the lender of death benefit proceeds equal to the contract loans, and tax free receipt by named beneficiaries of the leveraged death benefit proceeds exceeding contract loans. The 419 Plan distributions may be administered pursuant to the plan agreement so that they are received by the insurance investment contract owners in the form of tax free and interest free loans. At the death of the contract owner, any funds borrowed from the contract to finance lifestyle costs are repaid to the insurance company lender with a portion of the tax free death benefit. Unborrowed contract reserves actuarially guarantee a death benefit for doctors' family members that exceeds any loan balance borrowed for retirement spending purposes by the doctor during the doctor participant's lifetime. At the death of the doctor-owner-insured, tax free death benefits are provided to surviving family members, or other named beneficiaries including charitable institutions. * * *

   * * * * * * * *

419 Plans provide approximately 150% greater spendable retirement distributions from age 65 to age 85 than for equally funded qualified retirement plans for 35 year old participants, approximately 140% greater spendable retirement distributions than for equally funded qualified retirement plans for 45 year old participants, and approximately equal spendable retirement distributions for 55 year old participants making at least five years of annual contributions to the plan. * * *

Dr. and Mrs. White's Involvement With xélan

By 1999 Dr. White's medical practice had become very lucrative. Dr. White learned about xélan in 1999 when he attended a xélan seminar conducted by David Cline, a xélan financial counselor and Indianapolis Life insurance agent with an office in Tennessee. At the time Dr. White was 53 years old and Mrs. White was 47. Mr. Cline represented himself to Dr. and Mrs. White as a C.P.A. and a certified financial counselor and as holding a master of business administration degree. On the basis of the information that Dr. White obtained after he began to participate in the xélan 419 Plan, he now questions Mr. Cline's professional credentials. On March 5, 1999, Mr. Cline sent to Dr. White a letter regarding his attendance at the xélan seminar and the need to schedule a meeting to create a xélan tax reduction plan for Dr. White. Dr. White met with Mr. Cline on June 16, 1999, to discuss Dr. White's financial needs and the possibility of joining the Economic Association. Dr. White indicated his interest in the disability equity trust and the xélan 419 Plan. Dr. White's notes from the June 16, 1999, meeting with Mr. Cline indicate that Dr. White understood the xélan 419 plan to require five years of contributions with a "draw out" in the seventh year. After his initial meeting with Dr. White, Mr. Cline included S. Goldstein, of Goldstein & Associates, in the financial planning meetings with Dr. and Mrs. White.

On June 30, 1999, Dr. and Mrs. White met with Mr. Cline and Morris Loskove (who represented himself as a retired economics professor at the University of Memphis) at Dr. White's office to further discuss financial planning. Dr. White was interested only in the disability equity trust and the xélan 419 plan because he was interested only in disability and life insurance. At the meeting Dr. White, on behalf of Diogenes, which had not yet been incorporated, agreed to participate in the xélan Disability Equity Trust and the xélan 419 plan. Dr. White became a member of the Economic Association, designating Mr. Cline as his xélan financial counselor. Dr. White created and incorporated Diogenes at the recommendation of Mr. Cline and S. Goldstein.

Participation in the xélan 419 Plan

Diogenes was not incorporated until August 13, 1999. Nevertheless, on June 30, 1999, Dr. White signed a "Corporate Resolution and Application to Participate in the xélan Welfare Benefit Trust Program" (application) and provided a "Confidential Employee Census Data" form (census form). Diogenes initially committed to fund the program for at least five years at a fixed amount of $218,000 per year and to pay xélan a $600 annual administration fee for as long as it participated in the plan. As part of the application xélan was paid $2,500, which included a one-time setup fee of $1,900 and a first year administration fee of $600. On the census form the following individuals were identified as Diogenes employees as of June 30, 1999:

Name	Date of birth	Hire date1	W-2 Wages	Hours worked
Dr. White	11/7/45	1973	$700,000	2,000
Mrs. White	3/14/51	1976	118,000	2,000
Margaret	9/6/64	1997	5,000	1,000
Eric	5/12/84	1994	12,000	1,200

   1Diogenes was not incorporated until 1999. Eric was 10 years old in 1994.From 1999 through 2003 Dr. White never had wages of $700,000 and Mrs. White never had wages of $118,000 as employees of Diogenes. Neither Margaret nor Eric ever worked 1,000 or 1,200 hours, respectively, for Diogenes. For the years 2001, 2002, and 2003, Diogenes paid Dr. White wages of $15,000, $15,000, and $30,000, respectively, and paid Mrs. White wages of $30,000, $30,000, and $60,000, respectively. Neither Margaret nor Eric received any wages from

---

Diogenes during the years at issue.

Included in the setup fee was the cost of a tax opinion letter. On June 30, 1999, Dr. White signed a "Certificate of Diogenes Holdings, Inc." (certificate) in order to obtain a legal opinion from Williams Coulson regarding the tax consequences and risks associated with participating in the xélan 419 plan. In the certificate Dr. White represented, among other things, that the salaries of the employees of the corporation would not be reduced because of the participation in the xélan 419 plan.

On August 11, 1999, the xélan 419 plan sent a letter to Dr. White confirming Diogenes' payment of the setup fee and its commitment to fund the program for at least five years in the amount of $218,000 per year. Enclosed with the August 11, 1999, confirmation letter was a legal opinion from Mr. Lloyd to Dr. White dated July 9, 1999, regarding the xélan 419 plan. In the legal opinion from Mr. Lloyd, Dr. White was advised that "The Opinions are directed solely to Xélan and may be relied upon only by Xélan except that as part of our engagement with Xélan, we have agreed to provide a copy of the Opinions to you in the form of this letter" and that "The Opinions provided in this letter are based on the general fact pattern described below and documents which were provided to us by Xélan. Accordingly, these opinions may not apply to your company to the extent that your circumstances or the documents are different then those described below." Mr. Lloyd concluded the opinion letter by advising Dr. White to call him if he had "any questions regarding the application of the matters discussed in this letter to your specific case". Dr. White did not contact Mr. Lloyd or Williams Coulson and did not separately engage them or any other legal counsel to provide a legal opinion for Diogenes. Dr. White did not compare the fact patterns described in the opinion letter with the actual fact patterns of his business, and he sought counsel from neither his former attorney, Larry Banks, nor his longtime C.P.A., Ken Cozart. Rather, Dr. White relied "exclusively" upon the advice received from Mr. Cline and S. Goldstein. On the advice of Mr. Cline, Dr. White used Goldstein & Associates to prepare Diogenes' corporate tax returns for 1999 through 2003. On August 11, 1999, the xélan 419 plan sent to Dr. White a letter containing a Summary Plan Description. The Summary Plan Description explained the provisions of the xélan 419 plan, including a requirement that employees be age 21 with one year of service to be eligible to participate in the xélan 419 plan.

Dr. White subsequently reduced Diogenes' annual funding commitment to the xélan 419 plan to $200,000. On or about November 11, 1999, Mrs. White signed a $200,000 check from Diogenes to the xélan 419 plan to fund Diogenes' first year commitment to the program. On November 16, 1999, the xélan 419 plan sent Dr. White a letter confirming Diogenes' payment and requesting that he execute a new Corporate Resolution reflecting the change in a contribution amount to $200,000 per year. Mrs. White signed the new Corporate Resolution reflecting the annual commitment of $200,000.

As part of the xélan 419 plan, applications to Indianapolis Life were prepared for Dr. and Mrs. White on June 30, 1999, requesting the issuance of policies on each of them using an insurance product known as the Executive VIP policy. The Executive VIP policy is "an excess interest whole life plan" with its principal strategy such that the policy "is initially purchased and owned by an entity other than the insured--usually an employer or pension plan" and later "transferred to the insured by gift or by sale."

According to Indianapolis Life, the Executive VIP policy is targeted to executives, professionals, and business owners to address customer needs for tax favored retirement funds and for "[u]nlocking corporate retained earnings." The Executive VIP policy purports to provide a "[m]inimum fifth-year cash value to minimize tax on ownership transfer" together with "[s]trong tenth-year cash value".

The policies were designed with a nine-year surrender charge period. However, mortality and expense charges increase significantly in the eleventh year, and, therefore, the Executive VIP policy provides for the exchange of the policy after the 10th year without new evidence of insurability and without fees or sales expense deductions from the cash value of the new policy. After an exchange the new policy is a universal life policy and any existing loans are automatically transferred. Following an exchange the loan values of the new policy are available "without surrender charges, should you later choose to make systematic withdrawals to provide retirement income."

The Executive VIP policies were front loaded with high surrender charges to artificially suppress the value of the policies and designed specifically as investment vehicles to be used to build cash accumulations. Indianapolis Life described how the Executive VIP policy works as follows:

Generally, a policy will be purchased and owned by a corporation or individual which will pay premiums for five years. At the end of the fifth year, the policy will be transferred or sold to the insured or another entity. The recipient is responsible for any tax liability which may be generated on the value of the policy at the time of receipt. (Relatively speaking, this value will be minimal.)

Policy values may be used to pay premiums for the next five years, if the policy has sufficient values (changes in current interest rates, monthly expense and mortality charges may require additional out-of-pocket premiums to keep the policy in-force). At the end of the policy's tenth year, it is exchanged for a universal life policy and these values may be used to generate cash flow for retirement, estate liquidity or other purposes.

At Dr. White's direction the xélan 419 plan purchased from Indianapolis Life insurance policies in the following amounts:

Participant	Premium	Face amount
Dr. White	$175,326.69	$2,733,500
Mrs. White	23,693.82	460,790
Margaret	423.00	25,000
Eric	556.00	58,575

The amount of insurance coverage purchased through the xélan 419 plan was computed on the amount Dr. White had determined he wanted to contribute to the xélan 419 plan, $200,000, and the relative amounts of insurance Dr. White wished to purchase for each of his family members. The insurance policies purchased for Dr. and Mrs. White had face values equal to 3.905 times the amount of W-2 wages listed on the census form signed by Dr. White. The insurance policies purchased for Margaret and Eric had face values equal to approximately five times the amount of W-2 wages listed on the census form. As previously noted, the wages listed on the census form were grossly overstated.

In each of the years 1999, 2000, 2001, and 2002, Diogenes paid $200,000 to

the xélan 419 plan and the xélan 419 plan remitted equivalent payments to Indianapolis Life. Diogenes paid xélan the $600 annual administration fee to participate in the xélan 419 plan during 2000, 2001, and 2002 on September 2, 2000, December 26, 2001, and October 12, 2002, respectively. Diogenes claimed deductions on its Federal corporate income tax returns forth payments it made to the xélan 419 plan as follows:

Year	Classification of deduction	Amount
1999	Employee benefit programs	$200,000

2000	Employee benefit programs	200,000
2001	Employee benefit programs	200,000
2002	Pension, profit-sharing, etc.	200,000

On March 29, 2000, the xélan 419 plan provided Diogenes with an update with respect to the participation in the xélan 419 plan and copies of the first two pages of the insurance policies purchased. On January 30, 2002, and January 6, 2003, the xélan 419 plan provided information about the insurance policies issued on the lives of Dr. and Mrs. White, Eric, and Margaret together with letters notifying each of them of the insurance policies purchased as an employee benefit.

Termination of the xélan 419 Plan

On May 29, 2003, the xélan 419 plan sent a letter to Diogenes and Dr. White informing them that the trust had been terminated effective May 28, 2003 (termination letter). Enclosed with the termination letter were individual letters to Dr. White, Mrs. White, Margaret, and Eric, notifying them of their options as insured participants under the plan. The letters advised them that under the terms of the xélan 419 plan all participants would be given an opportunity to purchase the life insurance policies that were owned on their lives by the trust, and that all policies not purchased would be surrendered. The policy purchase prices for Dr. and Mrs. White, Margaret, and Eric were as follows:

Name	Purchase price
Dr. White	$43,794.05
Mrs. White	7,382.43
Margaret	400.53
Eric	938.44

By letter dated June 2, 2003, Mr. Cline informed Dr. White that xélan and its management had determined to terminate the xélan 419 plan. Mr. Cline advised Dr. White that "Since you have already completed 4 years of funding into the 419 Trust, there will be special provisions made to insure that you can complete the entire 5 year funding and also to insure that you will receive all of your anticipated return

within the Indianapolis Life policy." As of June 30, 2003, the accumulation value4 of Dr. and Mrs. White's Indianapolis Life policies was $642,220.87 ($564,655.36 for Dr. White's and $77,565.51 for Mrs. White's). The Indianapolis Life annual report indicates that as of September 15, 2003, the policy on Dr. White's life had a guaranteed cash and surrender value of $127,900.46. The Indianapolis Life annual report indicates that as of September 12, 2003, the policy on Mrs. White's life had a guaranteed cash and surrender value of $16,298.14.

In a memorandum dated June 27, 2003, Mr. Cline advised Dr. and Mrs. White with regard to their options regarding the termination of the xélan 419 plan. Mr. Cline recommended that Dr. and Mrs. White select one of two options: (1) "Purchase the policy from the Xélan Welfare Benefit Trust [($43,794.05 for Dr. White's policy and $7,382.43 for Mrs. White's policy)], pay the taxes on the Trust

---

4Accumulation value is defined by Indianapolis Life as "the base premium less the monthly deduction and any partial surrenders, plus interest", whereas the current cash value is defined as "the greater of the guaranteed cash value or the accumulation value less any surrender charge."

Distribution Amount in 2003, and then pay the final year premium for the policy with after-tax dollars"; or (2) "Transfer the policy to the Millennium Trust and pay the final year with tax-deductible dollars and then transfer the policy from the Millennium Trust to Dr. Jerald White [and Mrs. White] after the 5th year of contribution." Mr. Cline noted that under the first option, although Dr. and Mrs. White would initially have to pay additional money to the xélan 419 plan, "Upon receipt, the Trust will redistribute the assets back to the employees within 90 days, so each of you should receive a comparable amount in return plus your insurance contracts and your cash value." The xélan 419 plan's account records indicate that those participants who chose to purchase their policies from the xélan 419 plan after it terminated received distributions from the plan equal to or greater than the amounts they paid for the policies.

Dr. and Mrs. White did not elect to "purchase" the insurance policies acquired through the xélan 419 plan because Dr. White did not trust the people he was dealing with and he wanted to get the benefit of his original deal. Dr. White found it incredible that in order to purchase his policy from the xélan 419 plan he would have to pay them approximately $43,000 just to have them turn around and distribute the same back to him. Rather, Dr. and Mrs. White decided to "allow him to complete the contract he thought he had signed. Dr. and Mrs. White, Margaret, and Eric each signed a "Participant's Voluntary Election and Direction of Plan to Plan Transfer" by which they directed the xélan 419 plan to transfer their insurance policies to the Millennium plan. On September 19, 2003, the xélan 419 plan sent letters to Dr. and Mrs. White, Margaret, and Eric confirming that their requests to transfer their Indianapolis Life policies to the Millennium plan had been processed.

The Millennium Plan

Millennium Marketing Group, L.L.C. (MMG), was formed in 2002 by Norman Bevan5 and Scott Ridge6 to sponsor the Millennium plan. Mr. Bevan owns Innovus Financial Solutions, Inc. (Innovus), and has served as its president and chief executive officer. In 2002 Kathleen R. Barrow, an attorney admitted to practice law in Oklahoma in 1992 and Texas in 2002, was hired by Mr. Bevan and Mr. Ridge to provide legal advice regarding a proposed 419 plan. In 2003 Ms. Barrow joined the law firm Whitaker, Chalk, Swindle & Sawyer (Whitaker Chalk) and continued to provide legal advice regarding the Millennium plan.

5Mr. Bevan is a chartered life underwriter, a chartered financial consultant, and an accredited estate planner.

6Mr. Ridge is a chartered life underwriter and a chartered financial consultant.

On March 5, 2004, while employed by Whitaker Chalk, Ms. Barrow authored two opinion letters regarding the Millennium plan. On June 1, 2004, Ms. Barrow became an employee of Innovus and MMG, serving as president and chief counsel in their Houston, Texas, office. In July 2006 Ms. Barrow left the employ of Innovus and MMG, started her own law firm, and continued providing legal advice to the Millennium plan. In March 2007 Ms. Barrow joined the law firm Jackson Lewis LLP as a partner in its Houston, Texas, office.7

The Millennium plan was established on November 1, 2002, as a trust under the laws of the State of Mississippi. The Millennium plan provides eligible employees of participating employers with pre- and post-retirement death benefits and other pre- and post-retirement welfare benefits, the latter including medical expense reimbursement, disability benefits, and in certain limited circumstances involuntary severance benefits. In 2003 the plan also provided a benefit in the case of "hardship".

Republic Bank & Trust (Republic Bank) in Norman, Oklahoma, has served as the trustee of the Millennium plan since the plan's inception. The Millennium plan's assets are held by the trustee with the assistance of an independent financial adviser.

7At the time of trial Ms. Barrow, Mr. Bevan, and Mr. Ridge were the subjects of an IRS sec. 6700 investigation. Mr. Lloyd represented Ms. Barrow with regard to the sec. 6700 investigation.

The trustee is responsible for functions such as recordkeeping, including maintaining complete and accurate account records for all plan participants, allocating investment earnings, and posting distribution information to participant accounts.

The Millennium plan generally invests participating employer contributions in life insurance policies issued by State licensed A+ A.M. Best rated or better insurance carriers, including Indianapolis Life, to fund the benefits promised under the Millennium plan. All of the life insurance policies are owned and held in trust by the Millennium plan.

The General Product Information Guide (Guide) is a marketing brochure describing the Millennium plan. The Guide indicates that the Millennium plan allows participating employers to fund valuable welfare benefits for employees without having to limit deductions to current costs and to fund pre- and post- retirement death, life, medical, and disability benefits through the Millennium plan and presently deduct contributions for that purpose. Under the Millennium plan "Employers select the employees they want to become participants and they determine the targeted level of Death Benefit and Life Benefits for each participant. Employers choose their investment risk, by selecting the insurance product type (fixed, indexed or equity) to insure the selected benefits."

Under the terms of Diogenes' adoption agreement, the employer would become a covered employer for purposes of the plan upon the last to occur of four events: (1) the third-party administrator received the signed adoption agreement; (2) the board of directors of the employer authorized the execution and delivery of the adoption agreement and the third party administrator received the resolution/consent; (3) the initial contribution or other initial payment was placed into the escrow account; and (4) insurance on the lives of eligible employees was issued to the trust and received by the trustee. To be eligible to become a participant in the Millennium plan an employee must satisfy the following requirements: (1) the employee must work a total of one year (defined as 1,000 hours during the plan year) for the employer before the commencement of the plan year, and (2) the employee must be at least 25 years of age at the time of entry into the plan. Once the eligibility requirements are met, an eligible employee will become a plan participant upon the last to occur of the following events: (1) the qualifying employer of the eligible employee has become a covered employer; (2) the underwriter issues a policy of insurance on the life of the eligible employee;

(3) the eligible employee is assigned a rating group by the committee and notice of the assignment is sent to the employer by the third-party administrator; (4) the employer pays its contribution to the plan with respect to all eligible employees/participants of the employer; and (5) all insurance on the employer's eligible employee/participants and the fixed contribution of the covered employer are received by the trustee.

The master plan for the Millennium plan also provides that if, for any reason, no policy of insurance is issued by an underwriter on any eligible employee of a covered employer or no rating group assignment is made on any eligible employee of the covered employer, then any contribution made by the covered employer to the plan and/or trustee shall be refunded to the covered employer, minus the administration fee identified in the adoption agreement. Additionally, a covered employer may terminate participation in the plan and the fixed life benefits of the participants will be paid or transferred to a trust under section 419(e). Triggering events for the payment of fixed benefits include the death of a participant, a participant's termination of employment with the covered employer, termination of the participant's participation by the third-party administrator, withdrawal of the covered employer from the plan, or termination of the plan.

Although Mr. Cline was the only person Dr. White spoke to about transferring to the Millennium plan, Dr. White, as president of Diogenes, signed the adoption agreement for the Millennium plan effective July 11, 2003.

Even though Eric was only 19 years old at the time of the effective date of the adoption agreement, exhibit B to the agreement provided that the following employees of Diogenes were eligible to participate in the Millennium plan:

Name	Date of birth
Dr. White	11/7/1945
Mrs. White	3/14/1951
Margaret	9/6/1964
Eric	5/12/1984

Neither Eric nor Margaret worked the requisite 1,000 hours for Diogenes and neither of them received a salary from Diogenes in 2003. Although it was indicated in the adoption agreement that Diogenes elected to make fixed, annual contributions of $175,327 for class 1 employees (president), $23,649 for class 2 employees (office manager), and $979 for class 3 employees

(nonmanagement), Dr. and Mrs. White did not intend that Diogenes would make more than one final payment on each of the insurance policies in the amounts set forth in the adoption agreement.

Diogenes acknowledged and warranted that it had not relied upon any legal or tax advice of the sponsor, the committee, the third-party administrator, the underwriter, the trustee, or any agent of these, in executing the adoption agreement. In fact, Diogenes elected not to seek an individualized legal opinion pertaining to the Federal tax issues that may have arisen from participation in the Millennium plan.

On August 27, 2003, Sonya Siqueira and L. Donald Guess, on behalf of xélan, signed the Transfer of Ownership documents for the insurance policies for Dr. and Mrs. White, Margaret, and Eric. On September 23, 2003, a representative of Republic Bank signed the Transfer of Ownership documents for Dr. and Mrs. White, Margaret, and Eric. On October 3, 2003, a representative of Indianapolis Life signed the Transfer of Ownership documents for Dr. and Mrs. White, Margaret, and Eric. On November 28, 2003, Diogenes issued a $199,999.51 check payable to the Millennium plan. The check was used to pay premiums on Dr. and Mrs. White's,

Margaret's, and Eric's insurance policies as follows:

Name	Amount
Jerald White	$175,326.69
Claudia White	23,693.82
Margaret White	423.00
Eric White	556.00

However, by letter dated April 21, 2006, and signed by Ms. Barrow, the Millennium plan notified Dr. White that both his and Mrs. White's Indianapolis Life polices remained in extended term insurance mode because their insurance producer, Mr. Cline, had not submitted the paperwork necessary to cause the annual costs of the policies to be paid out of the policies' cash values after the fifth year. The letter further instructed Dr. and Mrs. White that if they were to complete the reinstatement paperwork provided by the Millennium plan trustee, then the life insurance policies would be reinstated to the form at which they were originally issued and would perform as illustrated when purchased in connection with their participation with xélan. Ms. Barrow also notified Dr. White that he could still void the transaction with respect to the Millennium plan. If the transaction was void, the contributed insurance policies would be returned.

Dr. and Mrs. White and Diogenes Join a Lawsuit Against Indianapolis Life and Mr. Cline On October 20, 2006, John B. Phillips, Catherine T. Phillips, and Phillips Management, Inc., filed a complaint for damages against Indianapolis Life and Mr. Cline in the U.S. District Court for the Southern District of Indiana, Indianapolis Division (lawsuit). On November 20, 2006, Dr. and Mrs. White and Diogenes, along with nine other plaintiffs, joined the lawsuit against Indianapolis Life and Mr. Cline.

In the lawsuit the plaintiffs accused Indianapolis Life and Mr. Cline of fraud, negligent misrepresentation, breach of common law fiduciary duty, and breach of insurers' duty of good faith with respect to their role in the promotion, marketing, and participation in employee benefit plans funded with life insurance. Dr. and Mrs. White's and Diogenes' prayer for relief included compensatory and punitive damages, rescission of the insurance policies and a return of their premiums, interest, costs, and other amounts.

OPINION

Pursuant to section 7491(a), petitioners have the burden of proof unless they introduce credible evidence relating to the issue that would shift the burden to respondent. See Rule 142(a). Our conclusions, however, are based on a preponderance of the evidence, and thus the allocation of the burden of proof is immaterial. See Martin Ice Cream Co. v. Commissioner, 110 T.C. 189, 210 n.16 (1998).

Section 419(a) generally provides that an employer's contributions paid or accrued to a welfare benefit fund are deductible, but only if they are otherwise deductible under chapter 1 of the Code. Section 419(b) further limits the deductibility of an employer's contributions to a welfare benefit fund to the fund's qualified cost for the taxable year. Section 419A(f)(6), however, provides that contributions paid by an employer to a multiple-employer welfare benefit fund are not subject to the deduction limitation of section 419(b).

Ordinary and Necessary Business Expenses

In general, section 162(a) provides that "There shall be allowed as a deduction all the ordinary and necessary expenses paid or incurred during the taxable year in carrying on any trade or business". There are five requirements a taxpayer must meet in order to deduct an item under this section. "The taxpayer must prove that the item claimed as a deductible business expense: (1) Was paid or incurred during the taxable year; (2) was for carrying on his, her, or its trade or business; (3) was an expense; (4) was a necessary expense; and (5) was an ordinary expense."

Neonatology Assocs., P.A. v. Commissioner, 115 T.C. 43, 88 (2000), aff'd, 299 F.3d 221 (3d Cir. 2002). A determination of whether an expenditure satisfies each of these requirements is a question of fact. See Commissioner v. Heininger, 320 U.S. 467, 475 (1943).

Petitioners argue that Diogenes' contributions to the xélan 419 plan and the Millennium plan satisfy the requirements of section 162 and are thus deductible under section 162(a). Petitioners contend that the contributions were paid to a fund for the benefit of employees, were intended to only directly benefit the employees, and were paid in amounts reasonably based upon the services the company expected to receive from its employees.

Respondent argues that although employers are generally not prohibited from funding term life insurance for employees and deducting the premiums paid as business expenses under section 162(a), *employers are not allowed to disguise investments in life insurance as deductible benefit-plan expenses when the investments accumulate cash value for the employees personally.*

Section 162(a)(1) specifies that a deduction for ordinary and necessary business expenses includes "a reasonable allowance for salaries or other compensation for personal services actually rendered". Where, as here, the case involves a closely held corporation with the controlling shareholders setting their own level of compensation as employees, the reasonableness of the compensation is subject to close scrutiny. Devine Bros., Inc. v. Commissioner, T.C. Memo. 2003-15 (citing Owensby & Kritikos, Inc. v. Commissioner, 819 F.2d 1315, 1324 (5th Cir. 1987), aff'g T.C. Memo. 1985-267).

We have found that contributions to plans similar to the xélan 419 plan and the Millennium plan were not deductible under section 162(a) in at least four previous cases: Neonatology Assocs., P.A. v. Commissioner, 115 T.C. 43, V.R. DeAngelis M.D.P.C. v. Commissioner, T.C. Memo. 2007-360, aff'd per curiam, 574 F.3d 789 (2d Cir. 2009), Curcio v. Commissioner, T.C. Memo. 2010-115, and Goyak v. Commissioner, T.C. Memo. 2012-13.

In Neonatology, Neonatology Associates deducted contributions to a voluntary employee's beneficiary association (VEBA) to provide life insurance for its employees. Neonatology Associates substantially overpaid the VEBA for term life insurance, and the Court found "incredible petitioners' assertion that the employee/owners of Neonatology * * * would have caused their respective corporations to overpay substantially for term life insurance with no promise or expectation of receiving the excess contributions back." Neonatology Assocs., P.A. v. Commissioner, 115 T.C. at 89. Because the plan participants could retrieve their policies from the plan, the Court concluded that "the purpose and operation of the Neonatology Plan * * * was to serve as a tax-free savings device for the owner/employees and not, as asserted by petitioners, to provide solely term life insurance to the covered employees." Id. at 92. The portions of the contribution that exceeded the cost of term life insurance were found to be "nondeductible

distributions of cash for the benefit of their employee/owners and do not constitute ordinary or necessary business expenses." Id. at 88-89. In V.R. DeAngelis M.D.P.C., a partnership named VRD/RTD enrolled in what purported to be a multiple-employer supplemental benefit plan and trust (STEP). The STEP was supposed to provide eligible employees with severance, and, if elected, life insurance benefits. Each year the partnership deducted the full amount of its contribution to the plan in that year as an ordinary and necessary business expense under section 162(a), and the plan invested the contributions in whole life insurance policies that accumulated cash for the doctors personally. The Court found that

The insurance premiums at hand pertained to the participating doctors' personal investments in whole life insurance policies that primarily accumulated cash value for those doctors personally. * * *

The use of whole life insurance policies and the direct interactions between the participating doctors and the STEP plan representatives support our finding that the participating doctors in their individual capacities fully expected to get their promised benefits and that any receipt of those benefits was not considered by anyone connected with the life insurance transaction to rest on any unexpected or contingent event. Each whole life insurance policy upon its issuance was in and of itself a separate account of the insured doctor, and the insured (rather than the STEP plan) dictated and directed the funding and management of the account and bore most risks incidental to the account's performance. The STEP plan in essence and in operation was simply an aggregation of separate plans for the participating doctors and not, as petitioners claim, one single plan in which various employers participated. * * *

V.R. DeAngelis M.D.P.C. v. Commissioner, T.C. Memo. 2007-360. The Court concluded that the contributions by VRD/RTD to the STEP plan were distributions to the partners and were not ordinary and necessary business expenses under section 162(a).

The facts in these cases are similar to those of Neonatology and V.R. DeAngelis M.D.P.C. The Indianapolis Life policies purchased with the contributions to the xélan 419 plan in 2001 and 2002 and to the Millennium plan in 2003 were nothing more than Dr. and Mrs. White's personal investment in whole life insurance policies that primarily accumulated cash value for Dr. and Mrs. White personally. Dr. White worked with Mr. Cline to develop an investment amount and strategy that was suitable to Dr. White. Dr. White determined the amount of contribution and coverage for himself, his spouse, and his children. Moreover, Dr. and Mrs. White believed that the investment would be "tax free in, tax free out". Dr. White knew the investment was into a cash value life insurance product and expected that, in addition to tax savings, his after-tax return on investment would equal or exceed the amount that would have to be contributed. The cash value of the insurance policies was suppressed during the initial years with high surrender charges. In 2003 when the xélan 419 plan terminated the "cash value" of the policies was approximately $127,000 but the total "accumulation value" was $642,220.87.8 Dr. White's decision to transfer the policies to the Millennium plan after the termination of the 8See supra note 4 and infra p. 52.

xélan 419 plan was to continue his original investment plan in order to "salvage the

$800 thousand that * * * [he] had already pumped into Xélan."

The xélan 419 plan permitted the employer (Diogenes) to terminate its participation and to withdraw from the plan at any time. Upon termination, the underlying insurance policies could be distributed to the participating employees. Dr. White had complete control over Diogenes and thus had the ability to cause the policies to be distributed.

In 2003 when the xélan 419 plan terminated, Dr. White was presented with the option of receiving the policies by "purchasing" the policies or transferring them to Millennium. He was told that if he chose to purchase the policies he would have to pay the xélan 419 plan approximately $43,000, but that the $43,000 would be returned to him. Since by then Dr. White no longer trusted xélan, he chose to have the policies transferred to Millennium.

The Millennium plan was selected by Dr. White to continue his original investment plan, and its operation was similar to that of the xélan 419 plan. While there were subtle differences in the insureds' ability to have the underlying insurance policies distributed to them upon the employer's termination of participation, it is clear from the record that Millennium, at least through 2006, was willing to allow Dr. White and Diogenes to "void" their participation in the Millennium plan and have the underlying insurance policies returned to them.

In Curcio v. Commissioner, T.C. Memo. 2010-115, and Goyak v. Commissioner, T.C. Memo. 2012-13, our decisions were largely based on the conclusion that the individual insureds always had the ability to receive the value of the underlying insurance policies purchased by the respective plans. Likewise, Dr. White had the ability to cause the policies to be distributed in these cases. After considering the facts and weighing the evidence, we conclude, as we did in the previously cited cases, that Diogenes' contributions to the xélan 419 plan in 2001 and 2002 and to the Millennium plan in 2003 were payments on behalf of Dr. and Mrs. White personally and were not ordinary and necessary business expenses. Because of our holding it is unnecessary for us to decide whether the contributions were subject to and limited by the rules of section 404(a)(5) or whether the arrangement was a welfare benefit fund to which the exceptions under section 419A(f)(6) apply.[9] See Neonatology Assocs., P.A. v. Commissioner, 115 T.C.

[9]Although Diogenes may arguably be entitled to deduct the costs of current life insurance protection for term life insurance, see Neonatology Assocs., P.A. v. Commissioner, 115 T.C. 43 (2000), aff'd, 299 F.3d 221 (3d Cir. 2002), petitioners have not requested any such deductions.

43; V.R. DeAngelis M.D.P.C. v. Commissioner, T.C. Memo. 2007-360.

Constructive Dividends

Section 61(a) generally provides: "gross income means all income from whatever source derived". The regulations under section 61 further provide that gross income "includes income realized in any form, whether in money, property, or services." Sec. 1.61-1(a), Income Tax Regs. However, section 301 provides that funds (or any other property) distributed by a corporation to a shareholder over which the shareholder has dominion and control are to be taxed under the provisions of section 301(c).

"Under section 301(c), a constructive distribution is taxable to the shareholder as a dividend only to the extent of the corporation's earnings and profits." Barnard v. Commissioner, T.C. Memo. 2001-242. Any portion of the constructive distribution that exceeds the corporation's earnings and profits is a nontaxable return of capital to the extent of the shareholder's basis in the corporation, and any remaining amount is taxable to the shareholder as long-term capital gain. Sec. 301(c)(2) and (3); Truesdell v. Commissioner, 89 T.C. 1280, 1295 (1987).

Diogenes was incorporated in 1999. Dr. White was the 100% owner and only shareholder of Diogenes. Diogenes' contributions to the xélan 419 plan in 2001 and 2002 and to the Millennium plan in 2003 conferred an economic benefit on Dr. and Mrs. White. See Neonatology Assocs., P.A. v. Commissioner, 115 T.C. at 91. The $200,000 annual contributions are constructive distributions of cash rather than payments of ordinary and necessary business expenses, and there is no indication that Diogenes expected any repayment of the cash underlying the conferred benefit.

See id.

The record supports the conclusion that after disallowing the deductions for its "contributions" to the xélan and Millennium plans, Diogenes had earnings and profits of at least $200,000 during each of the years in issue, and petitioners have not challenged respondent's determination that Diogenes had sufficient earnings and profits to characterize the subject distributions as dividends. Rather, petitioners assert that the Court need not consider the discussion because petitioners believe that Diogenes' contributions to xélan 419 plan in 2001 and 2002 and to the Millennium plan in 2003 were ordinary and necessary business expenses. We have already held that the subject contributions were not ordinary and necessary business expenses. Accordingly, we sustain respondent's determination that the distributions are taxable dividends to Dr. White. See Rule 142(a); Welch v. Helvering, 290 U.S. 111, 115 (1933). Because of our holding, it is unnecessary for us to reach the alternative arguments raised with respect to this issue.

Constructive Receipt of the Indianapolis Life Policies in 2003

Respondent determined that Dr. and Mrs. White received income of $642,220 in 2003 when the insurance policies purchased by the xélan 419 plan became available to them as a result of the termination of the xélan 419 plan. Respondent calculated those values in accordance with Rev. Proc. 2005-25, 2005-1 C.B. 962. This is the same as the "accumulated value" reported by Indianapolis Life. Petitioners argue that they transferred from one welfare benefit plan to another that both plans provided for similar benefits with similar restrictions on forfeiture and reversion of plan assets, and that Dr. and Mrs. White never had ownership, possession, or control of plan benefits either before or after the transfer. Respondent relies on section 402(b) (2), which provides that "The amount actually distributed or made available to any distributee by any trust described in paragraph (1) [a nonexempt trust] shall be taxable to the distributee, in the taxable year in which so distributed or made available, under section 72". Under section 72 any amount which is received under a life insurance contract and which is not received as an annuity shall be included in gross income to the extent it exceeds the investment in the contract. Sec. 72(e) (1) (A), (5) (A), (C), (E) (ii). The investment in the contract is defined generally as the aggregate amount of premiums or other consideration paid for the contract less amounts previously received under the contract, to the extent such latter amounts were excludable from gross income. Sec. 72(e) (6).10 Respondent cites no court opinions to support his position, and this issue appears to be one of first impression.

On May 29, 2003, Dr. and Mrs. White were notified that the xélan 419 plan was terminating and they were asked what they wanted to do with the Indianapolis Life policies. One of the options provided to Dr. and Mrs. White was to acquire the policies at no net cost to them other than the possible ensuing tax consequences. The up-front, out-of-pocket cost to acquire these two policies would have been

---

10Respondent calculated the value of the insurance contracts pursuant to Rev. Proc. 2005-25, 2005-1 C.B. 962. Petitioners have not contested respondent's method of computing the values of the insurance contracts using a variable premiums, earnings, and reasonable charges amount. See id. On brief respondent acknowledges that if the Court were to determine that the contributions to the xélan 419 plan in 2001 and 2002 are taxable income to Dr. and Mrs. White, then the income inclusion for premiums paid in 2001 and 2002 will create investment in the contract.

$51,176.48; however, as Dr. and Mrs. White had been informed, that amount or more would have been returned to them as a redistribution of assets within 90 days along with their insurance contracts. As of June 30, 2003, the total accumulation value of Dr. and Mrs. White's Indianapolis Life policies was $642,220.87. Under the annual accounting system of taxation, the amount of income for a taxable year is generally determined on the basis of triggering events during that year. Goyak v. Commissioner, T.C. Memo. 2012-13; see also Curcio v. Commissioner, T.C. Memo. 2010-115. A taxable event usually occurs when a

taxpayer acquires rights to property that he did not previously have. Respondent's

section 402(b)(2) argument is that a taxable event occurred when the xélan 419 plan

terminated in 2003 and the underlying insurance policies were made available for

distribution to Dr. and Mrs. White.

We have already determined that Diogenes' payments to the xélan 419 plan were not deductible and that they constitute dividend income to Dr. and Mrs. White. This was based in part on our finding that Dr. and Mrs. White always had the ability to terminate Diogenes' participation in the xélan 419 plan, which would have resulted in the distribution of the Indianapolis Life policies to Dr. and Mrs. White. Thus, the policies were always available for distribution. The taxable event that respondent argues occurred in 2003 gave Dr. and Mrs. White nothing in addition to what they always possessed; i.e., the power to have the policies distributed to them.11 Under these circumstances, we cannot agree that the termination of the xélan 419 plan was a taxable event.12 We therefore reject respondent's position that Dr. and Mrs. White received income of $642,220.87 when the xélan 419 plan terminated in 2003.

Accuracy-Related Penalty

Section 6662(a) and (b)(1) and (2) imposes a 20% accuracy-related penalty on any portion of an underpayment of tax required to be shown on a return attributable to a taxpayer's negligence or disregard of rules or regulations, or any substantial understatement of income tax.

Section 7491(c) provides that the Commissioner bears the burden of production with regard to penalties and must come forward with sufficient evidence 11Indeed, respondent argued on brief that the xélan 419 Plan was merely a conduit through which Dr. and Mrs. White held the insurance policies.

12Other than arguing that the termination of the xélan 419 plan in 2003 triggered the application of sec. 402(b)(2), resulting in a $642,220.87 increase in income with a possible adjustment for basis, respondent made no alternative arguments or calculations. See Gen. Star Nat'l Ins. Co. v. Administration Asigurarilor de Stat, 289 F.3d 434, 441 (6th Cir. 2002) (undeveloped legal arguments waived); Muhich v. Commissioner, 238 F.3d 860, 864 n.10 (7th Cir. 2001), aff'g T.C. Memo. 1999-192. indicating that it is appropriate to impose the penalty. See Higbee v. Commissioner, 116 T.C. 438, 446 (2001). Once the Commissioner meets his burden of production, however, the burden of proof remains with the taxpayer, including the burden of proving that the penalty is inappropriate because of reasonable cause or substantial authority under section 6664. See Rule 142(a); Higbee v. Commissioner, 116 T.C. at 446-447.

Respondent has met his burden of production in that he has shown that Dr. and Mrs. White caused Diogenes to improperly deduct hundreds of thousands of dollars used to purchase cash-accumulating whole life insurance policies which could later be distributed to Dr. and Mrs. White for free or for a small fraction of the value of the insurance policy. This is sufficient to indicate that it is appropriate to impose penalties under section 6662(a). See Curcio v. Commissioner, T.C. Memo. 2010 115.

There is a substantial understatement of income tax for any taxable year if the amount of the understatement for the taxable year exceeds the greater of 10 percent of the tax required to be shown on the return for the taxable year, or $5,000. Sec. 6662 (d) (1) (A). However, in the case of a corporation other than an S corporation or a personal holding company (as defined in section 542), there is a substantial understatement of income tax for any taxable year if the amount of the understatement for the taxable year exceeds the greater of 10% of the tax required to be shown on the return for the taxable year, or $10,000. Sec. 6662(d)(1)(B).

The understatements of tax on both Dr. and Mrs. White's Federal income tax returns and on Diogenes' corporate tax returns are substantial. Petitioners, however, argue that they had both reasonable cause and substantial authority for the deduction of contributions to the xélan 419 plan and the Millennium plan.

Reasonable Cause

"Reasonable cause requires that the taxpayer have exercised ordinary business care and prudence as to the disputed item." Neonatology Assocs., P.A. v. Commissioner, 115 T.C. at 98. The good-faith reliance on the advice of an independent, competent professional as to the tax treatment of an item may meet this requirement. See id. (citing United States v. Boyle, 469 U.S.

241 (1985)); sec. 1.6664-4(b), Income Tax Regs. Reliance on an opinion or advice must be based upon all pertinent facts and circumstances and the law as it relates to those facts and circumstances. Sec. 1.6664-4(c)(1)(i), Income Tax Regs.

To be reasonable, the professional tax advice must generally be from a competent and independent adviser unburdened with a conflict of interest and not from promoters of the investment. Mortensen v. Commissioner, 440 F.3d 375, 387 (6th Cir. 2006), aff'g T.C. Memo. 2004-279. "Courts have routinely held that taxpayers could not reasonably rely on the advice of promoters or other advisers with an inherent conflict of interest such as one who financially benefits from the transaction." Tigers Eye Trading, L.L.C. v. Commissioner, T.C. Memo. 2009-121 (citing Hansen v. Commissioner, 471 F.3d 1021, 1031 (9th Cir. 2006) ("a taxpayer cannot negate the negligence penalty through reliance on a transaction's promoters or on other advisors who have a conflict of interest"), aff'g T.C. Memo. 2004-269, Van Scoten v. Commissioner, 439 F.3d 1243, 1253 (10th Cir. 2006) ("To be reasonable, the professional adviser cannot be directly affiliated with the promoter; instead, he must be more independent"), aff'g T.C. Memo. 2004-275, Barlow v. Commissioner, 301 F.3d 714, 723 (6th Cir. 2002) (noting "that courts have found that a taxpayer is negligent if he puts his faith in a scheme that, on its face, offers improbably high tax advantages, without obtaining an objective, independent opinion on its validity"), aff'g T.C. Memo. 2000-339; Goldman v. Commissioner, 39 F.3d 402, 408 (2d Cir. 1994) (taxpayer could not reasonably rely on professional advice of someone known to be burdened with an inherent conflict of interest--a sales representative of the transaction), aff'g T.C. Memo. 1993-480, Pasternak v. Commissioner, 990 F.2d 893, 903 (6th Cir. 1993) (reliance on promoters or their agents is unreasonable because such persons are not independent of the investment), aff'g Donahue v. Commissioner, T.C. Memo. 991-181, and Illes v. Commissioner, 982 F.2d 163, 166 (6th Cir. 1992) (finding negligence where taxpayer relied on a person with financial interest in the venture), aff'g T.C. Memo. 1991-449). "A promoter's self-interest makes such 'advice' inherently unreliable." Id.

Petitioners did not seek independent advice regarding the deductibility of the contributions to the xélan 419 plan or the Millennium plan; rather, they relied on the advice of Mr. Cline and Mr. Lloyd. Mr. Cline was associated with xélan and involved in promoting the xélan 419 plan for his personal benefit and gains. As to Mr. Lloyd, petitioners did not hire him nor pay for the opinion letter he wrote; rather, xélan did. The opinion letter stated that Mr. Lloyd's law firm, Williams Coulson, had been engaged by xélan to prepare the opinion letter, that it was directed solely to xélan, and that it could be relied upon solely by xélan. When the xélan 419 plan terminated and the Indianapolis Life policies were made available to Dr. and Mrs. White, the only person they consulted was Mr. Cline. Mr. Cline's advice was relied upon by Dr. and Mrs. White in choosing to transfer the policies to the Millennium plan in 2003. In fact, it was not until August 2004 that petitioners received the administration manual containing the Millennium plan documents.

Accordingly, we hold that petitioners did not act with reasonable cause and in good faith when they entered into the xélan 419 plan and the Millennium plan relying primarily, if not solely, upon the advice of promoters and other interested parties that stood to benefit financially from the transactions.

Substantial Authority

The amount of an understatement is reduced by that portion of the understatement which is attributable to: (1) the tax treatment of any item by the taxpayer if there is or was substantial authority for such treatment, or (2) the taxpayer's adequately disclosing relevant facts in the return or in a statement attached to the return, with a reasonable basis for the tax treatment of such item by the taxpayer. Sec. 6662(d)(2)(B).

"In evaluating whether a taxpayer's position regarding treatment of a particular item is supported by substantial authority, the weight of authorities in support of the taxpayer's position must be substantial in relation to the weight of authorities supporting contrary positions." Antonides v. Commissioner, 91 T.C. 686, 702 (1988), aff'd, 893 F.2d 656 (4th Cir. 1990); see also sec. 1.6662-4(d) (3) (i), Income Tax Regs. The substantial authority standard is objective and, therefore, it is not relevant in determining whether the taxpayer believed substantial authority existed. Sec. 1.6662-4(d)(3)(i), Income Tax Regs.

In Booth v. Commissioner, 108 T.C. 524, 578 (1997), we stated that although legal opinions are not authority, the "authorities underlying a legal opinion, however, may give rise to substantial authority for the tax treatment of an item." Section 1.6662-4(d)(3)(iii), Income Tax Regs., provides that only the following are authority for purposes determining whether there is substantial authority for the tax treatment of an item:

[A]pplicable provisions of the Internal Revenue Code and other statutory provisions; proposed, temporary and final regulations construing such statutes; revenue rulings and revenue procedures; tax treaties and regulations thereunder, and Treasury Department and other official explanations of such treaties; court cases; congressional intent as reflected in committee reports, joint explanatory statements of managers included in conference committee reports, and floor statements made prior to enactment by one of a bill's managers; General Explanations of tax legislation prepared by the Joint Committee on Taxation (the Blue Book); private letter rulings and technical advice memoranda issued after October 31, 1976; actions on decisions and general counsel memoranda issued after March 12, 1981 (as well as general counsel memoranda published in pre-1955 volumes of the Cumulative Bulletin); Internal Revenue Service information or press releases; and notices, announcements and other administrative pronouncements published by the Service in the Internal Revenue Bulletin. * * *

In 1999 when Dr. and Mrs. White and Diogenes began their participation in the xélan 419 plan, the Court had issued Booth v. Commissioner, 108 T.C. 524 (1997), and the IRS had issued Notice 95-34, 1995-1 C.B. 309. In Booth the Court did not impose an accuracy-related penalty because the question of whether the Prime Plan was within the scope of section 419A (f) (6) was at the time a novel question. In Notice 95-34 the IRS provided guidance on the tax problems raised by certain trust arrangements in seeking to qualify for exemption from section 419.

Furthermore, before any of the years at issue, this Court issued Neonatology Assocs., P.A. v. Commissioner, 115 T.C. 43. We therefore conclude that there was not substantial authority supporting the deductions for the contributions to either the xélan 419 plan or the Millennium plan. In reaching our decision, we have considered all arguments made by the parties. To the extent not mentioned or addressed, they are irrelevant or without merit.

To reflect the foregoing,

Decisions will be entered under Rule 155

CASE OF THE YEAR 2011

INTRODUCTION

I had one case taken before the U.S. Supreme Court. Since I am licensed to practice before the court I sat next to the judges, the law firm that represented one of my companies gave oral arguments on appeal from a case I argued before the 9th Circuit. The attorney who gave the argument had argued many cases before the U.S. Supreme Court and was lead counsel at Ropes and Gray. We lost that battle-but won the war-if you can win a war. In any event, if you have a chance to visit the Supreme Court and listen to oral arguments you should do so-especially on a hot topic before the court. Pension are usually not one of them.

SUPREME COURT OF THE UNITED STATES

No. 09–804

CIGNA CORPORATION, ET AL., PETITIONERS v.

JANICE C. AMARA, ET AL., INDIVIDUALLY

AND ON BEHALF OF ALL OTHERS

SIMILARLY SITUATED

ON WRIT OF CERTIORARI TO THE UNITED STATES COURT OF

APPEALS FOR THE SECOND CIRCUIT

[May 16, 2011]

JUSTICE BREYER delivered the opinion of the Court. In 1998, petitioner CIGNA Corporation changed the nature of its basic pension plan for employees. Previously, the plan provided a retiring employee with a defined benefit in the form of an annuity calculated on the basis of his preretirement salary and length of service. The new plan provided most retiring employees with a (lump sum) cash balance calculated on the basis of a defined annual contribution from CIGNA as increased by compound interest. Because many employees had already earned at least some old-plan benefits, the new plan translated already earned benefits into an opening amount in the employee's cash balance account. Respondents, acting on behalf of approximately 25,000 beneficiaries of the CIGNA Pension Plan (which is also a petitioner here), challenged CIGNA's adoption of the new plan. They claimed in part that CIGNA had failed to give them proper notice of changes to their benefits, particularly because the new plan in certain respects provided them with less generous benefits. See Employee Retirement Income Security Act of 1974 (ERISA) §§102(a), 104(b), 204(h), 88 Stat. 841, 848, 862, as amended, 29 U. S. C. §§1022(a), 1024(b), 1054(h). The District Court agreed that the disclosures made by CIGNA violated its obligations under ERISA. In determining relief, the court found that CIGNA's notice failures had caused the employees "likely harm." The Court then reformed the new plan and ordered CIGNA to pay benefits accordingly. It found legal authority for doing so in ERISA §502(a) (1) (B), 29 U. S. C. §1132(a) (1) (B) (authorizing a plan "participant or beneficiary" to bring a "civil action" to "recover benefits due to him under the terms of his plan"). We agreed to decide whether the District Court applied the correct legal standard, namely, a "likely harm" standard, in determining that CIGNA's notice violations caused its employees sufficient injury to warrant legal relief. To reach that question, we must first consider a more general matter—whether the ERISA section just mentioned (ERISA's recovery-of-benefits-due provision, §502(a) (1) (B)) authorizes entry of the relief the District Court provided. We conclude that it does not authorize this relief. Nonetheless, we find that a different equity related ERISA provision, to which the District Court also referred, authorizes forms of relief similar to those that the court entered. §502(a) (3), 29 U. S. C. §1132(a) (3). Section 502(a) (3) authorizes "appropriate equitable relief" for violations of ERISA. Accordingly, the relevant standard of harm will depend upon the equitable theory by which the District Court provides relief. We leave it to the District Court to conduct that analysis in the first instance, but we identify equitable principles that the court might apply on remand.

3 Cite as: 563 U. S. ____ (2011)

Opinion of the Court

I

Because our decision rests in important part upon the circumstances present here, we shall describe those circumstances in some detail. We still simplify in doing so. But the interested reader can find a more thorough description in two District Court opinions, which set forth that court's findings reached after a lengthy trial. See 559 F. Supp. 2d 192 (Conn. 2008); 534 F. Supp. 2d 288 (Conn. 2008). A Under CIGNA's pre-1998 defined-benefit retirement plan, an employee with at least five years' service would receive an annuity annually paying an amount that depended upon the employee's salary and length of service. Depending on when the employee had joined CIGNA, the annuity would equal either (1) 2 percent of the employee's average salary over his final three years with CIGNA, multiplied by the number of years worked (up to 30); or (2) 12/3 percent of the employee's average salary over his final five years with CIGNA, multiplied by the number of years worked (up to 35). Calculated either way, the annuity would approach 60 percent of a longtime employee's final salary. A well-paid longtime employee, earning, say, $160,000 per year, could receive a retirement annuity paying the employee about $96,000 per year until his death. The plan offered many employees at least one other benefit: They could retire early, at age 55, and receive an only-somewhat-reduced annuity. In November 1997, CIGNA sent its employees a newsletter announcing that it intended to put in place a new pension plan. The new plan would substitute an "account balance plan" for CIGNA's pre-existing defined-benefit system. App. 991a (emphasis deleted). The newsletter added that the old plan would end on December 31, 1997, that CIGNA would introduce (and describe) the new plan sometime during 1998, and that the new plan would apply retroactively to January 1, 1998. Eleven months later CIGNA filled in the details. Its new plan created an individual retirement account for each employee. (The account consisted of a bookkeeping entry backed by a CIGNA-funded trust.) Each year CIGNA would contribute to the employee's individual account an amount equal to between 3 percent and 8.5 percent of the employee's salary, depending upon age, length of service, and certain other factors. The account balance would earn compound interest at a rate equal to the return on 5-year treasury bills plus one-quarter percent (but no less than 4.5 percent and no greater than 9 percent). Upon retirement the employee would receive the amount then in his or her individual account—in the form of either a lump sum or whatever annuity the lump sum then would buy. As promised, CIGNA would open the accounts and begin to make contributions as of January 1, 1998. But what about the retirement benefits that employees had already earned prior to January 1, 1998? CIGNA promised to make an initial contribution to the individual's account equal to the value of that employee's already earned benefits. And the new plan set forth a method for calculating that initial contribution. The method consisted of calculating the amount as of the employee's (future) retirement date of the annuity to which the employee's salary and length of service already (i.e., as of December 31, 1997) entitled him and then discounting that sum to its present (i.e., January 1, 1998) value. An example will help: Imagine an employee born on January 1, 1966, who joined CIGNA in January 1991 on his 25th birthday, and who (during the five years preceding the plan changeover) earned an average salary of $100,000 per year. As of January 1, 1998, the old plan would have entitled that employee to an annuity equal to $100,000 times 7 (years then worked) times 12/3 percent, or $11,667 per year—when he retired in 2031 at age 65. The 2031 price of an annuity paying $11,667 per year until death depends upon interest rates and mortality assumptions at that time. If we assume the annuity would pay 7 percent until the holder's death (and we use the mortality assumptions used by the plan, see App. 407a (incorporating the mortality table prescribed by Rev. Rul. 95–6, 1995–1 Cum. Bull. 80)), then the 2031 price of such an annuity would be about $120,500. And CIGNA should initially deposit in this individual's account on January 1, 1998, an amount that will grow to become $120,500, 33 years later, in 2031, when the individual retires. If we assume a 5 percent average interest rate, then that amount presently (i.e., as of January 1, 1998) equals about $24,000. And (with one further mortality-related adjustment that we shall describe infra, at 6–7) that is the amount, more or less, that the new plan's transition rules would have required CIGNA initially to deposit. Then CIGNA would make further annual deposits, and all the deposited amounts would earn compound interest. When the employee retired, he would receive the resulting lump sum. The new plan also provided employees a guarantee: An employee would receive upon retirement either (1) the amount to which he or she had become entitled as of January 1, 1998, or (2) the amount then in his or her individual account, whichever was greater. Thus, the employee in our example would receive (in 2031) no less than an annuity paying $11,667 per year for life. B 1 The District Court found that CIGNA's initial descriptions of its new plan were significantly incomplete and misled its employees. In November 1997, for example, CIGNA sent the employees a newsletter that said the new plan would "significantly enhance" its "retirement program," would produce "an overall improvement in . . . retirement benefits," and would provide "the same benefit security" with "steadier benefit growth." App. 990a, 991a, 993a. CIGNA also told its employees that they would "see the growth in [their] total retirement benefits from CIGNA every year," id., at 952a, that its initial deposit "represent[ed] the full value of the benefit [they] earned for service before 1998," Record E–503 (Exh. 98), and that "[o]ne advantage the company will not get from the retirement program changes is cost savings." App. 993a. In fact, the new plan saved the company $10 million annually (though CIGNA later said it devoted the savings to other employee benefits). Its initial deposit did not "represent[t] the full value of the benefit" that employees had "earned for service before 1998." And the plan made a significant number of employees worse off in at least the following specific ways: First, the initial deposit calculation ignored the fact that the old plan offered many CIGNA employees the right to retire early (beginning at age 55) with only somewhat reduced benefits. This right was valuable. For example, as of January 1, 1998, respondent Janice Amara had earned vested age-55 retirement benefits of $1,833 per month, but CIGNA's initial deposit in her new-plan individual retirement account (ignoring this benefit) would have allowed her at age 55 to buy an annuity benefit of only $900 per month. Second, as we previously indicated but did not explain, supra at 5, the new plan adjusted CIGNA's initial deposit downward to account for the fact that, unlike the old plan's lifetime annuity, an employee's survivors would receive the new plan's benefits (namely, the amount in the employee's individual account) even if the employee died before retiring. The downward adjustment consisted of multiplying the otherwise-required deposit by the probability that the employee would live until retirement—a 90 percent probability in the example of our 32-year-old, supra, at 4–5. And that meant that CIGNA's initial deposit in our example—the amount that was supposed to grow to $120,500 by 2031— would be less than $22,000, not $24,000 (the number we computed). The employee, of course, would receive a benefit in return—namely, a form of life insurance. But at least some employees might have preferred the retirement benefit and consequently could reasonably have thought it important to know that the new plan traded away one-tenth of their already-earned benefits for a life insurance policy that they might not have wanted. Third, the new plan shifted the risk of a fall in interest rates from CIGNA to its employees. Under the old plan, CIGNA had to buy a retiring employee an annuity that paid a specified sum irrespective of whether falling interest rates made it more expensive for CIGNA to pay for that annuity. And falling interest rates also meant that any sum CIGNA set aside to buy that annuity would grow more slowly over time, thereby requiring CIGNA to set aside more money to make any specific sum available at retirement. Under the new plan CIGNA did not have to buy a retiring employee an annuity that paid a specific sum. The employee would simply receive whatever sum his account contained. And falling interest rates meant that the account's lump sum would earn less money each year after the employee retired. Annuities, for example, would become more expensive (any fixed purchase price paying for less annual income). At the same time falling interest meant that the individual account would grow more slowly over time, leaving the employee with less money at retirement. Of course, interest rates might rise instead of fall, leaving CIGNA's employees better off under the new plan. But the latter advantage does not cancel out the former disadvantage, for most individuals are risk averse. And that means that most of CIGNA's employees would have preferred that CIGNA, rather than they, bear these risks. The amounts likely involved are significant. If, in our example, interest rates between 1998 and 2031 averaged 4 percent rather than the 5 percent we assumed, and if in 2031 annuities paid 6 percent rather than the 7 percent we assumed, then CIGNA would have had to make an initial deposit of $35,500 (not $24,000) to assure that employee the $11,667 annual annuity payment to which he had already become entitled. Indeed, that $24,000 that CIGNA would have contributed (leaving aside the life insurance problem) would have provided enough money to buy (in 2031) an annuity that assured the employee an annual payment of only about $8,000 (rather than $11,667). We recognize that the employee in our example (like others) might have continued to work for CIGNA after January 1, 1998; and he would thereby eventually have earned a pension that, by the time of his retirement, was worth far more than $11,667. But that is so because CIGNA made an additional contribution for each year worked after January 1, 1998. If interest rates fell (as they did), it would take the employee several additional years of work simply to catch up (under the new plan) to where he had already been (under the old plan) as of January 1, 1998—a phenomenon known in pension jargon as "wear away," see 534 F. Supp. 2d, at 303–304 (referring to respondents' requiring 6 to 10 years to catch up). The District Court found that CIGNA told its employees nothing about any of these features of the new plan— which individually and together made clear that CIGNA's descriptions of the plan were incomplete and inaccurate. The District Court also found that CIGNA intentionally misled its employees. A focus group and many employees asked CIGNA, for example, to "disclose details'" about the plan, to provide "'individual comparisons,'" or to show "'[a]n actual projection for retirement.'" Id., at 342. But CIGNA did not do so. Instead (in the words of one internal document), it "'focus[ed] on NOT providing employees before and after samples of the Pension Plan changes.'" Id., at 343. The District Court concluded, as a matter of law, that CIGNA's representations (and omissions) about the plan, made between November 1997 (when it announced the plan) and December 1998 (when it put the plan into effect) violated: (a) ERISA §204(h), implemented by Treas. Reg. §1.411(d)–6, 26 CFR §1.411(d)–6 (2000), which (as it existed at the relevant time) forbade an amendment of a pension plan that would "provide for a significant reduction in the rate of future benefit accrual" unless the plan administrator also sent a "written notice" that provided either the text of the amendment or summarized its likely effects, 29 U. S. C. §1054(h) (2000 ed.) (amended 2001); Treas. Reg. §1.411(d)–6, Q&A–10, 63 Fed. Reg. 68682 (1998); and (b) ERISA §§102(a) and 104(b), which require a plan administrator to provide beneficiaries with summary plan descriptions and with summaries of material modifications, "written in a manner calculated to be understood by the average plan participant," that are "sufficiently accurate and comprehensive to reasonably apprise such participants and beneficiaries of their rights and obligations under the plan," 29 U. S. C. §§1022(a), 1024(b) (2006 ed. and Supp. III). 2 The District Court then turned to the remedy. First, the court agreed with CIGNA that only employees whom CIGNA's disclosure failures had harmed could obtain relief. But it did not require each individual member of the relevant CIGNA employee class to show individual injury. Rather, it found (1) that the evidence presented had raised a presumption of "likely harm" suffered by the members of the relevant employee class, and (2) that CIGNA, though free to offer contrary evidence in respect to some or all of those employees, had failed to rebut that presumption. It concluded that this unrebutted showing was sufficient to warrant class-applicable relief. Second, the court noted that §204(h) had been interpreted by the Second Circuit to permit the invalidation of plan amendments not preceded by a proper notice, prior to the 2001 amendment that made this power explicit. 559 F. Supp. 2d, at 207 (citing Frommert v. Conkright, 433 F. 3d 254, 263 (2006)); see 29 U. S. C. §1054(h) (6) (2006 ed.) (entitling participants to benefits "without regard to [the] amendment" in case of an "egregious failure"). But the court also thought that granting this relief here would harm, not help, the injured employees. That is because the notice failures all concerned the new plan that took effect in December 1998. The court thought that the notices in respect to the freezing of old-plan benefits, effective December 31, 1997, were valid. To strike the new plan while leaving in effect the frozen old plan would not help CIGNA's employees. The court considered treating the November 1997 notice as a sham or treating that notice and the later 1998 notices as part and parcel of a single set of related events. But it pointed out that respondents "ha[d] argued none of these things." 559 F. Supp. 2d, at 208. And it said that the court would "not make these arguments now on [respondents'] behalf." Ibid. Third, the court reformed the terms of the new plan's guarantee. It erased the portion that assured participants who retired the greater of "A" (that which they had already earned as of December 31, 1997, under the old plan, $11,667 in our example) or "B" (that which they would earn via CIGNA's annual deposits under the new plan, including CIGNA's initial deposit). And it substituted a provision that would guarantee each employee "A" (that which they had already earned, as of December 31, 1997, under the old plan) plus "B" (that which they would earn via CIGNA's annual deposits under the new plan, excluding CIGNA's initial deposit). In our example, the District Court's remedy would no longer force our employee to choose upon retirement either an $11,667 annuity or his new plan benefits (including both CIGNA's annual deposits and CIGNA's initial deposit). It would give him an $11,667 annuity plus his new plan benefits (with CIGNA's annual deposits but without CIGNA's initial deposit). Fourth, the court "order[ed] and enjoin[ed] the CIGNA Plan to reform its records to reflect that all class members . . . now receive [the just described] 'A + B' benefits," and that it pay appropriate benefits to those class members who had already retired.

Id., at 222. Fifth, the court held that ERISA §502(a) (1) (B) provided the legal authority to enter this relief. That provision states that a "civil action may be brought" by a plan "participant or beneficiary . . . to recover benefits due to him under the terms of his plan." 29 U. S. C. §1132(a) (1) (B). The court wrote that its orders in effect awarded "benefits under the terms of the plan" as reformed. 559 F. Supp. 2d, at 212. At the same time the court considered whether ERISA §502(a) (3) also provided legal authority to enter this relief. That provision states that a civil action may be brought "by a participant, beneficiary, or fiduciary (A) to enjoin any act or practice which violates any provision of this subchapter or the terms of the plan, or (B) to obtain other appropriate equitable relief (i) to redress such violations or (ii) to enforce any provisions of this subchapter or the terms of the plan." 29 U. S. C. §1132(a) (3) (emphasis added). The District Court decided not to answer this question because (1) it had just decided that the same relief was available under §502(a)(1)(B), regardless, cf. Varity Corp. v. Howe, 516 U. S. 489, 515 (1996); and (2) the Supreme Court has "issued several opinions . . . that have severely curtailed the kinds of relief that are available under §502(a)(3)," 559 F. Supp. 2d, at 205 (citing Sereboff v. Mid Atlantic Medical Services, Inc., 547 U. S. 356 (2006); Great-West Life & Annuity Ins. Co. v. Knudson, 534 U. S. 204 (2002); and Mertens v. Hewitt Associates, 508 U. S. 248 (1993)). 3 The parties cross-appealed the District Court's judgment. The Court of Appeals for the Second Circuit issued a brief summary order, rejecting all their claims, and affirming "the judgment of the district court for substantially the reasons stated" in the District Courts "well-reasoned and scholarly opinions." 348 Fed. Appx. 627 (2009). The parties filed cross-petitions for writs of certiorari in this Court. We granted the request in CIGNA's petition to consider whether a showing of "likely harm" is sufficient to entitle plan participants to recover benefits based on faulty disclosures. II CIGNA in the merits briefing raises a preliminary question. Brief for Petitioners 13–20. It argues first and foremost that the statutory provision upon which the District Court rested its orders, namely, the provision for recovery of plan benefits, §502(a)(1)(B), does not in fact authorize the District Court to enter the kind of relief it entered here. And for that reason, CIGNA argues, whether the District Court did or did not use a proper standard for determining harm is beside the point. We believe that this preliminary question is closely enough related to the question presented that we shall consider it at the outset. A The District Court ordered relief in two steps. Step 1: It ordered the terms of the plan reformed (so that they provided an "A plus B," rather than a "greater of A or B" guarantee). Step 2: It ordered the plan administrator (which it found to be CIGNA) to enforce the plan as reformed. One can fairly describe step 2 as consistent with §502(a) (1) (B), for that provision grants a participant the right to bring a civil action to "recover benefits due . . . under the terms of his plan." 29 U. S. C. §1132(a) (1) (B). And step 2 orders recovery of the benefits provided by the "terms of [the] plan" as reformed. But what about step 1? Where does §502(a) (1) (B) grant a court the power to change the terms of the plan as they previously existed? The statutory language speaks of "enforc[ing]" the "terms of the plan," not of changing them. 29 U. S. C. §1132(a) (l) (B) (emphasis added). The provision allows a court to look outside the plan's written language in deciding what those terms are, i.e., what the language means. See UNUM Life Ins. Co. of America v. Ward, 526 U. S. 358, 377–379 (1999) (permitting the insurance terms of an ERISA-governed plan to be interpreted in light of state insurance rules). But we have found nothing suggesting that the provision authorizes a court to alter those terms, at least not in present circumstances, where that change, akin to the reform of a contract, seems less like the simple enforcement of a contract as written and more like an equitable remedy. See infra, at 18. Nor can we accept the Solicitor General's alternative rationale seeking to justify the use of this provision. The Solicitor General says that the District Court did enforce the plan's terms as written, adding that the "plan" includes the disclosures that constituted the summary plan descriptions. In other words, in the view of the Solicitor General, the terms of the summaries are terms of the plan. Even if the District Court had viewed the summaries as plan "terms" (which it did not, see supra, at 10–11), however, we cannot agree that the terms of statutorily required plan summaries (or summaries of plan modifications) necessarily may be enforced (under §502(a) (1) (B)) as the terms of the plan itself. For one thing, it is difficult to square the Solicitor General's reading of the statute with ERISA §102(a), the provision that obliges plan administrators to furnish summary plan descriptions. The syntax of that provision, requiring that participants and beneficiaries be advised of their rights and obligations "under the plan," suggests that the information about the plan provided by those disclosures is not itself part of the plan. See 29 U. S. C. §1022(a). Nothing in §502(a) (1) (B) (or, as far as we can tell, anywhere else) suggests the contrary. Nor do we find it easy to square the Solicitor General's reading with the statute's division of authority between a plan's sponsor and the plan's administrator. The plan's sponsor (e.g., the employer), like a trust's settlor, creates the basic terms and conditions of the plan, executes a written instrument containing those terms and conditions, and provides in that instrument "a procedure" for making amendments. §402, 29 U. S. C. §1102. The plan's administrator, a trustee-like fiduciary, manages the plan, follows its terms in doing so, and provides participants with the summary documents that describe the plan (and modifications) in readily understandable form. §§3(21) (A), 101(a), 102, 104, 29 U. S. C. §§1002(21) (A), 1021(a), 1022, 1024 (2006 ed. and Supp. III). Here, the District Court found that the same entity, CIGNA, filled both roles. See 534 F. Supp. 2d, at 331. But that is not always the case. Regardless, we have found that ERISA carefully distinguishes these roles. See, e.g., Varity Corp., 516 U. S., at 498. And we have no reason to believe that the statute intends to mix the responsibilities by giving the administrator the power to set plan terms indirectly by including them in the summary plan descriptions. See CurtissWright Corp. v. Schoonejongen, 514 U. S. 73, 81–85 (1995). Finally, we find it difficult to reconcile the Solicitor General's interpretation with the basic summary plan description objective: clear, simple communication. See §§2(a), 102(a), 29 U. S. C. §1001(a), 1022(a) (2006 ed.). To make the language of a plan summary legally binding could well lead plan administrators to sacrifice simplicity and comprehensibility in order to describe plan terms in the language of lawyers. Consider the difference between a will and the summary of a will or between a property deed and its summary. Consider, too, the length of Part I of this opinion, and then consider how much longer Part I would have to be if we had to include all the qualifications and nuances that a plan drafter might have found important and feared to omit lest they lose all legal significance. The District Court's opinions take up 109 pages of the Federal Supplement. None of this is to say that plan administrators can avoid providing complete and accurate summaries of plan terms in the manner required by ERISA and its implementing regulations. But we fear that the Solicitor General's rule might bring about complexity that would defeat the fundamental purpose of the summaries. For these reasons taken together we conclude that the summary documents, important as they are, provide communication with beneficiaries about the plan, but that their statements do not themselves constitute the terms of the plan for purposes of §502(a)(1)(B). We also conclude that the District Court could not find authority in that section to reform CIGNA's plan as written.

If §502(a) (1) (B) does not authorize entry of the relief here at issue, what about nearby §502(a) (3)? That provision allows a participant, beneficiary, or fiduciary "to obtain other appropriate equitable relief" to redress violations of (here relevant) parts of ERISA "or the terms of the plan." 29 U. S. C. §1132(a) (3) (emphasis added). The District Court strongly implied, but did not directly hold, that it would base its relief upon this subsection were it not for (1) the fact that the preceding "plan benefits due" provision, §502(a) (1) (B), provided sufficient authority; and (2) certain cases from this Court that narrowed the application of the term "appropriate equitable relief," see, e.g., Mertens, 508 U. S. 248; Great-West, 534 U. S. 204. Our holding in Part II–A, supra, removes the District Court's first obstacle. And given the likelihood that, on remand, the District Court will turn to and rely upon this alternative subsection, we consider the court's second concern. We find that concern misplaced. We have interpreted the term "appropriate equitable relief" in §502(a) (3) as referring to "'those categories of relief'" that, traditionally speaking (i.e., prior to the merger of law and equity) "'were typically available in equity.'" Sereboff, 547 U. S., at 361 (quoting Mertens, 508 U. S., at 256). In Mertens, we applied this principle to a claim seeking money damages brought by a beneficiary against a private firm that provided a trustee with actuarial services. We found that the plaintiff sought "nothing other than compensatory damages" against a nonfiduciary. Id., at 253, 255 (emphasis deleted). And we held that such a claim, traditionally speaking, was legal, not equitable, in nature. Id., at 255. In Great-West, we considered a claim brought by a fiduciary against a tort-award-winning beneficiary seeking monetary reimbursement for medical outlays that the plan had previously made on the beneficiary's behalf. We noted that the fiduciary sought to obtain a lien attaching to (or a constructive trust imposed upon) money that the beneficiary had received from the tort-case defendant. But we noted that the money in question was not the "particular" money that the tort defendant had paid. And, traditionally speaking, relief that sought a lien or a constructive trust was legal relief, not equitable relief, unless the funds in question were "particular funds or property in the defendant's possession." 534 U. S., at 213 (emphasis added). The case before us concerns a suit by a beneficiary against a plan fiduciary (whom ERISA typically treats as a trustee) about the terms of a plan (which ERISA typically treats as a trust). See LaRue v. DeWolff, Boberg & Associates, Inc., 552 U. S. 248, 253, n. 4 (2008); Varity Corp., 516 U. S., at 496–497. It is the kind of lawsuit that, before the merger of law and equity, respondents could have brought only in a court of equity, not a court of law. 4 A. Scott, W. Fratcher, & M. Ascher, Trusts §24.1, p. 1654 (5th ed. 2007) (hereinafter Scott & Ascher) ("Trusts are, and always have been, the bailiwick of the courts of equity"); Duvall v. Craig, 2 Wheat. 45, 56 (1817) (a trustee was "only suable in equity"). With the exception of the relief now provided by §502(a)(1)(B), Restatement (Second) of Trusts §§198(1)–(2) (1957) (hereinafter Second Restatement); 4 Scott & Ascher §24.2.1, the remedies available to those courts of equity were traditionally considered equitable remedies, see Second Restatement §199; J. Adams, Doctrine of Equity: A Commentary on the Law as Administered by the Court of Chancery 61 (7th Am. ed. 1881) (hereinafter Adams); 4 Scott & Ascher §24.2. The District Court's affirmative and negative injunctions obviously fall within this category. Mertens, supra, at 256 (identifying injunctions, mandamus, and restitution as equitable relief). And other relief ordered by the District Court resembles forms of traditional equitable relief. That is because equity chancellors developed a host of other "distinctively equitable" remedies—remedies that were "fitted to the nature of the primary right" they were intended to protect. 1 S. Symons, Pomeroy's Equity Jurisprudence §108, pp. 139–140 (5th ed. 1941) (hereinafter Pomeroy). See generally 1 J. Story, Commentaries on Equity Jurisprudence §692 (12th ed. 1877) (hereinafter Story). Indeed, a maxim of equity states that "[e]quity suffers not a right to be without a remedy." R. Francis, Maxims of Equity 29 (1st Am. ed. 1823). And the relief entered here, insofar as it does not consist of injunctive relief, closely resembles three other traditional equitable remedies. First, what the District Court did here may be regarded as the reformation of the terms of the plan, in order to remedy the false or misleading information CIGNA provided. The power to reform contracts (as contrasted with the power to enforce contracts as written) is a traditional power of an equity court, not a court of law, and was used to prevent fraud. See Baltzer v. Raleigh & Augusta R. Co., 115 U. S. 634, 645 (1885) ("[I]t is well settled that equity would reform the contract, and enforce it, as reformed, if the mistake or fraud were shown"); Hearne v. Marine Ins. Co., 20 Wall. 488, 490 (1874) ("The reformation of written contracts for fraud or mistake is an ordinary head of equity jurisdiction"); Bradford v. Union Bank of Tenn., 13 How. 57, 66 (1852); J. Eaton, Handbook of Equity Jurisprudence §306, p. 618 (1901) (hereinafter Eaton) (courts of common law could only void or enforce, but not reform, a contract); 4 Pomeroy §1375, at 1000 (reformation "chiefly occasioned by fraud or mistake," which were themselves concerns of equity courts); 1 Story §§152–154; see also 4 Pomeroy §1375, at 999 (equity often considered reformation a "preparatory step" that "establishes the real contract"). Second, the District Court's remedy essentially held CIGNA to what it had promised, namely, that the new plan would not take from its employees benefits they had already accrued. This aspect of the remedy resembles estoppel, a traditional equitable remedy. See, e.g., E. Merwin, Principles of Equity and Equity Pleading §910 (H. Merwin ed. 1895); 3 Pomeroy §804. Equitable estoppel "operates to place the person entitled to its benefit in the same position he would have been in had the representations been true." Eaton §62, at 176. And, as Justice Story long ago pointed out, equitable estoppel "forms a very essential element in . . . fair dealing, and rebuke of all fraudulent misrepresentation, which it is the boast of courts of equity constantly to promote." 2 Story §1533, at 776. Third, the District Court injunctions require the plan administrator to pay to already retired beneficiaries money owed them under the plan as reformed. But the fact that this relief takes the form of a money payment does not remove it from the category of traditionally equitable relief. Equity courts possessed the power to provide relief in the form of monetary "compensation" for a loss resulting from a trustee's breach of duty, or to prevent the trustee's unjust enrichment. Restatement (Third) of Trusts §95, and Comment a (Tent. Draft No. 5, Mar. 2, 2009) (hereinafter Third Restatement); Eaton §§211–212, at 440. Indeed, prior to the merger of law and equity this kind of monetary remedy against a trustee, sometimes called a "surcharge," was "exclusively equitable." Princess Lida of Thurn and Taxis v. Thompson, 305 U. S. 456, 464 (1939); Third Restatement §95, and Comment a; G. Bogert & G. Bogert, Trusts and Trustees §862 (rev. 2d ed. 1995) (hereinafter Bogert); 4 Scott & Ascher §§24.2, 24.9, at 1659–1660, 1686; Second Restatement §197; see also Manhattan Bank of Memphis v. Walker, 130 U. S. 267, 271 (1889) ("The suit is plainly one of equitable cognizance, the bill being filed to charge the defendant, as a trustee, for a breach of trust"); 1 J.

Perry, A Treatise on the Law of Trusts and Trustees §17, p. 13 (2d ed. 1874) (common-law attempts "to punish trustees for a breach of trust in damages, . . . w[ere] soon abandoned"). The surcharge remedy extended to a breach of trust committed by a fiduciary encompassing any violation of a duty imposed upon that fiduciary. See Second Restatement §201; Adams 59; 4 Pomeroy §1079; 2 Story §§1261, 1268. Thus, insofar as an award of make-whole relief is concerned, the fact that the defendant in this case, unlike the defendant in Mertens, is analogous to a trustee makes a critical difference. See 508 U. S., at 262–263. In sum, contrary to the District Court's fears, the types of remedies the court entered here fall within the scope of the term "appropriate equitable relief" in §502(a)(3). III Section 502(a) (3) invokes the equitable powers of the District Court. We cannot know with certainty which remedy the District Court understood itself to be imposing, nor whether the District Court will find it appropriate to exercise its discretion under §502(a)(3) to impose that remedy on remand. We need not decide which remedies are appropriate on the facts of this case in order to resolve the parties' dispute as to the appropriate legal standard in determining whether members of the relevant employee class were injured. The relevant substantive provisions of ERISA do not set forth any particular standard for determining harm. They simply require the plan administrator to write and to distribute written notices that are "sufficiently accurate and comprehensive to reasonably apprise" plan participants and beneficiaries of "their rights and obligations under the plan." §102(a); see also §§104(b), 204(h). Nor can we find a definite standard in the ERISA provision, §502(a) (3) (which authorizes the court to enter "appropriate equitable relief" to redress ERISA "violations"). Hence any requirement of harm must come from the law of equity. Looking to the law of equity, there is no general principle that "detrimental reliance" must be proved before a remedy is decreed. To the extent any such requirement arises, it is because the specific remedy being contemplated imposes such a requirement. Thus, as CIGNA points out, when equity courts used the remedy of estoppel, they insisted upon a showing akin to detrimental reliance, i.e., that the defendant's statement "in truth, influenced the conduct of" the plaintiff, causing "prejudice[e]." Eaton §61, at 175; see 3 Pomeroy §805. Accordingly, when a court exercises its authority under §502(a) (3) to impose a remedy equivalent to estoppel, a showing of detrimental reliance must be made. But this showing is not always necessary for other equitable remedies. Equity courts, for example, would reform contracts to reflect the mutual understanding of the contracting parties where "fraudulent suppression[s], omission[s], or insertion[s]," 1 Story §154, at 149, "material[ly] . . . affect[ed]" the "substance" of the contract, even if the "complaining part[y]" was negligent in not realizing its mistake, as long as its negligence did not fall below a standard of "reasonable prudence" and violate a legal duty. 3 Pomeroy §§856, 856b, at 334, 340–341; see Baltzer, 115 U. S., at 645; Eaton §307(b). Nor did equity courts insist upon a showing of detrimental reliance in cases where they ordered "surcharge." Rather, they simply ordered a trust or beneficiary made whole following a trustee's breach of trust. In such instances equity courts would "mold the relief to protect the rights of the beneficiary according to the situation involved." Bogert §861, at 4. This flexible approach belies a strict requirement of "detrimental reliance." To be sure, just as a court of equity would not surcharge a trustee for a nonexistent harm, 4 Scott & Ascher §24.9, a fiduciary can be surcharged under §502(a) (3) only upon a showing of actual harm—proved (under the default rule for civil cases) by a preponderance of the evidence. That actual harm may sometimes consist of detrimental reliance, but it might also come from the loss of a right protected by ERISA or its trust-law antecedents. In the present case, it is not difficult to imagine how the failure to provide proper summary information, in violation of the statute, injured employees even if they did not themselves act in reliance on summary documents—which they might not themselves have seen—for they may have thought fellow employees, or informal workplace discussion, would have let them know if, say, plan changes would likely prove harmful. We doubt that Congress would have wanted to bar those employees from relief. The upshot is that we can agree with CIGNA only to a limited extent. We believe that, to obtain relief by surcharge for violations of §§102(a) and 104(b), a plan participant or beneficiary must show that the violation injured him or her. But to do so, he or she need only show harm and causation. Although it is not always necessary to meet the more rigorous standard implicit in the words "detrimental reliance," actual harm must be shown. We are not asked to reassess the evidence. And we are not asked about the other prerequisites for relief. We are asked about the standard of prejudice. And we conclude that the standard of prejudice must be borrowed from equitable principles, as modified by the obligations and injuries identified by ERISA itself. Information-related circumstances, violations, and injuries are potentially too various in nature to insist that harm must always meet that more vigorous "detrimental harm" standard when equity imposed no such strict requirement. IV We have premised our discussion in Part III on the need for the District Court to revisit its determination of an appropriate remedy for the violations of ERISA it identified. Whether or not the general principles we have discussed above are properly applicable in this case is for it or the Court of Appeals to determine in the first instance. Because the District Court has not determined if an appropriate remedy may be imposed under §502(a) (3), we must vacate the judgment below and remand this case for further proceedings consistent with this opinion.

It is so ordered. JUSTICE SOTOMAYOR took no part in the consideration or decision of this case.

CASE OF THE YEAR-2010

INTRODUCTION

When this case came out-it made my enrolled actuaries smile. They are constantly haunted by potential computational errors (which are few) or interpretation errors…which can be many. This case has potential to be the case of the decade-and you can use it to fight IRS audits. I have cited the case many times before the IRS on audit-(of course they did not read it)-but there is great language you can and should use. I have highlighted some of them for you.

SUPREME COURT OF THE UNITED STATES

No. 08–810

SALLY L. CONKRIGHT, ET AL., PETITIONERS v. PAUL J. FROMMERT ET AL. ON WRIT OF CERTIORARI TO THE UNITED STATES COURT OF

APPEALS FOR THE SECOND CIRCUIT

[April 21, 2010]

CHIEF JUSTICE ROBERTS delivered the opinion of the Court. <u>People make mistakes. Even administrators of ERISA plans. That should come as no surprise, given that the Employee Retirement Income Security Act of 1974 is "an enormously complex and detailed statute,"</u> Mertens v. Hewitt Associates, 508 U. S. 248, 262 (1993), and the plans that administrators must construe can be lengthy and complicated. (The one at issue here runs to 81 pages, with 139 sections.) We held in Firestone Tire & Rubber Co. v. Bruch, 489 U. S. 101 (1989), <u>that an ERISA plan administrator with discretionary authority to interpret a plan is entitled to deference in exercising that discretion.</u> The question here is whether a single honest mistake in plan interpretation justifies stripping the administrator of that deference for subsequent related interpretations of the plan. We hold that it does not. I As in many ERISA matters, the facts of this case are exceedingly complicated. Fortunately, most of the factual details are unnecessary to the legal issues before us, so we cover them only in broad strokes. This case concerns Xerox Corporation's pension plan, which is covered by ERISA, 88 Stat. 829, as amended, 29 U. S. C. §1001 et seq. Petitioners are the plan itself (hereinafter Plan), and the Plan's current and former administrators (hereinafter Plan Administrator). See §1002(16) (A) (i); App. 32a. Respondents are Xerox employees who left the company in the 1980's, received lump-sum distributions of retirement benefits they had earned up to that point, and were later rehired. See 328 F. Supp. 2d 420, 424 (WDNY 2004); Brief for Respondents 9–10. The dispute giving rise to this case concerns how to account for respondents' past distributions when calculating their current benefits—that is, how to avoid paying respondents the same benefits twice. The Plan Administrator initially interpreted the Plan to call for an approach that has come to be known as the "phantom account" method. 328 F. Supp. 2d, at 424. Essentially, that method calculated the hypothetical growth that respondents' past distributions would have experienced if the money had remained in Xerox's investment funds, and reduced respondents' present benefits accordingly. See id., at 426–428; App. to Pet. for Cert. 146a. After the Plan Administrator denied respondents' administrative challenges to that method, respondents filed suit in federal court under ERISA, 29 U. S. C. §1132(a) (1) (B). See 328 F. Supp. 2d, at 428–429. The District Court granted summary judgment for the Plan, applying a deferential standard of review to the Plan Administrator's interpretation. See id., at 430–431, 439. The Second Circuit vacated and remanded, holding that the Plan Administrator's interpretation was unreasonable and that respondents had not been adequately notified that the phantom account method would be used to calculate their benefits. See 433 F. 3d 254, 257, 265–269 (2006). The phantom account method having been exorcised, the District Court on remand considered other approaches for adjusting respondents' present benefits in light of their past distributions. See 472 F. Supp. 2d 452, 456–458 (WDNY 2007). The Plan Administrator submitted an affidavit proposing an approach that, like the phantom account method, accounted for the time value of the money that respondents had previously received. But unlike the phantom account method, the Plan Administrator's new approach did not calculate the present value of a past distribution based on events that occurred after the distribution was made. Instead, the new approach used an interest rate that was fixed at the time of the distribution, thereby calculating the current value of the distribution based on information that was known at the time of the distribution. See App. to Pet. for Cert. 147a– 153a. Petitioners argued that the District Court should apply a deferential standard of review to this approach, and accept it as a reasonable interpretation of the Plan. See Defendants' Pre-Hearing

Brief Addressed to Remedies in No. 00–CV–6311 (WDNY), pp. 7–8; Defendants' PreHearing Reply Brief Addressing Remedies in No. 00–CV– 6311 (WDNY), p. 2. The District Court did not apply a deferential standard of review. Nor did it accept the Plan Administrator's interpretation. Instead, after finding the Plan to be ambiguous, the District Court adopted an approach proposed by respondents that did not account for the time value of money. Under that approach, respondents' present benefits were reduced only by the nominal amount of their past distributions—thereby treating a dollar distributed to respondents in the 1980's as equal in value to a dollar distributed today. See 472 F. Supp. 2d, at 457–458. The Second Circuit affirmed in relevant part, holding that the District Court was correct not to apply a deferential standard on remand, and that the District Court's decision on the merits was not an abuse of discretion. See 535 F. 3d 111, 119 (2008). Petitioners asked us to grant certiorari on two questions:

(1) Whether the District Court owed deference to the Plan Administrator's interpretation of the Plan on remand, and

 (2) Whether the Court of Appeals properly granted deference to the District Court on the merits. Pet. for Cert. i.

 We granted certiorari on both, 557 U. S. ___ (2009), but find it necessary to decide only the first. II A This Court addressed the standard for reviewing the decisions of ERISA plan administrators in Firestone, 489 U. S. 101. Because ERISA's text does not directly resolve the matter, we looked to "principles of trust law" for guidance. Id., at 109, 111. We recognized that, under trust law, the proper standard of review of a trustee's decision depends on the language of the instrument creating the trust. See id., at 111–112. If the trust documents give the trustee "power to construe disputed or doubtful terms, . . . the trustee's interpretation will not be disturbed if reasonable." Id., at 111. Based on these considerations, we held that "a denial of benefits challenged under §1132(a)(1)(B) is to be reviewed under a de novo standard unless the benefit plan gives the administrator or fiduciary discretionary authority to determine eligibility for benefits or to construe the terms of the plan." Id., at 115. We expanded Firestone's approach in Metropolitan Life Ins. Co. v. Glenn, 554 U. S. ___ (2008). In determining the proper standard of review when a plan administrator operates under a conflict of interest, we again looked to trust law, the terms of the plan at issue, and the principles of ERISA—plus, of course, our precedent in Firestone. See 554 U. S., at ___ (slip op., at 4, 6–7, 9–10). We held that, when the terms of a plan grant discretionary authority to the plan administrator, a deferential standard of review remains appropriate even in the face of a conflict. See id., at ___ (slip op., at 9). It is undisputed that, under Firestone and the terms of the Plan, the Plan Administrator here would normally be entitled to deference when interpreting the Plan. See 328 F. Supp. 2d, at 430–431 (observing that the Plan grants the Plan Administrator "broad discretion in making decisions relative to the Plan"). The Court of Appeals, however, crafted an exception to Firestone deference. Specifically, the Second Circuit held that a court need not apply a deferential standard "where the administrator ha[s] previously construed the same [plan] terms and we found such a construction to have violated ERISA." 535 F. 3d, at 119. Under that view, the District Court here was entitled to reject a reasonable interpretation of the Plan offered by the Plan Administrator, solely because the Court of Appeals had overturned a previous interpretation by the Administrator. Cf. ibid. (accepting the District Court's chosen method as one of "several reasonable alternatives"). B We reject this "one-strike-and-you're-out" approach. Brief for Petitioners 51. As an initial matter, it has no basis in the Court's holding in Firestone, which set out a broad standard of deference without any suggestion that the standard was susceptible to ad hoc exceptions like the one adopted by the Court of Appeals. See 489 U. S., at 111, 115. Indeed, we refused to create such an exception to Firestone deference in Glenn, recognizing that ERISA law was already complicated enough without adding "special procedural or evidentiary rules" to the mix. 554 U. S., at ___ (slip op., at 10). If, as we held in Glenn, a systemic conflict of interest does not strip a plan administrator of deference, see id., at ___ (slip op., at 9), it is difficult to see why a single honest mistake would require a different result. Nor is the Court of Appeals' decision supported by the considerations on which our holdings in Firestone and Glenn were based—namely, the terms of the plan, principles of trust law, and the purposes of ERISA. See supra, at 4–5. First, the Plan here grants the Plan Administrator general authority to "[c]onstrue the Plan." App. to Pet. for Cert. 141a–142a. Nothing in that provision suggests that the grant of authority is limited to first efforts to construe the Plan. Second, the Court of Appeals' exception to Firestone deference is not required by principles of trust law. Trust law is unclear on the narrow question before us. A leading treatise states that a court will strip a trustee of his discretion when there is reason to believe that he will not exercise that discretion fairly—for example, upon a showing that the trustee has already acted in bad faith: "If the trustee's failure to pay a reasonable amount [to the beneficiary of the trust] is due to a failure to exercise [the trustee's] discretion honestly and fairly, the court may well fix the amount [to be paid] itself. On the other hand, if the trustee's failure to provide reasonably for the beneficiary is due to a mistake as to the trustee's duties or powers, and there is no reason to believe the trustee will not fairly exercise the discretion once the court has determined the extent of the trustee's duties and powers, the court ordinarily will not fix the amount but will instead direct the trustee to make reasonable provision for the beneficiary's support." 3 A. Scott, W. Fratcher, & M. Ascher, Scott and Ascher on Trusts §18.2.1, pp. 1348–1349 (5th ed. 2007) (hereinafter Scott and Ascher) (footnote omitted) (citing cases). This is not surprising—if the settlor who creates a trust grants discretion to the trustee, it seems doubtful that the Court settlor would want the trustee divested entirely of that discretion simply because of one good-faith mistake.1 Here the lower courts made no finding that the Plan Administrator had acted in bad faith or would not fairly exercise his discretion to interpret the terms of the Plan. Thus, if the District Court had followed the trust law principles set out in Scott and Ascher, it should not have "act[ed] as a substitute trustee," Eaton v. Eaton, 82 N. H. 216, 218, 132 A. 10, 11 (1926), and stripped the Plan ————————

1The dissent is wrong to suggest a lack of case support for this interpretation of trust law. Post, at 10–12 (opinion of BREYER, J.). See, e.g., Hanford v. Clancy, 87 N. H. 458, 461, 183 A. 271, 272–273 (1936) ("Affirmative orders of disposition, such as the court made in this case, may only be sustained if, under the circumstances, there is but one reasonable disposition possible. If more than one reasonable disposition could be made, then the trustee must make the choice" (emphasis added)); In re Sullivan's Will, 144 Neb. 36, 40–41, 12 N. W. 2d 148, 150–151 (1943) (although trustees erred in not providing any support to plaintiff, "the court was without authority to determine the amount of support to which plaintiff was entitled from the trust fund" because "the court has no authority to substitute its judgment for that of the trustees" (emphasis added)); Eaton v. Eaton, 82 N. H. 216, 218–219, 132 A. 10, 11 (1926) ("[The trustee's] failure to administer the fund properly did not entitle the court to act as a substitute trustee. . . . [W]ithin the limits of reasonableness the trustee alone may exercise discretion, since that is what the will requires" (emphasis added) (cited in 3 A. Scott & W. Fratcher, Law of Trusts §187.1, pp. 30–31 (4th ed. 1988))); In re Marre's Estate, 18 Cal. 2d 184, 190, 114 P. 2d 586, 590– 591 (1941) (lower court erred in setting amount of payments to beneficiary after ruling that trustees had mistakenly failed to make payment; "[i]t is well settled that the courts will not attempt to exercise discretion which has been confided to a trustee unless it is clear that the trustee has abused his discretion in some manner. . . . The amounts to be paid should therefore be determined in the discretion of the trustees" (cited in 3 Scott and Ascher 1349, n. 4 (5th ed. 2007))); Finch v. Wachovia Bank & Trust Co., 156 N. C. App. 343, 348, 577 S. E. 2d 306, 310 (2003) (agreeing with lower court that trustee abused its discretion, but vacating the court's remedial order because it would "strip discretion from the trustee and replace it with the judgment of the court"). See also Brief for Petitioners 40–43. Administrator of the deference he would otherwise enjoy under Firestone and the terms of the Plan. Other trust law sources, however, point the other way. For example, the Restatement (Second) of Trusts states that "the court will control the trustee in the exercise of a power where he acts beyond the bounds of a reasonable judgment." Restatement (Second) of Trusts §187, Comment i, p. 406 (1957). Another treatise states that, after a trustee has abused his discretion, "[s]ometimes the court decides for the trustee how he should act, either by stating the exact result it desires to achieve, or by fixing some limits on the trustee's action and giving him leeway within those limits." G. Bogert & G. Bogert, Law of Trusts and Trustees §560, p. 223 (2d rev. ed. 1980). The unclear state of trust law on the question was perhaps best captured by the Texas Supreme Court: "There is authority for ordering a dismissal of the case to afford the trustee an opportunity to exercise a reasonable discretion in arriving at the amount of payments to be made in the light of our discussion of the problem and after a proper consideration of the many factors involved. On the other hand, there is authority for remanding the case to the trial court to hear evidence and in the exercise of its supervisory jurisdiction to fix the amount of such payments. There is still other authority for remanding the case to the trial court to hear evidence and fix the boundaries of a reasonable discretion to be exercised by the trustee within maximum and minimum limits." State v. Rubion, 158 Tex. 43, 54–55, 308 S. W. 2d 4, 11 (1957) (citations omitted). While we are "guided by principles of trust law" in ERISA cases, Firestone, 489 U. S., at 111, we have recognized before that "trust law does not tell the entire story," Varity Corp. v. Howe, 516 U. S. 489, 497 (1996); see ibid. ("In some instances, trust law will offer only a starting point, after which courts must go on to ask whether, or to what extent, the language of the statute, its structure, or its purposes require departing from common-law trust requirements"); Brief for Respondents 50 (pressing same view as the dissent but concluding that the dispute over trust law "need not be resolved"). Here trust law does not resolve the specific issue before us, but the guiding principles we have identified underlying ERISA do. Congress enacted ERISA to ensure that employees would receive the benefits they had earned, but Congress did not require employers to establish benefit plans in the first place. Lockheed Corp. v. Spink, 517 U. S. 882, 887 (1996). We have therefore recognized that ERISA represents a "'careful balancing' between ensuring fair and prompt enforcement of rights under a plan and the encouragement of the creation of such plans." Aetna Health Inc. v. Davila, 542 U. S. 200, 215 (2004) (quoting Pilot Life Ins. Co. v. Dedeaux, 481 U. S. 41, 54 (1987)). Congress sought "to create a system that is [not] so complex that administrative costs, or litigation expenses, unduly discourage employers from offering [ERISA] plans in the first place." Varity Corp., supra, at 497. ERISA "induc[es] employers to offer benefits by assuring a predictable set of liabilities, under uniform standards of primary conduct and a uniform regime of ultimate remedial orders and awards when a violation has occurred." Rush Prudential HMO, Inc. v. Moran, 536 U. S. 355, 379 (2002). Firestone deference protects these interests and, by permitting an employer to grant primary interpretive authority over an ERISA plan to the plan administrator, preserves the "careful balancing" on which ERISA is based. Deference promotes efficiency by encouraging resolution of benefits disputes through internal administrative proceedings rather than costly litigation. It also promotes predictability, as an employer can rely on the expertise of the plan administrator rather than worry about unexpected and inaccurate plan interpretations that might result from de novo judicial review. Moreover, Firestone deference serves the interest of uniformity, helping to avoid a patchwork of different interpretations of a plan, like the one here, that covers employees in different jurisdictions—a result that "would introduce considerable inefficiencies in benefit program operation, which might lead those employers with existing plans to reduce benefits, and those without such plans to refrain from adopting them." Fort Halifax Packing Co. v. Coyne, 482 U. S. 1, 11 (1987). Indeed, a group of prominent actuaries tells us that it is impossible even to determine whether an ERISA plan is solvent (a duty imposed on actuaries by federal law, see 29 U. S. C. §§1023(a) (4), (d)) if the plan is interpreted to mean different things in different places. See Brief for Chief Actuaries as Amici Curiae 5–11. Respondents and the United States as amicus curiae do not question that deference to plan administrators serves these important purposes. Rather, they argue that deference is less important once a plan administrator has issued an interpretation of a plan found to be unreasonable. But the interests in efficiency, predictability, and uniformity—and the manner in which they are promoted by deference to reasonable plan construction by administrators— do not suddenly disappear simply because a plan administrator has made a single honest mistake. This case illustrates the point. Consider first the interest in efficiency, an interest that Xerox has pursued by granting the Plan Administrator authority to construe the Plan. On remand from the Court of Appeals, if the District Court had applied a deferential standard of review under Firestone, the question before it would have been whether the Plan Administrator's interpretation of the Plan was reasonable. After answering that question, the case might well have been over. Instead, the District Court declined to defer, and therefore had to answer the more complicated question of how best to interpret the Plan. The prospect of increased litigation costs inherent in respondents' approach does not end there. Under respondents' and the Government's view, the question whether a deferential standard of review was required in this case turns on whether the Plan Administrator was interpreting the "same terms" or deciding the "same issue" on remand. See Brief for Respondents 43, 46–48, 53, and n. 13; Brief for United States as Amicus Curiae 13–15, 23. Whether that condition is satisfied will not always be clear. Indeed, petitioners dispute that question here, arguing that the Plan Administrator confronted an entirely new issue on remand— how to interpret the Plan, knowing that specific provisions requiring use of the phantom account method could not be applied to respondents due to a lack of notice. See Brief for Petitioners 50–

51. Respondents would force the parties to litigate this potentially complicated "same issue" or "same terms" question before a district court could even decide whether deference is owed to a plan administrator's view. As we recognized in Glenn, there is little place in the ERISA context for these sorts of "special procedural rules [that] would create further complexity, adding time and expense to a process that may already be too costly for many of those who seek redress." 554 U. S., at ___ (slip op., at 10). The position of respondents and the Government could interject other additional issues into ERISA litigation. For example, even under their view, the District Court here could have granted deference to the Plan Administrator; the court merely was not required to do so. See Brief for Respondents 43, 49–50, 52–53; Brief for United States as Amicus Curiae 23–24. That raises the question of how a court is to decide between the two options; respondents' answer is to weigh an indeterminate number of factors, which would only further complicate ERISA proceedings. See Tr. of Oral Arg. 34, 40–45. This case also demonstrates the harm to the interest in predictability that would result from stripping a plan administrator of Firestone deference. After declining to apply a deferential standard here, the District Court adopted an interpretation of the Plan that does not account for the time value of money. 472 F. Supp. 2d, at 458; 535 F. 3d, at 119. In the actuarial world, this is heresy, and highly unforeseeable. Indeed, the actuaries tell us that they have never encountered an ERISA plan resembling this one that did not include some adjustment for the time value of money. Brief for Chief Actuaries as Amici Curiae 12. Respondents' own actuarial expert testified before the District Court that fairness would require recognizing the time value of money in some fashion. See App. 127a, 130a. And respondents and the Government do not dispute that the District Court's approach, which does not account for the fact that respondents were able to use their past distributions as they saw fit for over 20 years, would place respondents in a better position than employees who never left the company. Cf. Brief for Respondents 42–43; Brief for United States as Amicus Curiae 32–33. Deference to plan administrators, who have a duty to all beneficiaries to preserve limited plan assets, see Varity Corp., 516 U. S., at 514, helps prevent such windfalls for particular employees. Finally, this case demonstrates the uniformity problems that arise from creating ad hoc exceptions to Firestone deference. If other courts were to adopt an interpretation of the Plan that does account for the time value of money, Xerox could be placed in an impossible situation. Similar Xerox employees could be entitled to different benefits depending on where they live, or perhaps where they bring a legal action. Cf. 29 U. S. C. §1132(e) (2) (permitting suit "where the plan is administered, where the breach took place, or where a defendant resides or may be found"). In fact, that may already be the case. In similar litigation over the Plan, the Ninth Circuit also rejected the use of the phantom account method, but held that the Plan Administrator should utilize actuarial principles in accounting for rehired employees' past distributions—which would presumably include taking some cognizance of the time value of money. See Miller v. Xerox Corp. Retirement Income Guarantee Plan, 464 F. 3d 871, 875–876 (2006); Brief for ERISA Industry Committee and American Benefits Council as Amici Curiae 8–9. Thus, failing to defer to the Plan Administrator here could well cause the Plan to be subject to different interpretations in California and New York. "Uniformity is impossible, however, if plans are subject to different legal obligations in different States." Egelhoff v. Egelhoff, 532 U. S. 141, 148 (2001). Firestone deference serves to avoid that result and to preserve the "careful balancing" of interests that ERISA represents. Pilot Life Ins. Co., 481 U. S.,

at 54. C In spite of all this, respondents and the Government argue that requiring the District Court to apply Firestone deference in this case would actually disserve the purposes of ERISA. They argue that continued deference would encourage plan administrators to adopt unreasonable interpretations of plans in the first instance, as administrators would anticipate a second chance to interpret their plans if their first interpretations were rejected. And they argue that plan administrators would be able to proceed seriatim through several interpretations of their plans, each time receiving deference, thereby undermining the prompt resolution of disputes over benefits, driving up litigation costs, and discouraging employees from challenging the decisions of plan administrators at all. All this is overblown. There is no reason to think that deference would be required in the extreme circumstances that respondents foresee. Under trust law, a trustee may be stripped of deference when he does not exercise his discretion "honestly and fairly." 3 Scott and Ascher 1348. Multiple erroneous interpretations of the same plan provision, even if issued in good faith, might well support a finding that a plan administrator is too incompetent to exercise his discretion fairly, cutting short the rounds of costly litigation that respondents fear. Applying a deferential standard of review does not mean that the plan administrator will prevail on the merits. It means only that the plan administrator's interpretation of the plan "will not be disturbed if reasonable." Firestone, 489 U. S., at 111; see also ibid. ("'Where discretion is conferred upon the trustee with respect to the exercise of a power, its exercise is not subject to control by the court except to prevent an abuse by the trustee of his discretion'" (quoting Restatement (Second) of Trusts §187)). Thus, far from "impos[ing] [a] rigid and inflexible requirement" that courts must defer to plan administrators, post, at 8, we simply hold that the lower courts should have applied the standard established in Firestone and Glenn. III The Court of Appeals erred in holding that the District Court could refuse to defer to the Plan Administrator's interpretation of the Plan on remand, simply because the Court of Appeals had found a previous related interpretation by the Administrator to be invalid. Because we reverse on that ground, we do not reach the question whether the Court of Appeals also erred in applying a deferential standard of review to the decision of the District Court on the merits.2 The judgment of the Court of Appeals for the Second Circuit is reversed, and the case is remanded for further proceedings consistent with this opinion. It is so ordered. JUSTICE SOTOMAYOR took no part in the consideration or decision of this case.

The Government raises an additional argument—that the District Court should not have deferred to the Plan Administrator's second interpretation of the Plan because that interpretation would have violated ERISA's notice requirements. See Brief for United States as Amicus Curiae 25–26. That is an argument about the merits, not the proper standard of review, and we leave it to be decided, if necessary, on remand.

JUSTICE BREYER, with whom JUSTICE STEVENS and JUSTICE GINSBURG join, dissenting. I agree with the Court that "people make mistakes," ante, at 1, but I do not share its view of the law applicable to those mistakes. To explain my view, I shall describe the three significant mistakes involved in this case. I

A

The first mistake is that of Xerox Corporation's pension plan (Plan) and its administrators (collectively, Plan Administrator), petitioners here. The Plan, as I understand it, pays employees the highest of three benefits upon retirement. App. 29a–31a. These benefits are calculated as follows (I simplify and use my own words, not those of the Plan): (1) "The Pension": Take your average salary for your five highest salary years at Xerox; multiply by 1.4 percent; and multiply again by the number of years you worked at Xerox (up to 30). Id., at 7a–11a, 29a–30a. Thus, if the average salary of your five highest paid years was $50,000 and you worked at Xerox for 30 years, you would be entitled to receive $21,000 per year ($50,000×1.4 percent×30). (2) "The Cash Account": Every year, Xerox credits 5

BREYER, J., dissenting percent of your salary to a cash account. Id., at 40a. This account accrues interest at a yearly fixed rate 1 percent above the 1-year Treasury bill rate. Id., at 41a. To determine your benefits under this approach, take the balance of your cash account and convert the final amount to an annuity. Id., at 31a. Thus, if you have accrued, say, $200,000 in your account and the relevant annuity rate at the time of your retirement is 7 percent, you would be entitled to receive approximately $14,000 per year upon your retirement (approximately $200,000×7 percent). (3) "The Investment Account": Before 1990, Xerox contributed to an employee profit sharing plan. Id., at 33a–34a. Thus, all employees who were hired by the end of 1989 have an investment account that consists of all of the contributions Xerox made to this profit sharing plan (prior to its discontinuation) and the investment returns on those contributions. Id., at 33a– 36a. To determine your benefits under this approach, take the balance of your investment account and convert the final amount to an annuity. Id., at 31a. Thus, just like the cash account, if you have accrued $400,000 in your account and the relevant annuity rate at the time of your retirement is 7 percent, you would be entitled to receive approximately $28,000 per year upon your retirement (approximately $400,000×7 percent). Given these three examples, the retiring employee's pension would come from the investment account, and the employee would receive $28,000 per year. This case concerns one aspect of Xerox's retirement plan, namely, the way in which the Plan treats employees who leave Xerox and later return, working for additional years before their ultimate retirement. The Plan has long treated such leaving-and-returning employees as follows (again, I simplify and use my own words): First, when an employee initially leaves, she is paid a lump-sum distribution equivalent to the benefits she has accrued up to that point (i.e., the highest of her pension, her cash account, or, if she was hired before the end of 1989, her investment account). See ante, at 2. Second, when the employee returns, she again begins to accrue amounts in her cash account, App. 40a–41a, starting from scratch. (She accrues nothing in her investment account, because Xerox no longer makes profit sharing contributions. Id., at 34a.) Thus, by the time of her retirement the employee may not have accrued much money in this account. Third, a rehired employee's pension is calculated in the way I have set forth above, with her entire tenure at Xerox (both before her departure and after her return) taken into account. See Brief for Petitioners 9–10. Fourth, the employee's benefits calculation is adjusted to take account of the fact that the employee has already received a lump-sum distribution from the Plan. See App. 32a; Brief for Petitioners 10–11. This case is about the adjustment that takes place during step four. It concerns the way in which the Plan Administrator calculates that adjustment so as to reflect the fact that a retiring leaving-and-returning employee has already received a distribution when she initially left Xerox. Before 1989, the Plan Administrator calculated the adjusted amount by taking the benefits distribution previously received (say, $100,000) and adjusting it to equal the amount that would have existed in the investment account had no distribution been made. Ibid. Thus, if an employee had not left Xerox, and if the $100,000 had been left in her investment account for, say, 20 years, that amount would likely have increased dramatically—perhaps doubling, tripling, or quadrupling in amount, depending upon how well the Plan's investments performed.

It is this hypothetical sum—termed the "phantom account," ante, at 2—that is at issue in this case. Xerox's pre-1989 Plan assumed that a rehired employee had this hypothetical sum on hand at the time of her final retirement from the company, and in effect subtracted the amount from the employee's benefits upon her departure. Brief for Petitioners 10–11; cf. ante, at 2. Depending on how the Plan's investments did over time, the Administrator's use of this "phantom account" could have a substantial impact on a rehired employee's benefits. (See Appendix, infra, for an example of how this "phantom account" works.) When the Plan Administrator amended Xerox's Employee Retirement Income Security Act of 1974 (ERISA) Plan in 1989, however, it made what it tells us was an "inadvertent[t]" omission. Brief for Petitioners 11, n. 3. In a section of the 1989 Plan applicable to the roughly 100 leaving-and-returning employees who are plaintiffs here, the Plan said that it would "offset" the retiring employees' "accrued benefit" (as ordinarily calculated) "by the accrued benefit attributable" to the prior lump-sum "distribution" those employees received when they initially left Xerox. App. 32a. But the Plan said nothing about how it would calculate this "offset." In other words, the Plan said nothing about the Administrator's use of the "phantom account." This led to the first mistake in this case. Despite the Plan's failure to include language explaining how the Administrator would take into account an employee's prior distribution, the Plan Administrator continued to employ the "phantom account" methodology. In essence, the Administrator read the 1989 Plan to include the language that had been omitted—an interpretation that, as described below, see Part I–B, infra, the Court of Appeals found to be arbitrary and capricious and in violation of ERISA.

The District Court committed the second mistake in this case. In 1999, the respondents, nearly 100 employees who left and were later rehired by Xerox, brought this lawsuit. Ante, at 2; Brief for Petitioners ii–iii, 12. They pointed out that the 1989 Plan said that it would decrease their retirement benefits to reflect the fact that they had already received a lump-sum benefits distribution when they initially left Xerox. But, they added, neither the 1989 Plan, nor the 1989 Plan's Summary Plan Description, said anything about whether (or how) the Administrator would adjust their previous benefits distribution to take into account that they had received the distribution well before their retirement. They thus claimed that the Plan Administrator could not use the "phantom account" methodology to adjust their previous distributions. See Brief for

United States as Amicus Curiae 4–5. The District Court, however, rejected respondents' claims. 328 F. Supp. 2d 420 (WDNY 2004). The court accepted the Administrator's argument that the 1989 Plan implicitly incorporated the "phantom account" approach that had previously been part of Xerox's retirement plan. Id., at 433–434. And the court thus held in favor of petitioners— thereby committing the second mistake in this case. Id., at 439. On appeal, the Second Circuit disagreed with the District Court and vacated the District Court's decision in relevant part. 433 F. 3d 254 (2006). The Court of Appeals concluded that, because the 1989 Plan said nothing about how the Administrator would adjust the previous benefits distributions, it was "arbitrary and capricious" for the Administrator to interpret the 1989 Plan as if it still incorporated the "phantom account." Id., at 265–266, and n. 11. And the Court of Appeals thus held that the language of the Plan and the Summary Plan Description, at the least, violated ERISA by failing to provide respondents with fair notice that the Administrator was going to use the "phantom account" approach. See id., at 265 (discussing 29 U. S. C. §1022); see also 433 F. 3d, at 263, 267–268 (holding that the Administrator's attempt to apply the "phantom account" to respondents violated two other ERISA provisions: 29 U. S. C. §1054(h)'s notice requirement and §1054(g)'s prohibition on retroactive benefit cutbacks). Rather, the court noted, respondents "likely believed"—based on the language of the Plan—"that their past distributions would only be factored into their [current] benefits calculations by taking into account the amounts they had actually received." 433 F. 3d, at 267. In light of these conclusions, the Court of Appeals recognized the need to devise a remedy for the Administrator's abuse of discretion and ERISA violations—a remedy that took into account the previous benefits distributions respondents had received in a manner consistent with the 1989 Plan. The court therefore remanded the case to the District Court, with the following instructions: "On remand, the remedy crafted by the district court for those employees [in the respondents' situation] should utilize an appropriate [pre-1989 Plan] calculation to determine their benefits. We recognize the difficulty that this task poses . . . . As guidance for the district court, we suggest that it may wish to employ equitable principles when determining the appropriate calculation and fashioning the appropriate remedy." Id., at 268. On remand, the District Court invited the parties to submit remedial recommendations. Brief for Petitioners 14. The Plan Administrator proposed an approach that would adjust respondents' previous benefits distributions by adding interest, and, as a fallback, the Administrator suggested that the Plan should treat respondents as new hires. Ante, at 3; Brief for United States as Amicus Curiae 6–7. The District Court rejected these suggestions and concluded that the "appropriate" remedy was the one suggested by the Second Circuit: no adjustment to the prior distributions received by respondents. 472 F. Supp. 2d 452, 458 (WDNY 2007). The court stated that this remedy was "straightforward; it adequately prevent[ed] employees from receiving a windfall[;] and . . . it most clearly reflect[ed] what a reasonable employee would have anticipated based on the not-very-clear language in the Plan." Ibid. And the Court of Appeals, finding that the District Court did not abuse its discretion in crafting a remedy, affirmed. 535 F. 3d 111 (CA2 2008). II The third mistake, I believe, is the Court's. As the majority recognizes, ante, at 4, "principles of trust law" guide this Court in "determining the appropriate standard" by which to review the actions of an ERISA plan administrator. Firestone Tire & Rubber Co. v. Bruch, 489 U. S. 101, 111–113 (1989); see also Metropolitan Life Ins. Co. v. Glenn, 554 U. S. ___, ___ (2008) (slip op., at 4); Aetna Health Inc. v. Davila, 542 U. S. 200, 218–219 (2004);

Central States, Southeast & Southwest Areas Pension Fund v. Central Transport, Inc., 472 U. S. 559, 570 (1985). And, as the majority also recognizes, ante, at 4, where an ERISA plan grants an administrator the discretionary authority to interpret plan terms, trust law requires a court to defer to the plan administrator's interpretation of plan terms. See, e.g., Glenn, supra, at ____ (slip op., at 4). But the majority further concludes that trust law "does not resolve the specific issue before" the Court in this case—i.e., whether a court is required to defer to an administrator's second attempt at interpreting plan documents, even after the court has already determined that the administrator's first attempt amounted to an abuse of discretion. Ante, at 9. In my view, this final conclusion is erroneous, as trust law imposes no such rigid and inflexible requirement. The Second Circuit found the Administrator's interpretation of the Plan to be arbitrary and capricious and in violation of ERISA, and it made clear that the District Court's task on remand was to "craf[t]" a "remedy." See 433 F. 3d, at 268. Trust law treatise writers say that in these circumstances a court may (but need not) exercise its own discretion rather than defer to a trustee's interpretation of trust language. See G. Bogert & G. Bogert, Law of Trusts and Trustees §560, pp. 222–223 (2d rev. ed. 1980) (hereinafter Bogert & Bogert) (after finding an abuse of discretion, a court may "decide for the trustee how he should act," possibly by "stating the exact result" the court "desires to achieve"); see also 2 Restatement (Third) of Trusts §50, p. 258 (2001) (hereinafter Third Restatement) ("A discretionary power conferred upon the trustee . . . is subject to judicial control only to prevent misinterpretation or abuse of the discretion by the trustee"); 1 Restatement (Second) of Trusts §187, p. 402 (1957) (hereinafter Second Restatement) ("Where discretion is conferred upon the trustee . . . , its exercise is not subject to control by the court, except to prevent an abuse by the trustee of his discretion"); see also Firestone, supra, at 111. Judges deciding trust law cases have said the same. See, e.g., Colton v. Colton, 127 U. S. 300, 322 (1888) (stating that it was the "duty of the court" to determine the trust payments due after rejecting the trustee's interpretation); State v. Rubion, 158 Tex. 43, 55, 308 S. W. 2d 4, 11 (1957) ("Considering that we have held that there has already been an abuse of discretion by the trustee . . . , we have concluded that a remand of the case to the trial court for the definite establishment of amounts to be paid will better promote a speedy administration of justice and a final termination of this litigation"); Glenn, supra, at ____ (SCALIA, J., dissenting) (slip op., at 5) (court may exercise discretion under trust law when a "trustee had discretion but abused it"). In short, the controlling trust law principle appears to be that, "[w]here the court finds that there has been an abuse of a discretionary power, the decree to be rendered is in its discretion." Bogert & Bogert §560, at 222. Of course, the fact that trust law grants courts discretion does not mean that they will exercise that discretion in all instances. The majority refers to the 2007 edition of Scott on Trusts, ante, at 6, which says that, if there is "no reason" to doubt that a trustee "will . . . fairly exercise" his "discretion," then courts "ordinarily will not fix the amount" of a payment "but will instead direct the trustee to make reasonable provision for the beneficiary's support," 3 A. Scott, W. Fratcher, & M. Ascher, Scott and Ascher on Trusts §18.2.1, pp. 1348–1349 (5th ed. 2007) (emphasis added). As this passage demonstrates, there are situations in which a court will typically defer to a trustee's remedial suggestion. The word "ordinarily" confirms, however, that the Scott treatise writers recognize that there are instances in which courts will not defer. And other treatises indicate that black letter trust law gives the district courts authority to decide which instances are which. See Bogert & Bogert §560, at 222–

223 (when there is an abuse of discretion, a court "may set aside the transaction," "award damages to the beneficiary," or "order a new decision to be made in the light of rules expounded by the court"); 2 Third Restatement §50, and Comment b, at 261 (discussing similar remedial options); 1 Second Restatement §187, and Comment b, at 402 (same); see also 3 Third Restatement §87, and Comment c, at 244–245 (noting that "judicial intervention on the ground of abuse" is allowed when a "good-faith," yet "unreasonable," decision is made by a trustee); Rubion, supra, at 54–55, 308 S. W. 2d, at 11 (discussing a court's remedial options).

Nevertheless, the majority reads the Scott treatise as establishing an absolute requirement that courts defer to a trustee's fallback position absent "reason to believe that [the trustee] will not exercise [his] discretion fairly—for example, upon a showing that the trustee has already acted in bad faith." Ante, at 6. And based on this reading, the majority further concludes that the existence of the Scott treatise creates uncertainty as to whether, under basic trust law principles, a court has the power to craft a remedy for a trustee's abuse of discretion. Ante, at 6–9. It is unclear to me, however, why the majority reads the passage from Scott as creating a war among treatise writers, compare ante, at 6 (discussing Scott) with ante, at 8 (discussing Bogert), when the relevant passages can so easily be read as consistent with one another. I simply read the Scott treatise language as identifying circumstances in which courts typically choose to defer to an administrator's fallback position. The treatise does not suggest that the law forbids a court from acting on its own in the exercise of its broad remedial authority—authority that trust law plainly grants to supervising courts. See supra, at 8–9. A closer look at the Scott treatise confirms this understanding. The treatise cites seven cases in support of the passage upon which the majority relies. See 3 Scott §18.2.1, at 1349, n. 4. Three of these cases explicitly state that a court may exercise its discretion to craft a remedy if a trustee has previously abused its discretion. See Old Colony Trust Co. v. Rodd, 356 Mass. 584, 589, 254 N. E. 2d 886, 889 (1970) ("A court of equity may control a trustee in the exercise of a fiduciary discretion if it fails to observe standards of judgment apparent from the applicable instrument"); In re Marre's Estate, 18 Cal. 2d 184, 190, 114 P. 2d 586, 590–591 (1941) ("It is well settled that the courts will not attempt to exercise discretion which has been confided to a trustee unless it is clear that the trustee has abused his discretion in some manner" (emphasis added)); In re Ferrall's Estate, 92 Cal. App. 2d 712, 716–717, 207 P. 2d 1077, 1079–1080 (1949) (following In re Marre's Estate). Three other cases are inapposite because their circumstances do not involve any allegation of abuse of discretion by the trustee. See In re Ziegler's Trusts, 157 So. 2d 549, 550 (Fla. Dist. Ct. App. 1963) (per curiam) ("There is no contention here that the court . . . would not retain its rights, upon appropriate petition or other pleadings by an interested party, to review an alleged abuse, if any, of the discretion exercised by the trustees"); In re Grubel's Will, 37 Misc. 2d 910, 911, 235 N. Y. S. 2d 21, 23 (Surr. Ct. 1962) (stating that "in the first instance" it is the "proper function of the trustees" to set an amount to be paid (emphasis added)); Orr v. Moses, 94 N. H. 309, 312, 52 A. 2d 128, 130 (1947) (declining to construe will because none "of the parties now assert claims adverse to any position taken by the trustee"). In the final case, the court decided that, on the facts before it, it did not need to control the trustees' discretion. See Estate of Stillman, 107 Misc. 2d 102, 111, 433 N. Y. S. 2d 701 (Surr. Ct. 1980) ("The fine record of the trustees in enhancing the equity of these trusts while earning substantial income, also persuades the court of the wisdom of retaining their services as fiduciaries"). Which of these cases says that, after the trustee has abused its discretion, a district court must still defer to the trustee? None of them do. I repeat: Not a single case cited by the Scott treatise writers supports the majority's reading of the treatise. The majority seeks to justify its reading of the Scott treatise by referring to four cases that Scott does not cite. See ante, at 7, n. 1. I am not surprised that the treatise does not refer to these cases. In the first three, a court thought it best, when a trustee had not yet exercised judgment about a particular matter, to direct the trustee to do so. See In re Sullivan's Will, 144 Neb. 36, 40–41, 12 N. W. 2d 148, 150–151 (1943) (finding that the trustees' "failure to act" was erroneous, and directing the trustees to exercise their discretion in setting a payment amount); Eaton v. Eaton, 82 N. H. 216, 218, 132 A. 10, 11 (1926) (same); Finch v. Wachovia Bank & Trust Co., 156 N. C. App. 343, 347–348, 577 S. E. 2d 306, 309–310 (2003) (hold ing trustee erred by "[f]ail[ing] to exercise judgment," and directing it to do so). The fourth case concerns circumstances so distant from those before us that it is difficult to know what to say. (The question was whether the beneficiary of a small trust had title in certain trust assets or whether the trustee had discretionary power to allocate them in her best interest; the court held the latter, adding that, if the trustee acted unreasonably, the lower court in that particular case should seek to have the trustee removed rather than trying to administer the trust funds itself.) See Hanford v. Clancy, 87 N. H. 458, 460–461, 183 A. 271, 272–273 (1936). I cannot read these four cases, or any other case to which the majority refers, as holding that a court, as a general matter, is required to defer to a trust administrator's second attempt at exercising discretion. And I am aware of no such case. In contrast, the Restatement and Bogert and Scott treatises identify numerous cases in which courts have remedied a trustee's abuse of discretion by ordering the trustee to pay a specific amount. See 2 Third Restatement §50, Reporter's Note, at 283 (citing cases such as Coker v. Coker, 208 Ala. 354, 94 So. 566 (1922)); Bogert & Bogert §560, at 223, n. 19 (citing cases such as Rubion); 3 Scott §18.2.1, at 1348–1349, nn. 3–4 (citing cases such as Emmert v. Old Nat. Bank of Martinsburg, 162 W. Va. 48, 246 S. E. 2d 236 (1978)); see also Brief for United States as Amicus Curiae 18 (listing cases). I thus do not find trust law "unclear" on this matter. Ante, at 6. When a trustee abuses its discretion, trust law grants courts the authority either to defer anew to the trustee's discretion or to craft a remedy. See, e.g., 3 A. Scott & W. Fratcher, Scott on Trusts §187, pp. 14–15 (4th ed. 1988) ("This ordinarily means that so long as [the trustee] acts not only in good faith and from proper motives, but also within the bounds of reasonable judgment, the court will not interfere; but the court will interfere when he acts outside the bounds of a reasonable judgment"). Nor does anything in the present case suggest that the District Court abused its remedial authority. The Second Circuit stated that the interpretive problem on remand was in essence a remedial problem. See 433 F. 3d, at 268. It added that the remedial problem was "difficul[t]" and that "the district court . . . may wish to employ equitable principles when determining the appropriate calculation and fashioning the appropriate remedy." Ibid. The Administrator had previously abused his discretionary power. Id., at 265–268. And the District Court found that the Administrator's primary remedial suggestion on remand—adjusting respondents' previous benefits distributions by adding interest—probably would have violated ERISA's notice provisions. 472 F. Supp. 2d, at 457. Under these circumstances, the District Court reasonably could have found a need to use its own remedial judgment, rather than rely on the Administrator's—which is just what the Second Circuit said. 535 F. 3d, at 119. Moreover, even if the "narrow" trust law "question before us" were difficult, ante, at 6—which it is not—this difficulty would not excuse the Court from trying to do its best to work out a legal solution that nonetheless respects basic principles of trust law. "Congress invoked the common law of trusts" in enacting ERISA, and this Court has thus repeatedly looked to trust law in order to determine "the particular duties and powers" of ERISA plan administrators. Central States, Southeast & Southwest Areas Pension Fund v. Central Transport, Inc., 472 U. S. 559, 570–572 (1985); see also, e.g., Glenn, 554 U. S., at ___ (slip op., at 4); Davila, 542 U. S., at 218–219; Firestone, 489 U. S., at 111–113. While, as the majority recognizes, ante, at 8, trust law may "not tell the entire story," Varity Corp. v. Howe, 516 U. S. 489, 497 (1996), I am aware of no other case in which this Court has simply ignored trust law (on the basis that it was unclear) and crafted a legal rule based on nothing but "the guiding principles we have identified underlying ERISA," ante, at 9. See Varity, supra, at 497 ("In some instances, trust law will offer only a starting point, after which courts must go on to ask whether, or to what extent, the language of the statute, its structure, or its purposes require departing from common law trust requirements" (emphasis added)). In any event, it is far from clear that the Court's legal rule reflects an appropriate analysis of ERISA-based policy. To the contrary, the majority's absolute "one free honest mistake" rule is impractical, for it requires courts to determine what is "honest," encourages appeals on the point, and threatens to delay further proceedings that already take too long. (Respondents initially filed this retirement benefits case in 1999.) See Glenn, supra, at ___ (slip op., at 10). It also ignores what we previously have pointed out—namely, that abuses of discretion "arise in too many contexts" and "concern too many circumstances" for this Court "to come up with a one-size-fits-all procedural [approach] that is likely to promote fair and accurate" benefits determinations. Ibid. And, finally, the majority's approach creates incentives for administrators to take "one free shot" at employer-favorable plan interpretations and to draft ambiguous retirement plans in the first instance with the expectation that they will have repeated opportunities to interpret (and possibly reinterpret) the ambiguous terms. I thus fail to see how the majority's "one free honest mistake" approach furthers ERISA's core purpose of "promot[ing] the interests of employees and their beneficiaries in employee benefit plans." Shaw v. Delta Air Lines, Inc., 463 U. S. 85, 90 (1983); see also, e.g., 29 U. S. C. §1001(b) (noting that ERISA was enacted "to protect . . . employee benefit plans and their beneficiaries"); Curtiss-Wright Corp. v. Schoonejongen, 514 U. S. 73, 83 (1995) (discussing ERISA's central "goa[l]" of "enab[ing] plan beneficiaries to learn their rights and obligations at any time"); Massachusetts Mut. Life Ins. Co. v. Russell, 473 U. S. 134, 148 (1985) (ERISA was enacted "to protect contractually defined benefits"). The majority does identify ERISA-related factors—e.g., promoting predictability and uniformity, encouraging employers to adopt strong plans—that it believes favor giving more power to plan administrators. See ante, at 9– 13. But, in my view, these factors are, at the least, offset by the factors discussed above—e.g., discouraging administrators from writing opaque plans and interpreting them aggressively—that argue to the contrary. At best, the policies at issue—some arguing in one direction, some the other—are far less able than trust law to provide a "guiding principle." Thus, I conclude that here, as elsewhere, trust law ultimately provides the best way for courts to approach the administration and interpretation of ERISA. See, e.g., Firestone, supra, at 111–113. And trust law here, as I have said, leaves to the supervising court the decision as to how much weight to give to a plan administrator's remedial opinion. III Since the District Court was not required to defer to the Administrator's fallback position, I should consider the second question presented, namely, whether the Court of Appeals properly reviewed the District Court's decision under an "abuse of discretion" standard. Ante, at 4 (acknowledging, but not reaching, this issue). The answer to this question depends upon how one characterizes the Court of Appeals' decision. If the court deferred to the District Court's interpretation of Plan terms, then the Court of Appeals most likely should have reviewed the decision de novo. See Firestone, supra, at 112; cf. Davila, supra, at 210 ("Any dispute over the precise terms of the plan is resolved by a court under a de novo review standard"). If instead the Court of Appeals deferred to the District Court's creation of a remedy, in significant part on the basis of "equitable principles," then it properly reviewed the District Court decision for "abuse of discretion." See, e.g., Cook v. Liberty Life Assurance Co., 320 F. 3d 11, 24 (CA1 2003); Zervos v. Verizon N. Y., Inc., 277 F. 3d 635, 648 (CA2 2002); Grosz-Salomon v. Paul Revere Life Ins. Co., 237 F. 3d 1154, 1163 (CA9 2001); Halpin v. W. W. Grainger, Inc., 962 F. 2d 685, 697 (CA7 1992). The District Court opinion contains language that supports either characterization. On the one hand, the court wrote that its task was to "interpret the Plan as written." 472 F. Supp. 2d, at 457. On the other hand, the court said that "virtually nothing is set forth in either the Plan or the [Summary Plan Description]" about how to treat prior distributions; and, in describing its task, it said that the Court of Appeals had directed it to use "equitable principles" in fashioning a remedy. Ibid. Ultimately, the District Court appears to have used both the Plan language and equitable principles to arrive at its conclusion. See id., at 457–459. The Court of Appeals, too, used language that supports both characterizations. Compare 535 F. 3d, at 117 (noting that the District Court "applied [Plan] terms" in crafting its remedy), with id., at 117–119 (describing the District Court's decision as the "craft[ing]" of a "remedy" and acknowledging that it had directed the District Court to use "equitable principles" in doing so). But the Court of Appeals ultimately treated the District Court's opinion as if it primarily created a fair remedy. Ibid. Given the prior Court of Appeals opinion's language, supra, at 6 (quoting 433 F. 3d, at 268), I believe that view is a fair, indeed a correct, view. And I consequently believe the Court of Appeals properly reviewed the result for an "abuse of discretion." Petitioners argue that, because respondents were seek ing relief under 29 U. S. C. §1132(a)(1)(B), the Court of Appeals was, in effect, prohibited from treating the remedy as anything other than an application of a plan's terms. Brief for Petitioners 55–56; Reply Brief for Petitioners 3, and n. 8, 16–17. While this provision allows plaintiffs only to "enforce" or "clarify" rights or to "recover benefits" "under the terms of the plan," §1132(a)(1)(B) (emphasis added), it does not so limit a court's remedial authority, Great-West Life & Annuity Ins. Co. v. Knudson, 534 U. S. 204, 221 (2002) (In §1132(a)(1)(B), "Congress authorized 'a participant or beneficiary' to bring a civil action . . . without referenc[ing] whether the relief sought is legal or equitable"). The provision thus does not prohibit a court from shaping relief through the application of equitable principles, as trust law plainly permits. See, e.g., 2 Third Restatement §50, and Comment b, at 261 (discussing remedial options); Bogert & Bogert §870, at 123–126 (2d rev. ed. 1995). Indeed, a court that finds, for example, that an administrator provided employees with inadequate notice of a plan's terms (as was true here) may have no alternative but to rely significantly upon those principles. Cf. 29 U. S. C. §1104(a)(1)(D) (plan fiduciary must "discharge his dut[y] . . . in accordance with the documents and instruments governing the plan insofar as such documents and instruments are consistent" with ERISA). For these reasons I would affirm the decision of the Court of Appeals. And I therefore respectfully dissent from the majority's contrary determination.

The "Phantom Account"

This Appendix provides a simplified and illustrative example of, as I understand it, how the "phantom account" works. For the purposes of this Appendix, I make the following assumptions: John worked at Xerox for 10 years from 1970 to 1980. At the time of his departure from Xerox, he was issued a lump-sum benefits distribution of $140,000. He was then rehired in January 1989, and he worked for Xerox for 5 more years before retiring (until December 1993), earning $50,000 each year of his second term of employment. I also assume that (1) Xerox's contribution to John's investment account was $2,500 in 1989 (the last year such accounts were offered), (2) Xerox's contributions to John's cash and investment accounts are always made on the final day of the year, (3) the rate of return in John's cash and investment accounts is always 5 percent, and (4) annuity rates are also always 5 percent. (For the sake of simplicity, I treat all annuities as perpetuities, meaning that I calculate the present value of the annuities thusly: Present Value = Annual Payment/Annuity Rate.) Given the above assumptions, John's pension upon his retirement would be $10,500 per year ($50,000×1.4 per cent×15 years), which has a present value of $210,000 ($10,500/5 percent). John's cash and investment accounts at the end of his fifth year would look as follows (While Xerox's ERISA Plan did not include cash accounts until 1990, each employee's opening cash account balance was credited with the balance of his investment account at the end of 1989. The figures for John's cash account in 1989 thus reflect the performance of his investment account. In addition, all numbers are rounded to the nearest hundred):

Year (A) Inv. Account: Xerox Contributions

(B) Inv. Account: Accrued Since Return

(C) Inv. Account: Phantom Account

(D) Inv. Account: Total (Columns B+C)

(E) Cash Account: Xerox Contributions

(F) Cash Account: Accrued Since Return

(G) Cash Account: Phantom Account

(H) Cash Account: Total (Columns F+G)

Year	(A)	(B)	(C)	(D)	(E)	(F)	(G)	(H)
1989	2,500	2,500	217,200	219,700	2,500	2,500	217,200	219,700
1990	0	2,600	228,000	230,700	2,500	5,100	228,000	233,200
1991	0	2,800	239,400	242,200	2,500	7,900	239,400	247,300
1992	0	2,900	251,400	254,300	2,500	10,800	251,400	262,200
1993	0	3,000	264,000	267,000	2,500	13,800	264,000	277,800

Now, as far as I understand it, John's retirement benefits are calculated as follows, see 433 F. 3d, at 260: First, the Plan Administrator would choose which of John's three accounts would yield him the greatest benefits. In making this comparison, the Plan Administrator would assume that John had never left Xerox when calculating John's pension. The Plan Administrator would also assume, when calculating the value of John's cash and investment accounts, that the lump-sum distribution John had received from Xerox had remained invested in his accounts. (In other words, the Plan Administrator would include the "phantom account" in his calculations. The total value of this phantom account in 1989, when John rejoined Xerox, is equal to John's lump-sum distribution of $140,000×1.059, or approximately $217,200.) The Plan Administrator would thus compare John's pension, column D, and column H to determine John's benefit. As you can see above, column H provides the greatest benefit, so John's cash account would be used to calculate the benefits he would receive upon retirement. Second, the Plan Administrator would "offset" John's prior distribution against his current benefits to determine the amount of benefits John would actually receive. Thus, the Plan Administrator would take the "total" value of John's cash account, including the "phantom account" ($277,800), and subtract out the value of the "phantom account" ($264,000). The total present value of the benefits John would receive upon his second retirement would thus be $13,800. This means that John would receive approximately $690 annually ($13,800×5 percent) upon retirement under the Plan Administrator's "phantom account" approach. In comparison, if John had simply been treated as a new employee when he was rehired, his pension would have entitled him to at least $3,500 annually ($50,000×1.4 percent×5 years) upon his retirement. And the impact of the "phantom account" may have been even more dramatic with respect to some of the respondents in this case. See Brief for Respondents 24 (describing how respondent Paul Frommert erroneously received a report claiming that his retirement benefits were $2,482.00 per month, before later discovering that, because of the "phantom account," his actual monthly pension was $5.31 per month).

THE DOL FIDUCIARY RULE

MUCH can be said about the DOL fiduciary rule-however-this has now become political football and is not settled yet. In fact, this may not be settled for a long time as the rule does not have objective test. The rule is "subjective". For example, the rule could have stated "reasonable compensation is 3.00 for assets held in plans less than $100,000, 2.00 for assets in plans from $100,000-$500,000 and 1% for assets over $500,000.

Not much litigation in this case, but it is not the rule.

The rule is….. "reasonable compensation" which will be determined by a "reasonable judge" somewhere in the future of litigation.

The rule is 1032 pages. The rule is directed at advisor compensation. The reason is after a study of studies which were NOT peer reviewed, the DOL concluded that investors are losing 17 Billion a year in their qualified plans. The advisor would select high cost funds over low cost funds. The advisor did not operate in the best interest of the plan etc. etc.

In general, the advisor was making too much money from these plans.

Solution-make all advisors Fiduciaries and create 1032 pages of regulation that is not following objective standards or miss any substantive guidance.

Reading 1032 pages-additional pages may not help until the rule becomes final. In addition, the rule could dominate an entire book of material.

T.C. Memo. 2016-28

UNITED STATES TAX COURT
RAYMOND S. MCGAUGH, Petitioner v.
COMMISSIONER OF INTERNAL REVENUE, Respondent

Docket No. 13665-14. Filed February 24, 2016.

P had a self-directed IRA of which M was the custodian and
which held stock in corporation X. P requested that M purchase
additional stock in X for the IRA. Although the investment in X was
not a prohibited investment for the IRA, M refused to purchase the
stock directly. At P's request M issued a wire transfer directly to X;
and more than 60 days thereafter, X in turn issued the stock in the
name of P's IRA. M reported the transaction to the IRS because M
had determined that the wire transfer was a distribution to P not
followed by a rollover investment within the period permitted under
I.R.C. sec. 408(d)(3). R consequently determined that there was a
distribution from the IRA to P and a deficiency in P's income tax for
the 2011 taxable year.

Held: There was no distribution from the IRA to P.

Eric C. Onyango, for petitioner.
Michael C. Dancz and Kathryn E. Kelly, for respondent.

MEMORANDUM OPINION

GUSTAFSON, Judge: The Internal Revenue Service ("IRS") issued to
petitioner, Raymond S. McGaugh, a statutory notice of deficiency pursuant to
section 6212 1 on March 17, 2014, for Mr. McGaugh's 2011 Federal income tax.
In the notice the IRS determined a deficiency in tax of $13,538 arising from a
distribution from Mr. McGaugh's individual retirement account ("IRA") and an
accuracy-related penalty of $2,708 under section 6662(a). The matter is currently
before the Court on Mr. McGaugh's motion for summary judgment pursuant to
Rule 121, which the Commissioner has opposed.

The issue for decision is whether a transaction involving the removal of
$50,000 from Mr. McGaugh's IRA to purchase stock for his IRA constituted a
distribution that was not rolled over within the 60-day period allowed in section

---

1Unless otherwise indicated, all section references are to the Internal

Revenue Code (26 U.S.C.; "the Code"), as amended, and all Rule references are to the Tax Court Rules of Practice and Procedure. All amounts are rounded to the nearest dollar.

408(d)(3) and is thus taxable income. For the reasons stated below, we will grant summary judgment in Mr. McGaugh's favor.

Background

The facts set forth below are based on the pleadings and other pertinent materials in the record and are not in dispute. See Rule 121(b). Mr. McGaugh's petition alleges an address in Illinois.

Since 2002 Mr. McGaugh has maintained a self-directed IRA with custodian Merrill Lynch, and the IRA held 10,000 shares of stock in First Personal Financial Corp. ("FPFC"). The Commissioner asserts, and we assume, that Mr. McGaugh is a member of the board of directors of FPFC, but the Commissioner has not denied that FPFC stock is permitted to be an asset in the IRA. In the summer of 2011, Mr. McGaugh requested that Merrill Lynch use funds from his IRA to purchase an additional 7,500 shares of FPFC stock. However, for reasons the record does not show, Merrill Lynch would not purchase the shares directly on Mr. McGaugh's behalf.

Consequently, Mr. McGaugh requested that Merrill Lynch initiate a wire transfer of $50,000 directly to FPFC. On October 7, 2011, Merrill Lynch initiated and FPFC received the wire transfer. (There is no evidence that Mr. McGaugh requested an IRA distribution to himself.) On November 28, 2011, FPFC issued the stock certificate not in Mr. McGaugh's name but instead in the name of "Raymond McGaugh IRA FBO Raymond McGaugh", as Mr. McGaugh had requested. FPFC claims that the stock certificate was mailed to Merrill Lynch on or about the same day as the November 28, 2011, issuance date on the certificate; but because Merrill Lynch states that the stock certificate was not received until "early 2012", we treat the timing of the transmittal of the stock certificate to Merrill Lynch as being in dispute and assume it was in 2012. Thereafter Merrill Lynch attempted to mail the stock certificate to Mr. McGaugh, but it was returned by the postal service at least twice. The record does not show where the original stock certificate is currently located; but we assume (as the IRS asserts) that Mr. McGaugh holds it (an assertion he denies).2

For purposes of Mr. McGaugh's motion, we assume that Merrill Lynch received the stock certificate from FPFC more than 60 days after the wire transfer, which Merrill Lynch therefore reckoned to be outside the 60-day limitation period

---

2 The stock certificate evidently remains in limbo. Mr. McGaugh insists that Merrill Lynch is obliged to hold the stock as an asset of the IRA, but Merrill Lynch denies that it possesses the stock certificate. In early 2015 FPFC stated that, before it could issue a replacement certificate, it would need "a lost certificate

affidavit with a hold harmless from Merrill Lynch * * * since that is the party that we issued the original certificate to". The year at issue is 2011, and we do not address the tax effects, if any, of the later dealings among Mr. McGaugh, FPFC, and Merrill Lynch.

---

for a qualified rollover transaction under section 408(d)(3). Believing the transaction to be subject to the rollover rules, and believing the transfer to be outside the 60-day limit, Merrill Lynch reported the $50,000 transaction as a taxable distribution on Form 1099-R, "Distributions From Pensions, Annuities, Retirement or Profit-Sharing Plans, IRAs, Insurance Contracts, etc." and refuses to treat the FPFC stock as an asset of the IRA. Mr. McGaugh continues to object to the refusal.

The IRS determined that the wire transfer issued by Merrill Lynch constituted a "distribution" from Mr. McGaugh's IRA and was includible in gross income under sections 408(d) and 72 and that, because he had not yet reached age 59-1/2, it was an "early distribution" subject to the 10% additional tax of section 72(t). The IRS issued a notice of deficiency for the 2011 tax year determining a $13,538 deficiency in tax as well as an accuracy-related penalty of $2,708. Mr. McGaugh timely filed his petition on June 11, 2014, seeking redetermination of the liability and filed a motion for summary judgment on May 26, 2015, to which the Commissioner responded.3

The Commissioner filed a 3 response on June 24, 2015, and a supplemental response on September 8, 2015. At the Commissioner's request, this case was called at the Court's session in Chicago, Illinois, on October 19, 2015, so that a subpoena that the Commissioner had issued to Merrill Lynch could be enforced.

Discussion

I. Standard for summary judgment

Under Rule 121 (the Tax Court's analog to Rule 56 of the Federal Rules of Civil Procedure), the Court may grant summary judgment where there is no genuine dispute as to any material fact and a decision may be rendered as a matter of law. The moving party (here, Mr. McGaugh) bears the burden of showing that no genuine dispute of material fact exists, and the Court will view any factual material and inferences in the light most favorable to the non-moving party. Dahlstrom v. Commissioner, 85 T.C. 812, 821 (1985); cf. Anderson v. Liberty Lobby, Inc., 477 U.S. 242, 255 (1986) (same standard under Fed. R. Civ. P. 56). "The opposing party is to be afforded the benefit of all reasonable doubt, and any inference to be drawn from the underlying facts contained in the record must be viewed in a light most favorable to the party opposing the motion for summary judgment." Espinoza v. Commissioner, 78 T.C. 412, 416 (1982). Since we consider Mr. McGaugh's motion for summary judgment, we draw all inferences in

---

3 Attorneys for Merrill Lynch produced documents to the Commissioner and appeared at the calendar call. The Commissioner's counsel stated that she would review the documents and discuss them with Merrill Lynch's attorneys. In the months that have elapsed since then, the Commissioner has not filed any motion to compel nor filed any further response to Mr. McGaugh's motion for summary judgment.

---

favor of the Commissioner. That is, we assume the facts as shown by the Commissioner, the non-moving party, or as shown by Mr. McGaugh and not disputed by the Commissioner.

II. General IRA principles

As we previously explained in Peek v. Commissioner, 140 T.C. 216, 222-223 (2013):

A taxpayer who invests his money in the hope of making a gain over a period of years--whether to fund his retirement or for any other purpose--normally must pay tax on that gain as he realizes it. Sec. 1001(a), (c). His payment of the tax from time to time diminishes the size of his investment and thereby, to some extent, diminishes his future gains. However, a taxpayer may create an "individual retirement account", which is exempt from tax under section 408(e)(1) and in which his investment can therefore increase until his retirement without being diminished by income tax liability. As long as the account qualifies as an IRA, the taxpayer-investor is not liable for income tax on the gains, so that the undiminished investment account can earn maximum returns until the time comes for payout, when the taxpayer will finally owe income tax on those greater gains. Under section 408, the benefit of the traditional IRA is thus deferral of income tax liability on retirement investment gains. * * *

Generally, under section 72, amounts distributed to the taxpayer from an IRA are includible in the taxpayer's gross income, see sec. 408(d)(1), and those amounts are subject to a "10-Percent Additional Tax" if the taxpayer has not yet "attain[ed] age 59-1/2", see sec. 72(t).

The IRA must be a trust or a custodial account, administered by a trustee or custodian (here, Merrill Lynch) who acts as a fiduciary for that IRA. Sec. 408(a), (h); 26 C.F.R. sec. 1.408-2(a), (d), Income Tax Regs. The fiduciary is responsible for the investment and disposition of the property held in the IRA. 26 C.F.R. sec. 1.408-2(e).

An amount will not be treated as a taxable distribution from an IRA if it is a qualified rollover. Sec. 408(d)(3). A distribution is considered a qualified rollover contribution if the entire amount an individual receives is paid into a qualifying IRA or other eligible retirement plan within 60 days of the distribution. Id.; see also Schoof v. Commissioner, 110 T.C. 1, 7 (1998).

Because the IRA paid out $50,000 (to FPFC) at Mr. McGaugh's request and for his ultimate benefit, and because (as we assume for purposes of the pending motion) that amount was not repaid to the IRA (in the form of the FPFC stock) until after the 60-day rollover period, Merrill Lynch and the IRS treated the transaction as a taxable distribution.

III. The occurrence of a distribution

A. There was no literal distribution of IRA funds to Mr. McGaugh.

Section 408(d)(1) provides that "any amount paid or distributed out of an individual retirement plan shall be included in gross income by the payee or distributee". Construing t 4 he facts in the Commissioner's favor, the evidence shows that Merrill Lynch wired money to FPFC for which FPFC issued shares to the IRA. No cash, check, or wire transfer ever passed through Mr. McGaugh's hands, and he was therefore not a literal "payee or distributee" of any amount.

B. Mr. McGaugh was, at most, a conduit of the IRA funds.

The Commissioner evidently reckons that the foregoing account is an oversimplified description of the transaction, since Merrill Lynch declined to make a direct purchase and instead simply wired funds at Mr. McGaugh's instruction, thus arguably putting the funds at Mr. McGaugh's discretion. But if we adopt this perspective on the transaction and acknowledge Mr. McGaugh as the director of the transaction, the outcome does not change. The owner of an IRA is entitled to direct the investment of the funds without forfeiting the tax benefits of an IRA. Even acknowledging that Mr. McGaugh pulled all the strings, it remains true that the funds the IRA released went straight to the investment and resulted in the stock shares' being issued straight to the IRA.

4The regulations elaborate slightly by providing that "any amount actually paid or distributed or deemed paid or distributed * * * shall be included in the gross income of the payee or distributee", 26 C.F.R. sec. 1.408-4(a)(1), Income Tax Regs. (emphasis added); but it appears that a "deemed distribution" occurs when an IRA ceases to qualify because of a prohibited transaction or where the taxpayer uses the IRA's assets as collateral for a loan, id. para. (d). Thus, the regulations shed no light on the issue in this case.

If we analyze the situation for possible "constructive receipt" of the funds from Merrill Lynch by Mr. McGaugh (and constructive transfer of the funds by him to FPFC), the outcome still does not change. "It is well established that the mere receipt and possession of money does not by itself constitute gross income." Liddy v. Commissioner, T.C. Memo. 1985-107, aff'd, 808 F.2d 312 (4th Cir. 1986). "We accept as sound law the rule that a taxpayer need not treat as income moneys which he did not receive under a claim of right, which were not his to keep, and which he was required to transmit to someone else as a mere conduit." Diamond v. Commissioner, 56 T.C. 530, 541 (1971), aff'd, 492 F.2d 286 (7th Cir. 1974).

Thus, money received as a mere agent or conduit is not includible in gross income. Liddy v. Commissioner, 808 F.2d at 314; Diamond v. Commissioner, 56 T.C. at 541. We have held that this principle may apply in the case of a taxpayer and an IRA, see Ancira v. Commissioner, 119 T.C. 135, 138 (2002); and the IRS so acknowledges. 5 The question at issue here is whether, in the wire

---

5As the Commissioner states in his supplemental opposition (at 7-8) to the motion for summary judgment, "if Merrill Lynch, as custodian of petitioner's IRA, purchased the shares with funds from petitioner's IRA, either through petitioner as an agent/conduit or otherwise, then there may not have been a distribution. See Ancira v. Commissioner, 119 T.C. 135, 137-40 (2002) (the withdrawal of funds from an IRA did not give rise to a distribution, where the withdrawal was in the

---

transfer and subsequent stock purchase, Mr. McGaugh acted as a conduit to or an agent of the IRA fiduciary and custodian, Merrill Lynch.

Neither the Code nor the applicable regulations provide specific guidance on whether or when an amount is considered to have been "paid or distributed out of an individual retirement plan" through the use of the beneficiary as a conduit from the custodian to the investment. This Court has, however, addressed a case involving facts similar to Mr. McGaugh's: In Ancira v. Commissioner, 119 T.C. at 136, the taxpayer maintained a self-directed IRA, and during the year at issue he requested that his IRA custodian purchase a particular company's stock for his IRA. While the issuing company's stock was a permissible asset that could be held by the IRA, company policy of the custodian of the account did not permit it to directly purchase stock that was not publicly traded. Id. The taxpayer therefore requested a check made payable to the non-public issuing company, and the custodian sent the taxpayer the requested check. Id. The taxpayer forwarded the check to the issuing company, and the issuing company issued the stock certificate. Id. at 136-137. The certificate stated that the taxpayer's IRA was the owner of the shares of the stock, and the taxpayer presumed that the issuing

---

5(...continued)
form of a check that could not be negotiated by the account owner, and the funds were used by the IRA custodian to acquire stock)."

[*12] company had sent the stock certificate to the IRA custodian as instructed.

Id. at 137. However, for unspecified reasons the certificate was not delivered to the custodian, and the taxpayer did not discover the mistake until after receiving a notice of deficiency from the IRS. Id. After learning of the error, the taxpayer directed the issuing company to send the stock certificate to him, and he then delivered it directly to the custodian. Id.

In Ancira we held that no distribution from the IRA to the taxpayer occurred when the custodian delivered the check to him. Id. at 139. We observed that no distribution would have occurred if the custodian had either purchased stock directly from the issuing company or sent a check to a broker who then purchased the stock for the IRA. Id. at 137-138. We held that the taxpayer acted as an agent or conduit for the custodian because the taxpayer arranged the purchase but was not in constructive receipt of the check and the ownership of the stock was directly assumed by the IRA. Id. at 138. Moreover, we determined that the delay of the delivery of the stock certificate to the custodian was a bookkeeping error, which "did not alter the ownership of the stock by the IRA and certainly did not transfer the ownership to * * * [the taxpayer]." Id. at 140.

Like the taxpayer in Ancira, Mr. McGaugh wished to acquire for his IRA stock that apparently could not be purchased directly by the custodian, Merrill Lynch. Mr. McGaugh therefore arranged the purchase of FPFC stock, instructed Merrill Lynch to make the wire transfer to FPFC, and instructed FPFC to deliver the certificate directly to Merrill Lynch. Moreover, unlike the taxpayer in Ancira, who received a check from the IRA and delivered it to the issuing company, Mr. McGaugh never personally handled any check by which the IRA funds were transmitted to FPFC. Instead, he requested that Merrill Lynch transfer the funds via wire transfer directly to the issuing company, and that transfer was duly made without Mr. McGaugh's interposition. And unlike the stock in Ancira, the FPFC stock certificate was sent directly to the custodian.

The Commissioner emphasizes that "[i]t appears that petitioner is in possession of the purported stock certificate." Even if Mr. McGaugh had physical possession of the stock certificate, he was not in constructive receipt of the asset. The "essence [of constructive receipt] is that funds which are subject to a taxpayer's unfettered command and which he is free to enjoy at his option are constructively received by him whether he sees fit to enjoy them or not." Ancira v. Commissioner, 119 T.C. at 138 (quoting Estate of Brooks v. Commissioner, 50 T.C. 585, 592 (1968)). Here, the stock was issued not in Mr. McGaugh's name but in the name "Raymond McGaugh IRA FBO Raymond McGaugh". Even with physical possession of the stock certificate, Mr. McGaugh could not have realized any practical utility or benefit from the certificate in the name of the IRA. (And if Merrill Lynch's attempts to mail the IRA's stock certificates to Mr. McGaugh in "early 2012" (contrary to his instructions and intention) gave him ownership of the shares, then that was a distinct 2012 transaction that would not affect his 2011 income tax liability.)

We are not persuaded by the Commissioner's argument that Mr. McGaugh's circumstances are similar to that of the taxpayer in Dabney v. Commissioner, T.C. Memo. 2014-108. In Dabney this Court found a taxable distribution from the taxpayer's IRA when the taxpayer explicitly requested an IRA distribution (to himself) with the goal of purchasing land for his IRA but failed to return the distribution (or any other property) to the account within the 60-day rollover period of section 408(d)(3). Id. at *5. The policies of the custodian, Charles Schwab, did not permit real property to be an asset of its IRAs, id. at *4, *11, so in March 2009 Mr. Dabney requested a distribution of his IRA funds and a transfer of those funds to the title company handling the property sale. Contrary to Schwab's policies, Mr. Dabney directed the company to issue title in the name of the IRA, but it failed to do so and put the property in his name. He tried to sell the property and finally succeeded in January 2011 and wired the proceeds to Schwab as a purported "rollover contribution". We held that the transfer of the funds from the IRA to Mr. Dabney constituted a taxable distribution.

Here, by contrast, Merrill Lynch previously permitted FPFC stock as an asset to be held in Mr. McGaugh's IRA, and its subsequent correspondence seems to indicate that if the stock at issue had been received within the 60-day period, it would have been accepted. And here the stock certificate bears the name of the IRA as its owner; and it is therefore not like the real property in Dabney that, for more than a year, was titled in the name of the individual taxpayer. Mr. Dabney requested a distribution in order to conduct a real estate transaction not permitted by the IRA, whereas Mr. McGaugh directed the IRA to make a permissible investment. This case is not like Dabney.

Rather, this case resembles Ancira. We hold that Mr. McGaugh did not receive a distribution when Merrill Lynch made the wire transfer to FPFC; and to the extent that he had control over the wired funds, he at most acted as a conduit for the IRA custodian. Consequently, the 60-day limitation on a rollover under section 408(d)(3) does not really come into play in this case. The timing of the mailing of the shares (i.e., more than 60 days after the wire transfer) does not alter our conclusion that there was no distribution from the IRA to Mr. McGaugh. We will therefore grant Mr. McGaugh's motion for summary judgment.

To reflect the foregoing,
An appropriate order and decision
will be entered.